THE COMPLETE TRAINING OF HORSE AND RIDER

In the Principles of Classical Horsemanship

THE COMPLETE TRAINING OF

HORSE & RIDER

ALOIS PODHAJSKY

Foreword by Sylvia Loch

THE SPORTSMAN'S PRESS
LONDON

First published in Great Britain 1967
Reprinted: 1969 (twice); 1971; 1972; 1973; 1975; 1977; 1978; 1981; 1982; 1983; 1991

Published originally under the title
"Die Klassische Reitkunst"
by Nymphenburger Verlagshandlung GmbH, München

English translation by Eva Podhajsky and Colonel V. D. S. Williams

Published by arrangement with Doubleday, a division of Bantam Doubleday Dell Publishing Group, Inc.

British Library Cataloguing in Publication Data

Podhajsky, Alois *1898–1973*
The complete training of horse and rider.
1. Dressage
I. Title II. Die klassische Reitkunst. *English*
798.23

ISBN 0–948253–51–7

Printed in Great Britain by
Redwood Press Limited
Melksham, Wiltshire

CONTENTS

PHOTOGRAPHS

Drawings by Anton Haug

PHOTOGRAPHIC CREDITS

Fritz Kern, Vienna: 11, 15, 17, 18, 32
Werner Menzendorf, Berlin: 3, 4, 5, 6, 7, 10, 12, 21, 22, 23, 27, 31, 33, 34, 35, 37, 38
Bruno Kerschner, Salzburg: 16, 19, 25, 26, 30, 36

This is to express my deep gratitude
to my friend Colonel V. D. S. Williams,
who is responsible for the development of dressage in England
and without whose special knowledge and experience
this book could not have been translated.

FOREWORD

By SYLVIA LOCH

I have always felt very humble watching the dedicated work of the Spanish Riding School of Vienna and its 'dancing white horses', the name so aptly given by Alois Podhajsky to describe his beloved Lipizzaners. The old masters claimed that the art of training horses ennobled the soul; amidst the practical brilliance of *The Complete Training of Horse and Rider*, there is clearly an inspired quality which will appeal to all horse lovers.

This fundamental training book has already sold thousands of copies worldwide and percipient riders rank it first amongst equals as the definitive dressage handbook. Whether schooling a young horse for general safe riding or bringing on the mature horse to the highest levels of dressage competition, there has to be a total balanced comprehension of the horse's physical and mental aspects. What is particularly encouraging is the clarity and simplicity of the language and the easily understood similes.

After explaining the principles of classical riding, including an important section on reward, Podhajsky leads the reader through an understanding of the basic gaits and natural balance of the horse to lungework and the progressive exercises which will supple and prepare the horse for the turns, lateral movements, canter changes and finally the airs.

The author emphasises that the head and neck of the horse must only be raised through the correct action of the hindquarters. His definition of collection is clear cut and should be read and returned to again and again; this aspect of training is too often misunderstood today. Only through adhering to the classical precepts can the horse enjoy the lightness of the forehand which produced Xenophon's 'divine sensation' of truly uniting horse and rider as one.

This fine book has rightly earned its place as an equestrian classic.

THE COMPLETE TRAINING OF HORSE AND RIDER

CHAPTER I

REVIEW AND PRINCIPLES OF RIDING

1. *Historical Review*

In ancient days the art of riding was developed to a high degree, as may be seen from the book of the Greek statesman and general, Xenophon, written about 380 B.C. Even before him Simon of Athens had written a thorough and detailed book about the art of riding which Xenophon mentions more than once. Unfortunately, this book by Simon has been lost, as has one by the Roman writer Pliny, *De Iaculatione Equestri.*

Any horse expert who has studied this book of Xenophon's written 2400 years ago cannot fail to be impressed by the preciseness of his explanations and by his insight into the feelings of the horse. His training was based on intuition and kind treatment, a policy that, unfortunately, was not always followed by riding masters in later years. This attitude of kindness is best expressed by his own words: "Anything forced and misunderstood can never be beautiful. And to quote the words of Simon: 'If a dancer was forced to dance by whip and spikes, he would be no more beautiful than a horse trained under similar conditions.'"

With the fall of the Greek empire and, later, with the great migration, the cultural value of many arts was lost. That of riding declined more and more and finally ceased to exist. To Xenophon's book must be given the credit for preserving the ideas of equestrian art to the present day, because it was this book that formed the basis of its renaissance.

Nearly 2000 years later, in the sixteenth century, the long forgotten art of riding, together with other artistic accomplishments, came to light again. As the great masters of painting and sculpture began to flourish under the Italian sun, so the newly awakened art of riding was reintroduced by the Neapolitan nobleman Grisone, who was known to his contemporaries as the "father of the art of equitation."

Grisone had thoroughly studied Xenophon's book. He quotes, almost word for word, the instruction about the rider's seat and aids. His idea, however, was to control the horse by force, as is proved by the numerous severe bits he invented.

The best known of Grisone's many pupils was Pignatelli. He was the director of the famous Riding Academy at Naples to which Pluvinel came as a student from France. Pluvinel, who later became riding master to Louis XIII, followed the instructions of Pignatelli, but added to them from his own experience. Unlike his teacher and predecessor, he advocated individual treatment for the horse and substituted humane principles for the force in current use. His ideas were circulated in his book *Manège du Roi,* which appeared in 1623. This book was ridiculed to begin with, but in course of time Pluvinel's principles were accepted and he prepared the path for François Robichon de la Guérinière, who later became the greatest riding master of France.

As a result of this development of humaneness, the doctrines of the Duke of Newcastle, published in his elaborate book in 1657, failed to create a durable basis for the art of riding in England, partly because of the cruelty of his methods. For the same reason Georg Engelhardt von Löhneysen's book, published in 1588, also failed to get a following.

The influence built up by Grisone, Pignatelli, and their pupils was soon lost. At the beginning of the eighteenth century the art of riding was almost exclusively influenced by France. And it was the great riding master de la Guérinière who produced the most revolutionary book on riding of all times. Unlike the writings of his predecessors, his book is clear and easy to understand. He based it on simplicity and facts in order to be completely understood by his readers. There is no need to discuss Guérinière's teachings in detail in this work, not because they are not sufficiently interesting, but because they are applied unaltered at the Spanish Riding School and may be seen there in daily use.

With the French Revolution the doctrines of Guérinière were lost to France. Moreover, the Napoleonic wars brought to an end the riding academies of the various courts of Europe. Only the Spanish Riding School in Vienna has faithfully preserved up to the present day the methods of Guérinière. This was due chiefly to the influence of Max Ritter von Weyrother, an outstanding horseman who was head rider at the School during the early part of the nineteenth century. His influence, which spread far beyond the confines of his country, was particularly felt in Germany, where Seidler, and, even more so, Seeger and Oeynhausen were his disciples. They were powerful enough to withstand the teachings of Baucher and to establish their methods so firmly that, later, Plinzner and Fillis could not influence the riding in that country. Steinbrecht's book, published in 1885, was also based on their teaching.

Plinzner, who worked in the Royal Stables in Berlin from 1874 onwards, overbent his horses, as Baucher did, and destroyed any forward urge. His followers made excuses for his methods because he trained horses for Emperor William II of Germany, who had a withered arm and had to ride with one hand.

James Fillis was introduced to Baucher's methods in France. He then spent twelve years as a riding master at the Military Academy in Petrograd and made his first appearance in Germany in a circus in 1892. He captivated the spectators at the circus and found many followers among riders who would have liked to see his methods employed in the training of military chargers. Without doubt Fillis was a great artist, but interested more in the field of circus riding than in the art of classical equitation, in which all movements are based on the laws of nature. The proof of this is shown by the many unnatural movements which he practised, such as the canter on three legs, the canter backward, and the Spanish walk. In 1913 Fillis died in Paris, as forgotten as his teacher, Baucher, while the methods of the Spanish Riding School still flourish.

Up to the beginning of the First World War the German Cavalry School at Hanover was under the influence of the Spanish Riding School through its former head rider Gebhart.

This historical development of riding reveals that the art is not confined to any special country. It flourishes wherever human beings dedicate themselves to horsemanship and know how to cultivate and develop its practice, wherever there are experts, and wherever such skill brings pleasure to those who love beauty. The art of riding is indeed international; it belongs to the civilised world, and it is the duty of every nation to preserve and foster it in the interest of culture.

2. *Principles of Training*

No book of instruction can explain riding by generalities alone. If it is to be of value a method must be laid down. Every detail must be explained, even at the risk of being long-winded, if the method is to be described with absolute clarity.

Ideas with regard to the importance of theory over practice will always differ, but they will agree on one point, namely, that the one is not complete without the other. Theory without practice is of little value, whereas practice is the proof of theory. It is the theoretical knowledge that will show the way to perfection. Theory is the knowledge, practice the ability. Knowledge must always take precedence over action. This thesis is especially true of the art of riding. In spite of initial success, the self-taught person can never become more than a workman; only on a foundation of theory can riding develop to the realm of art.

Equestrian art, perhaps more than any other, is closely related to the wisdom of life. Many of the same principles may be applied as a line of conduct to follow. The horse teaches us self-control, constancy, and the ability to understand what goes on in the mind and the feelings of another creature, qualities that are important throughout our lives. Moreover, from this relationship with his horse the rider will learn that only kindness and mutual understanding will bring about achievements of highest perfection. Many roads lead to Rome. The question is which is the best and shortest. With riding, only theoretical knowledge and practical ability will help the student to select the best road to success. Once selected it must be followed to the end; changes of direction will lead to confusion and failure to reach the goal.

To be successful the rider must be able to distinguish between cause and effect. The effect will be easy to see, but the cause will be recognised only through knowledge, which is supplied by theory.

3. *Sources of the Methods of Training*

The sources of training in the classical art of riding can best be found by following the method employed at the Spanish Riding School. Unfortunately this method has been based almost exclusively on oral tradition, as the few existing records are incomplete.

The most valuable reference is given in *Directives,* published by H. E. von Holbein in 1898. These, although they only give general outlines, reveal the extraordinary knowledge of the author as he points out the method of training to be followed at the School.

> Beginning with the principle that working to a fixed pattern will be detrimental to any art, this book does not lay down fixed rules but gives a line to follow which should help a rider to maintain a methodical system while training his horse. As a guide the following books are recommended; they do not contradict each other but follow the same line of thought:
>
> de la Guérinière 1751
> Max Ritter von Weyrother 1814
> Louis Seeger 1844
> Baron von Oeynhausen 1845–1865
> and the Regulations for the Austro-Hungarian Cavalry.

A short description of these books and their authors seems necessary. *François Robichon de la Guérinière,* whose importance has already been mentioned, was master of horse to King

Louis XV of France. He is heard of for the first time in 1716 when he took over the famous Riding Academy of Paris, which previously had been directed by his teacher François Anne de Vendeuil. From 1730 till his death in 1751 Guérinière directed the royal stables in the Tuileries, which had been founded by Pluvinel, the teacher of Louis XIII one hundred years before.

Guérinière's book, *Ecole de Cavalerie,* was published for the first time in 1733 and republished between the years 1740 and 1802 under various titles. Because of its clarity and importance it was mentioned by von Holbein as a basis for the fundamental training at the Spanish Riding School. In the introduction to his book Guérinière says that he not only gives his own ideas and methods, but also that he has studied the books by the best authors and has supplemented their teachings by his own experiences and the advice of his teacher de Vendeuil and his predecessors du Plessis and de la Vallée.

The *Ecole de Cavalerie* consists of three chapters:

(1) Knowledge of the horse in and out of the stable
(2) Training
(3) Treatment of illness

This classification clearly shows what knowledge he expected from a rider, which should also apply to riders of the present day.

Guérinière's aim was to obtain by systematic work a riding horse that was quiet, supple, and obedient, pleasant in his movements and comfortable for his rider. These are requirements for any school horse, hunter, or charger, and as we have said, the methods employed by this famous riding master have been preserved at the Spanish Riding School.

Max Ritter von Weyrother was the most outstanding member of a family of outstanding riders. He came to the Spanish Riding School in 1813, was made head rider in 1825, and died in 1833. There are no records of his age. In 1814 Weyrother published a small book on *How to Select the Proper Curb Bit.* After his death a book was published in 1836 under the title *Extracts From Papers Collected by Friends of Max Ritter von*

Weyrother and Published After His Death. These extracts give some idea of the reputation of this man, and they show that he was asked to prepare a plan of training for the Austro-Hungarian Cavalry School. In this little book we find the principles of training employed at the School today, which is the best proof of the quality of his teaching and the heritage he handed down to the successive head riders who followed him.

Weyrother, who strictly followed Guérinière's teachings, deals in his papers mainly with the training of the rider. He has coined the phrase "the thinking rider," still in use at the School, underlining the necessity of reinforcing practical ability with theoretical knowledge. His reputation has spread far beyond the frontiers of Austria. The German Baron Biel in his book *The Noble Horse,* published in 1830, states that he was much distressed to find that the noble art of riding was no longer to be found in Germany inasmuch as the horses were overbent in an exaggerated and unnatural way. On visiting the Spanish Riding School in Vienna he found the training based on very different methods. Head rider Weyrother made it clear to him what those methods were, and he came to the conclusion that any breeder would be lucky to have his horses trained under those principles. No one would then dare to state that the noble English horse is not suitable for the art of riding.

Louis Seeger opened the first private riding school in Berlin, and in 1844 published his book *System of the Art of Riding,* for which he received the gold medal. He also published in 1852 *Monsieur Baucher and His Methods,* which was a serious warning to German riders, expressing his opinion of the harm being done to the art of riding by the French riding master.

Seeger was a pupil of Max von Weyrother. His system was completely under the influence of his teacher and in accordance with the principles taught at the Spanish Riding School, which maintains that a school horse must always be a perfect horse for everyday purposes. In this book the reader will find complete sentences from Weyrother's extracts, supplemented by the author's experiences and more fully explained. He lays down the principles of Guérinière and Weyrother in a methodical sequence. He also allocates considerable space to the laws of balance and proves his theories by the laws of physics. Unfortunately his instructions about raising the head and neck of the horse and the use of the spur were often misunderstood. It is to Seeger's credit that, unlike his contemporaries, he wrote a simple book which gives valuable information even today.

Baron von Oeynhausen came from an aristocratic family of riders in the north of Germany. He received training at various German riding schools and for many years was instructor and second in command of the Military Equitation School in Salzburg. Oeynhausen published several books between 1850 and 1869 based on the theoretical lectures he gave at the military school. In the preface to one of his early books he states that it has been his object to collect and spread all principles that might be of use in the training of the horse, and as a result, he quotes from many other writers. Weyrother's influence is particularly evident throughout these books, for he is quoted word for word. It is not known whether Oeynhausen was a pupil of Weyrother or ever at the Spanish Riding School, but in his writings he shows a great knowledge of the methods employed at the School and of the schocl jumps, which he was unlikely to have seen anywhere else.

The last reference to the training at the Spanish Riding School mentioned by H. E. von Holbein is to the *Instructions for the Austrian Cavalry*, which coincides almost completely with the books of Weyrother, Seeger, and Oeynhausen. If the editions of these *Instructions* published from 1873 to 1898 are compared, no alterations will be found except for a few expressions. The 1898 edition was used for the cavalry in Austria until 1938.

H. E. von Holbein himself can claim the credit for having first laid down the instructions for training at the Spanish Riding School. He published these *Directives* in 1898 and the same year was appointed Director of the School, a position he held until October 1901. In the introduction to his *Directives* he points to the fact that the shorter time allowed for training and the universal demand for speed have caused a decline in the art of riding throughout the various armies.

In view of this situation, it seems more necessary than ever to preserve an institution such as the Spanish Riding School, where the equestrian art is cultivated to the highest perfection. The deeper purpose of the High School is to preserve the principles and experiences of the art of riding as a means of showing how best and most quickly to train a rider and to teach the horse to submit himself to the rider's will.

Every rider at the School must have a thorough understanding of his purpose, and to reach his goal he must give to it all his mental and physical abilities. The High School must never be practised as an art on its own, allowing the training to become unbalanced. It must be built up on all three phases of riding, each of which has an equally important part to play.

Phase One. Riding the horse with a natural carriage on straight lines in the ordinary paces in free forward movement with the rein in contact and on a long rein. This is known as riding straight forward. This kind of riding may be practised for itself alone.

Phase Two. Riding the collected horse in turns and circles at all paces (in America commonly called "gaits") and in perfect balance. This is known as the Campaign School. It improves the natural impulsion of the horse, cultivates his carriage and paces, strengthens his muscles, and makes his joints supple and flexible. The proficiency and stamina of the horse will be increased, his intelligence and understanding awakened, and the rider is given a line of conduct to be followed for further training. In the Campaign School the ordinary natural paces and cross-country jumping will be developed; the horse will be given the necessary bend in ribs, neck, and gullet, as well as the correct position appropriate for his conformation.

This second phase of riding has to be developed from the first and presents the only possible preparation for the third, namely the High School. Only on this foundation can the rider proceed to art, that is, to High School, because nature can exist without art, but art can never exist without nature.

Phase Three. Riding the horse in greater collection with regularity, suppleness, and proficiency, and with an increased bend in the joints of the hind legs in all ordinary paces, as well as the less ordinary paces and jumps that can be copied from nature. These movements developed by training to the highest perfection are called High School.

This phase of riding cannot exist without the first two and especially without the Campaign School. It unites all three phases. In principle the fully trained school horse must always be able to show the same standard of excellence as an all-purpose horse as he does as a school horse.

H. E. von Holbein points out that by making High School so artificial, a gap has been created between school riding and campaign riding to the disadvantage of both. There is no reason to separate the movements of campaign riding from those of the High School. Every effort must be made to clarify and simplify the instructions and theories that have been handed down by word of mouth, and to follow the doctrines of only those masters who have proved themselves by showing that the horse can be trained to the highest proficiency, even of the High School, by natural methods and without constraint.

Every rider at the Spanish Riding School should strive to bring campaign and school riding closer together, at the same time preserving the independence of both. Every rider must be perfectly clear in his own mind as to which phase of training his horse is in, as well as the method to be followed in his lessons and the goal he wishes to achieve. Every rider must not only ride but also think, as only a thinking rider will be able to attain his goal in relatively short time without spoiling his horse. As a conclusion H. E. von Holbein states in his *Directives* that the art of riding must be divorced from all mystery by simplicity and truth. The rebirth of the High School will then be possible and free from all false doctrines and medieval conceptions, so that riding may be again acknowledged as an art within the reach of every serious rider.

Enumerated above are the sources from which the training at the Spanish Riding School has been developed. It has seemed necessary to draw attention to these sources in order to emphasise the purity of the method of training and to underline the fact that the principles of the art of riding have not been altered although they have largely been handed down by word of mouth from one generation to another. On the contrary, the study of the sources proves that the School still cultivates the classical art of riding in spite of the upheavals that Europe has undergone in the present century and that it has strived to live up to its great tradition.

One more fact that this study has revealed is that the art of training the horse based on the laws of nature has not outlived itself, that it has not been replaced by modern methods but has been preserved and still remains alive.

CHAPTER II

THE DEFINITIONS OF THE CLASSICAL ART OF RIDING

As the artist must know what he wishes to convey by his completed work and the workman must understand how best to use his tools, so must the rider have an exact knowledge of his aim and the ways and means to obtain it.

The object of the classical art of riding is to train a horse not only to be brilliant in the movements and exercises of the High School, but also to be quiet, supple, and obedient, and by his smooth movements to make riding a true pleasure. This clearly shows that in every kind of riding we strive for the same objective. Whether it is a dressage horse, a jumper, a hunter or charger, he should always be quiet, supple, and obedient. These qualities are the basis for every kind of riding. Performances of the greatest brilliance can be built up only on this foundation.

A successful teacher must have a thorough knowledge of his pupils. The rider must know his horse physically as well as mentally. He should have not only a thorough knowledge of the horse's anatomy and of the functions of his joints and muscles but also be able to understand his feelings and anticipate his reactions. With this knowledge he will ensure that his horse enjoys his work and does not become sour. It would be beyond the scope of this book to discuss hippology, but any rider would be well advised to study the conformation of the horse he proposes to train.

The daily work should be divided into periods of varying duration interrupted by periods of rest. Those of work should not be too long and at the end of the daily work the horse should be as lively in his steps as he was at the beginning. The rider should not wait to bring the exercises to an end when the horse shows signs of fatigue, but try to finish the lesson on a good note. The good memory of the horse may be used to advantage; a successful exercise should be rewarded by the rider's dismounting and leading the horse back to the stable. The rider should also prevent the horse from anticipating his aids; therefore, a frequent change of the order of the exercises is advisable. Meanwhile, the horse must be given time to understand his rider and to develop the necessary proficiency that will enable him to obey.

The principles of classical riding can be laid down, but there is no definite rule as to how to put them into practice. In the course of centuries the riding masters of the past have studied thoroughly these principles and have accumulated experiences that will serve as instructions for the riders of today and prevent them from wasting their time with unnecessary experiments. On the other hand, there are no rules for any difficulties that may appear. Remedies that are successful with one horse may prove unsuccessful with another. As is the way with other things in life, riding cannot be learned from books alone. Only by trying out the various possibilities will the rider obtain success.

Besides a knowledge of the physiology and psychology of the horse, the rider must have a clear notion of the theory of movement and balance. The former means an exact knowledge of the sequence of the steps; the latter, a knowledge of how the steps should be executed and what form a horse should adopt to be able to move in balance. So it is necessary to give a number of exact definitions every rider is expected to know.

1. The Paces (or Gaits)

The ordinary natural paces of the horse are walk, trot, and canter. The less ordinary paces are lateral movements, rein-back, piaffe, and passage. While the pace defines the sequence of steps, the tempo gives the measure of speed within the movements of the various paces, i.e., the number of metres (or yards) covered per minute. The tempo may be lengthened or shortened, but one of the main objects of training is to be able to maintain a regular tempo.

The Walk. In the walk the horse moves his legs one after the other so that four hoof beats may be heard. For example: first, left forefoot; second, right hind foot; third, right forefoot; fourth, left hind foot. Two or three feet are always on the ground at the same time; the horse steps from one leg to the other and there is no moment of suspension. Therefore, the rider will find it easiest to ride at this pace. The sequence of steps remains unchanged in ordinary, collected, or extended walk; the length and elevation of the strides change with the different tempos. In the ordinary walk the horse should cover a distance of 100 metres in one minute. It is a bad fault if the horse

Sequence of steps at the walk

moves forward with both legs of one side at the same time, when only two hoof beats will be heard. It is also a fault when the legs are not put forward in the same rhythm and the same length of stride, or the horse makes hasty steps. As with any other pace, regularity is necessary for a good walk. A school horse should never drag his feet; he must lift them from the ground and put them forward in a full stride.

Incorrect walk

The Trot. In the trot the diagonal legs must be raised from the ground simultaneously and be replaced on the ground together, making two hoof beats. For instance, after the left diagonal (left fore and right hind) leaves the ground, the right diagonal (right fore and left hind) is raised before the left diagonal has touched the ground again, so that the horse is suspended with all four legs in the air for a moment. This moment is called *suspension.* As is it not easy to maintain the correct seat in the moment of suspension, the trot will make higher demands on the rider than the walk. In the trot the horse carries his own and his rider's weight with the two diagonal legs or in the suspension. The sequence remains unchanged in the collected, ordinary, or extended tempos; only the length of stride and the duration of suspension will change. The duration of suspension is shortest in the shortened tempo and longest in extension; therefore, the young rider will find it easier to maintain his seat in the short trot than in the extended.

The regular hoof beats of the diagonal legs, interrupted by the moment of suspension, give the rhythm of the movement, as

1 Head rider Max Ritter von Weyrother, after an engraving by Perger 1815

2 Longeing of a young stallion, after an engraving by Ridinger

3 Young horse at the walk

4 Trot in the first phase of training

5 Young horse at the canter

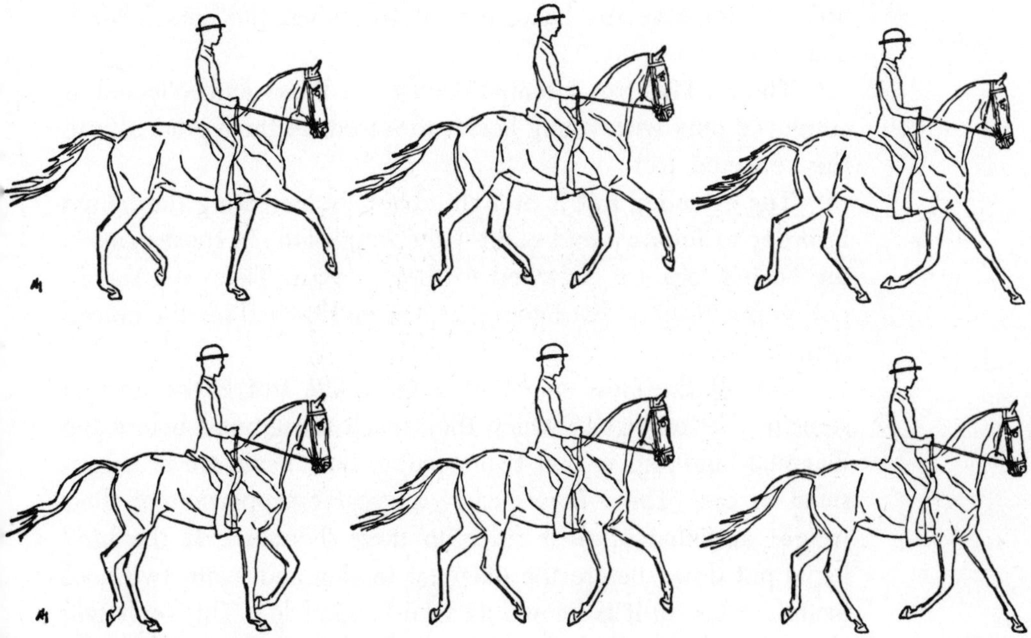

Sequence of steps at the trot

it were, the music of riding. It is of great importance that the rhythm remains the same in all tempos and it is only the length of stride that changes. The shortening of the stride in the same rhythm will require the legs to be raised higher. These lively, elevated steps are known as cadence. It would be wrong, however, to allow the steps to become slower and hovering in the shortened trot.

Rhythm and cadence do not have the same meaning. Rhythm denotes the regularity of the steps. Even the horse with dull and stiff steps can trot in rhythm but without showing cadence. Cadence without rhythm, on the contrary, is inconceivable. If the rhythm is lost, the trot will become unlevel and the horse will lose his brilliance and beauty.

In the ordinary trot the horse should cover a distance of 225 metres in one minute. This trot is generally used when riding in the country, and the collected trot employed in the arena in order to improve the balance and strengthen the horse's hindquarters.

The working trot, a tempo between ordinary and collected, is employed only with young horses to introduce them gradually to the collected trot.

The extended trot is brought about by increasing the tempo in order to improve and control the impulsion; in the extension the horse's legs are stretched to their utmost. This pace should not be practised on hard going, as it would be bad for the horse's legs.

One of the most common faults in the trot is the hurried steps of the forelegs in which they reach the ground before the diagonal hind leg, so that two separate hoof beats are heard instead of one. These horses carry a greater proportion of their weight and that of their rider on their shoulders. If the hind leg is put down before the diagonal foreleg and again two hoof beats are heard, it is known as a hasty hind leg. This fault will also occur when the horse does not bend his joints sufficiently and drags his hind legs along the ground. It is also a fault when the horse does not bring his hind legs sufficiently under the body and appears to make a longer stride with his forelegs, which accordingly have to be withdrawn to equal the stride of the hind legs. In terms of riding the horse promises more in front than he can show with his hindquarters. Another fault is when one hind leg steps more under the body than the other, thus making the strides uneven.

The trot is the most important pace for the training of the horse and rider; faults that creep in at the trot will most likely have a bad influence on the other paces.

The Canter. The canter consists of a series of bounds. In the correct canter three hoof beats should be heard. It is known as the right or left canter according to which foreleg is leading. In the right canter the left hind leg is placed on the ground (first hoof beat), then the right hind leg and left foreleg together at the same time (second hoof beat), followed by the right foreleg (third hoof beat). The left hind leg should leave the ground before the right foreleg is put down, then comes the left diagonal; finally the right foreleg, followed by its suspension. In the correct canter the entire weight is carried in the following sequence: one hind leg–two hind legs and one foreleg–one hind leg and the diagonal foreleg–one hind leg and two fore-legs–one foreleg–all four legs in the air, moment of suspension.

This sequence of steps must be maintained at all tempos. The canter is incorrect if four hoof beats can be heard, which happens when the hind leg is put down before the corresponding diagonal foreleg. This fault appears when the horse loses impulsion by incorrect collection and does not canter with sufficient elevation. Some people are of the opinion that a four-beat canter is a collected canter, but this is incorrect; in this case the horse does not execute correct bounds of canter but "hobbles" along. Therefore, the so-called canter in four-time is a bad fault; only in the racing gallop should there be four hoof beats.

The working canter, in which the horse covers 225 metres

Sequence of steps at the canter

Canter in four-time

in a minute, is a pace between the collected and ordinary canter and is generally used only in the arena. The ordinary canter, in which the horse covers a distance of 375 metres in one minute, is the tempo for cross-country riding and can be increased into the extended canter. With the perfect canter the onlooker must have the impression that the horse bounds elastically from the ground and returns to it in the same manner.

A common fault with weak horses is the disunited canter, in which the horse canters with the left leg leading in front and the right leg leading behind, or vice versa. The rider will be able to recognise the fault by an uncomfortable feeling through the horse's back.

In the "false" canter, the horse canters to the right with the near-fore leading, or to the left with the off-fore leading. If this is performed on purpose it is known as a counter canter. The renvers canter differs from the counter canter by the fact that in the former the horse moves on two tracks.

Lateral Work. In lateral work the sequence of steps in walk, trot, and canter remains unchanged, and the horse moves forward and sideways. The legs that are in movement cross over in front of those that are on the ground.

The Rein-back. In the rein-back the legs do not move in the sequence of the walk, but in that of the trot; for instance, the right diagonal followed by the left diagonal so that only two hoof beats can be heard. The rein-back is correct if the horse

Sequence of steps at the rein-back

lifts his diagonal feet off the ground and puts them down again together; he should not creep back dragging his feet along the ground.

The Piaffe. The piaffe is a cadenced trot on the spot. The horse steps from one diagonal pair of legs to the other with a moment of suspension in between. If the horse lifts the diagonal legs only when the other pair has reached the ground, the piaffe is incorrect and appears stiff and the impression of dancing in the movement is lost.

The piaffe used to be and sometimes still is called passage on the spot; this definition lays emphasis on the moment of suspension. In my opinion this is not correct, because in the piaffe the moment of suspension is the shortest, while it becomes increasingly longer in the collected, ordinary, and extended trot, and attains the longest duration in the passage.

In the ideal piaffe the forelegs are raised so that the forearm becomes almost horizontal to the ground and the hoof of the suspended hind leg is raised above the fetlock of the leg on the ground.

The piaffe is incorrect if the legs are not raised diagonally or regularly or when only the forelegs are lifted while the hind legs remain touching the ground. It is equally incorrect if the hind legs are raised in an exaggerated manner while the forelegs are hardly moved at all. In none of these cases will the horse be able to make an immediate transition into the trot, which is the surest sign that the piaffe was incorrect. The correct piaffe is developed from a forward urge which has been checked, as may be seen with excited horses at liberty. When the obstruction has been removed the horse will immediately cease the piaffe and move forward in a trot.

Another fault occurs when the horse moves his legs sideways instead of in the direction of the movement. This is called balancé and may be seen in the circus. The piaffe is still more incorrect if the horse crosses his forelegs and weaves from one side to the other. This movement could not even be described as "Piaffe balancé" as it shows nothing of the dancing rhythm.

The Passage. In the passage the horse swings proudly forward from one pair of diagonal legs to the other and, according to his conformation and talent, suspends the pair of diagonal legs in the air higher and for a longer period than in the trot. In this pace the suspension attains the longest duration. In the ideal passage the horse gives the impression of floating above the ground, free from weight and borne on invisible wings. The classical passage demands a strong, thoroughly trained horse, master of his balance and free from any tension. If this is not the case numerous faults will occur. For instance, if the hind legs do not step sufficiently under the body and do not carry enough weight, they will come to the ground before the diagonal forelegs and the brilliance of the movement will be lost. A pas-

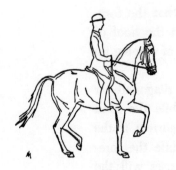

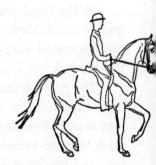

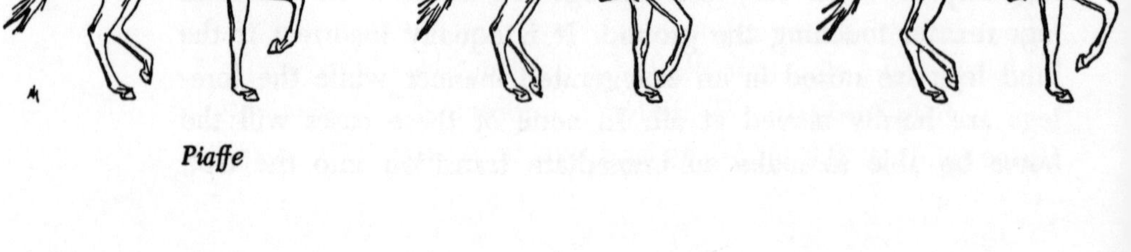

Piaffe

Passage

sage of this kind may be seen in the circus. Or the steps of the hind legs may be uneven or one hind leg step higher under the body than the other.

The type of trot which appears to hover and does not go sufficiently forward must never be mistaken for a passage. In the classical passage the movement of the horse should appear as the collected trot in slow motion.

It has become the habit nowadays to demand spectacular movements like the passage before the horse has had enough training in the basic exercises. This may result in the classical passage being lost.

2. *Halt and Half-halt*

The halt should always be performed in the direction of the movement and without loss of balance. When halted, the horse should carry his own weight and that of his rider equally on all four legs; this will occur only if the hind legs are brought sufficiently under the body. The horse must remain on the bit and be ready to move off immediately into any pace demanded by his rider.

When reducing the pace to the halt, the transition should be smooth, fluid, and level, which is possible only if it is brought about by the correct application of the rider's back, leg, and rein aids, thus ensuring that the horse does not lose his balance.

A halt correctly executed will improve the bending of the three joints of the hind legs, and will be a test of the degree of balance, of suppleness, and of the action of the rein going through the body that the horse has attained by his training.

The half-halt may be described as a "call to attention" to prepare the horse for the next command of his rider. It can be employed to shorten the stride, improve the contact and collection, and give notice to the horse that an exercise requiring greater proficiency is about to be demanded.

The same aids are employed as for a full halt but to a lesser degree and are discontinued the moment the horse has responded. The half-halt will help the horse to carry himself better and take a lighter contact with the bit. It may be used as a corrective, especially with a horse that is inclined to lie heavily on the reins.

3. *Balance*

A horse will be able to master the various paces in full harmony only if he has been blessed with good natural paces and is in balance. Perfect balance is given partly by nature but can be improved by systematic training.

Even a human being needs gymnastic training for smooth and supple athletic action, although it is easier for him than it is for a horse as he is not hampered with a weight on his back and the direction of gravity is vertical over his feet. Nevertheless the first movements are difficult for a child and the average adolescent must learn by exercises to move and dance with grace. Only very few creatures can produce perfect harmonious movements without any assistance from gymnastics.

The horse carries his weight on all four legs; the centre of gravity is not directly supported, and the weight is unequally distributed over all four legs. By nature the forelegs have to bear the greater proportion as they have to carry the neck and head. Therefore, it is more difficult for the horse than for the human to obtain and maintain balance, but balance is the basic requirement for pure and impulsive paces. Moreover, the weight of the rider throws additional weight on the forehand, which makes matters still more difficult for the horse.

It is the rider's art to balance the centres of gravity of horse and rider so that the former is not disturbed in his movements. Any rider who has had the opportunity to break in a young horse will know how clumsily he moves when first mounted. The reason is that the horse must readjust his balance to the unaccustomed weight of the rider.

Few horses are naturally balanced, that is to say, carry an even proportion of their weight on forehand and hindquarters. Such horses make work much easier for the rider. Most horses, however, will carry a greater proportion of their weight on the forehand, a fact which will be still more noticeable when the rider mounts. The hind legs will push the weight more than they carry it, a fault which must be corrected if the paces are to be made as light and elastic as is expected from a school horse.

The object of training will be to correct the balance by making the hindquarters carry a greater proportion of the weight and to relieve the forehand by transferring the weight from the shoulders to the quarters. The former will be obtained by collection; the latter, by raising the forehand through lowering the quarters. Both will be possible only when the horse accepts the bit and is straight. Besides physical balance, mental balance is necessary in order to allow the horse to work consistently and quietly.

4. Contact with the Bit

The connection between the rider's hands and the horse's mouth is called "contact with the bit." This contact governs the guidance and collection of the horse.

The expression has its origin in the fact that the horse should seek a soft connection with the bars of his mouth on the bit, that is to say, a contact. To be correct this contact should be consistent. The rider should have the feeling that he is connected to the horse's mouth by means of an elastic ribbon. As the reins are made of leather and have no spring, this elastic connection can be brought about only by the supple flexion of the horse's jaw combined with the sensitive and light touch of the rider's hands, which depends on flexible wrists. A perfect contact is possible only when the horse is in absolute balance, carries himself, and does not seek support from the reins. It may then be said that the horse is "on the bit."

Balance and contact are complementary to each other: the better the balance the better the contact. On the other hand, correct contact will improve the balance and suppleness of the horse.

Contact will depend on the conformation and temperament of the horse. Horses with weak hindquarters, which develop a greater pushing than carrying force, will in most cases have too strong a contact; it will be hard or even tough. These horses will have an inclination to rush off or lie too much on the reins (pullers). The contact is considered tough if neither the giving nor the taking action of the reins gives any change in the connection with the horse's mouth. In most cases this will be due to a dullness or general stiffness of the horse, or a consequence of incorrect training. The horse will appear to have a dead mouth, which is more difficult to cure than too strong a contact, which may be improved by repeated actions of the reins and increased activity of the hindquarters.

Above the Bit. A horse is said to be above the bit when the head is too high and the angle of the face too far in front of the perpendicular. In this case the pressure of the bit comes on the corners of the lips instead of the bars of the mouth. It frequently occurs with horses that are weak in the back and are caused discomfort by the weight of the rider. These horses must be given plenty of time to become accustomed to carrying the weight with a lowered head and arched back. On no account must an attempt be made to lower the head by pulling at the reins, or by any other incorrect method.

Behind the Bit. In this case the horse brings the angle of the face too far back behind the perpendicular and may drop the bit. This will often be caused by asking collection too soon without first obtaining the necessary impulsion or because the rider's hands are too strong.

Excitable horses may have an irregular contact, that is to say, change from above the bit to behind the bit, and vice

LEFT: *correct contact* CENTRE: *behind the bit* RIGHT: *above the bit*

versa. To cure this the rider should ride quietly forward, applying the reins with a light hand.

Apart from the different kinds of contact, a horse may not accept the bit evenly on both sides. He will make himself stiff on one side and will follow the slightest action of the rein on the other by turning his head. He will take a firmer contact and only reluctantly follow the action of the rein on the side on which he is stiff. On the other side he will anticipate the action of the rein and bend this way; that is to say, he becomes hollow on this side. When the reins are applied evenly the horse will bend his neck to the hollow side, on which he will not accept the rein. The rider will be able to recognise this as the rein will not touch the neck on this hollow side, whereas it lies close to the neck on the side on which the horse makes himself stiff and does not follow the action of the rein. It is the rider's task to try to achieve the same contact with the bit on both sides by demanding more contact on the hollow and less on the stiff side.

Improvement of the contact will coincide with the general progress. The training will be successful only if the horse's ability is improved and increased by suppleness and proficiency. Attention must be drawn to a common fault: the rider should not try to seek contact with the horse's mouth by pulling at the reins, which would check impulsion. The horse should seek the contact from the rider's hands.

5. *Position of the Head*

The immediate success of the contact is shown in the position of the horse's head, and the position and carriage of the head are of the utmost importance for balance.

The position of the head depends on the degree of training and on the tempo of the movement. Much also depends on the conformation of the horse; a horse with strong neck muscles and tight in the gullet will have to overcome certain difficulties, and will be able to follow the rider's demands only after the muscles have become accustomed to the work. Time must be allowed for these horses in the course of their training. The position of the head must be allowed more freedom in the first stage of training and in the faster paces, that is to say, the neck must become longer, must stretch forward more and become lower. With horses in an advanced stage of training and in the collected paces the line of the face should be more or less vertical while the neck should be more arched. The face line must never come behind the vertical, as in this case the horse would be overbent and not go sufficiently forward.

The young horse should be allowed to adopt that position of the head in which he finds it easiest to contact the bit and carry the rider's weight quietly and willingly without excitement. As the strength and proficiency increase, the horse's head and neck will be raised to a position in which a line drawn from the nose to the hip will be parallel to the ground, and the poll

Correct position of the head

will be the highest point of the arched neck. This must not be considered a strict rule, as the amount the neck will be raised will depend on the conformation of the horse, that is to say, the length of his back and the length and shape of his neck. The poll, however, must be the highest point of the horse's head regardless of his conformation.

Since a horse is unable to place his forelegs on the ground at a point in front of a line drawn straight downward continuing the line of his face, it will be a false extension when the horse shoots his forelegs farther to the front than this point inasmuch as they will have to be withdrawn before touching the ground, which would detract from the beauty of the movement. This points to the necessity of sufficient freedom for the head in the extended paces.

When moving on a straight line the position of the head and neck must be straight. In a turn the horse must be bent from head to tail in the degree defined by the arc of the circle or turn. The position of the head should be such that the rider is just able to see the horse's inside eye. It is of great importance that the neck is not bent more than the whole body and that the horse yields in the gullet and not in the muscles of his neck. Both ears must be at the same level, otherwise the horse's head will be tilted. In the arena a well-trained horse should have a slight position to the inside when on a straight line.

It must be emphasised that the correct position of the head cannot be obtained by strong action of the reins, which would only shorten the neck.

The position of the head is the means, the paces the object, of dressage. The correct position of the head will be the result of contact and balance, both developed by riding briskly forward, and will make it easier for the horse to follow the commands of the rider given through the reins.

6. *Straightening*

Balance can be obtained and collection possible only if the horse is straight.

Most green horses, especially if they are naturally balanced, will be straight. That is to say, the hind feet will follow the tracks of the forefeet. Under the weight of the rider, when working in the arena or when incorrectly collected, the horse will show an inclination to be crooked; the hind feet will no longer follow the tracks of the forefeet but step to the side, and the horse will not have an even contact on both sides.

It has often been said that the crookedness of the horse is caused by the position of the foal in the womb, but this theory remains to be proved. On the other hand, the fact must be recognised that the forehand is narrower than the hindquarters and that the horse will be crooked if his shoulder is allowed to be taken too close to the wall. This will be observed especially with a young horse who will try to move with the forehand and hindquarters at the same distance from the wall, and sometimes push his shoulders towards the wall, seeking support for his balance. As a consequence he will become crooked. The forehand, therefore, must be brought away from the wall to bring the shoulders in front of the hindquarters. Only when the horse is straight will it be possible, by collection, to make the hindquarters carry a greater proportion of the weight, and by making him bend the three joints of the hind legs cause him to carry out the appropriate gymnastic exercises which will improve his balance and suppleness and strengthen the hindquarters for further demands.

The importance of straightness is emphasised in one of the most fundamental rules of equitation: Straighten your horse and ride him forward.

7. *Collection*

The horse in collection must step with his hind legs well under his body, which can be recognised by the fact that the tracks of the hind feet come into or in front of those of the forefeet. This will make the horse arch his back correctly and carry his head higher thus becoming shorter in his body.

Collection is necessary for work in the shortened tempo of the paces, and for the performance of short turns and smooth halts. It requires an increased bend of the joints of the hind legs and furthers the physical training of the horse. Collection is necessary for advanced training as it makes the hindquarters carry a greater proportion of the weight and thus relieves the forehand. In this way it will also prevent the horse from wearing out his forelegs prematurely. Correct collection will be possible only when the horse is straight, balanced, and in contact with the bit. On the other hand, collection increases balance (thus improving contact), develops the paces, and establishes obedience.

Collection must be obtained by pushing the hindquarters towards the reins, which remain applied. The compression (shortening) of the horse must be produced by pushing forward from behind and not by pulling back with the reins. The latter would create an incorrect collection and the hind feet of the horse would not track up to the forefeet. Only when collection is obtained from rear to front will the horse step under the body with his hind legs in such a way that the rider can feel it in the reins. This is called "the horse steps into the rein." In general the horse should be collected only when in movement; collection at a halt should be practised only to make the horse understand the aids or as a test in the course of advanced training.

8. *Action of the Rein Going Through the Body*

The action of the rein goes through the body of the horse when it passes through his neck and back, thus bending and putting more weight on the hind leg of the same side. This is possible only when the horse is straight and takes an even contact with the bit. At the same time the action of the rein passes through the hand, shoulder, and back of the rider and influences the horse's back. The horse steps with his hind legs under the elastic back and through the elastic neck into the rein of the same side. In order to obtain this action the correct seat of the rider is of the utmost importance. If the upper part of his body falls behind the vertical, the horse's hind legs will push the weight instead of carrying it. If his body leans forward it will check the forward movement, push the forehand into the ground, and fail to activate the hind legs.

If the horse is overbent the action of the rein does not pass through the body but goes out through the withers. If the horse is above the bit the action of the rein will come to an end at the neck. If the horse accepts the bit on one side only, the action of the rein will escape on the opposite side and lose its effect.

9. *Raising the Head and Neck by the Action of the Hindquarters*

To improve the balance of the horse it is necessary to raise the head and neck. This can be achieved only with the increase of correct collection. The rider must never try to achieve it by forcing the head up with the reins. The position of the head must be maintained while the forehand is carried higher by the lowering of the hindquarters. This will make the horse appear higher in front, his movements will be freer, and the hindquarters will be lowered by the bending of the three joints of the hind legs. The hind legs, on which the brilliance of the paces depends, must act with more energy and the tracks of the hind feet must step into or in front of those made by the forefeet. In fact, the hind legs may be compared to the engine of a motor car which produces the power for movement.

The connection between raising the head and neck and collection has been one of the most misinterpreted notions of equestrian art. Throughout the whole of the development of this art, up to the present day, misunderstanding of this subject has been the cause of mistakes which have had the opposite effects to those that were required.

Impulsion and the purity of the paces is the ultimate object of dressage, which can be obtained only by the correct position of the head and the raising of the forehand brought about by collection. This cannot be repeated too often and must be the guiding line throughout the whole training. The position of the head and neck will develop in the same ratio as the progress in training and will show the degree of training the horse has reached.

The degree to which the neck can be raised will be decided by the conformation of the horse. It will be less with a horse that is weak in the hindquarters and back. In this case, if the rider demands too much the horse will drop his back and will not be able to bring his hind legs under the body. Horses with weak backs will be inclined to raise their heads too high and will drop their backs under the weight of their riders, which will cause them to make incorrect paces and show signs of nervousness through discomfort.

At first the horse should learn to carry his rider with a straight back and seek contact with the bit by lowering his head. Only then will the rider, by use of the pushing aids, be able to make the horse step more under the body with his hind legs and, by restraining him with the reins, cause him to round his back and raise his neck so that his crest comes nearer to the rider. Care must be taken that the under part of the neck does not become convex, producing a bulge as with a goitre, which can occur when the reins are incorrectly applied.

In the collected paces and with advanced horses the degree to which the forehand should be raised will be greater than in the extended paces. As already stated, misconceived methods of raising the forehand have always led to confusion, but the conscientious rider who follows the correct principles of classical equitation will reap his reward. The rider who concentrates on riding his horse forward on the bit and makes him step well under the body with his hind legs, thus making him raise his forehand correctly, will achieve much greater success than a rider who thinks only of raising his horse's head with the reins without pushing him forward.

10. Bending

Bending will increase the horse's suppleness and proficiency and help to eliminate stiffness. The horse may be bent laterally

ABOVE: *straight horse with correct bend* BELOW: *crooked horse, his hind legs not stepping into the tracks of the forelegs*

as well as longitudinally. The *lateral bend* is easier to obtain and, therefore, should be practised first. This bend consists of a regular and even curve from the poll to the tail. The ribs on the inside will be somewhat compressed and the body arched to the outside.

Different degrees of this bend are necessary when riding large or small circles or turns in order to enable the horse to perform these exercises not only with suppleness and with his centre of gravity below that of his rider, but also with regularity and in full balance.

A slight bend to the rein on which the horse is being ridden should always be demanded from a trained horse in an arena even when on a straight line. In a lateral bend the inside leg of the rider is the centre round which the horse is bent. As a rule the horse should be bent only when he is in motion, but to begin with a young horse may be bent when at the halt to introduce him to the rein aids for bending.

The lateral bend is correct when the horse is bent in the neck not more than in the whole body and when he flexes at the gullet. Every horse will allow himself to be bent more easily to one side than to the other, even exaggerating the bend on this side and making himself stiff on the other. The rider must try, by systematic training, to make his horse equally supple and elastic on both sides.

The *longitudinal bend* is of the utmost importance for the suppleness and elasticity of the paces, but it should not be attempted until the horse has mastered the lateral bend. It consists of bending all three joints of the hind legs accompanied by flexing the gullet equally on both sides.

The correct bend of the hind legs must be brought about by all three joints being bent equally and to the same degree. If the hocks only are bent, as is often the case, the bend will be of little value and the horse will be prematurely worn out as in all likelihood it will lead to spavins or thorough-pins. In this case, in spite of the appearance of activity in the hindquarters, these horses will move with tense and wooden steps and will be uncomfortable for the rider.

Horses with normal conformation will find no difficulty in correctly bending the three joints of the hind legs. Those with overbent hocks (sickle hocks) will tend to bend this joint too much to the neglect of the others, which will not become elastic, with the result that the strides will not go sufficiently forward. Horses with straight hocks will have greater difficulty in bending them and, therefore, the increased bend should be asked only gradually. The exercises to increase the bend of the joints of the hind legs should not be asked until the muscles and sinews have been strengthened and made supple. Forcing a horse to bend his hind legs before he is properly prepared will lead only to resistance.

As a car without springs would give an uncomfortable ride over a bumpy road, so would the movements of a horse be un-

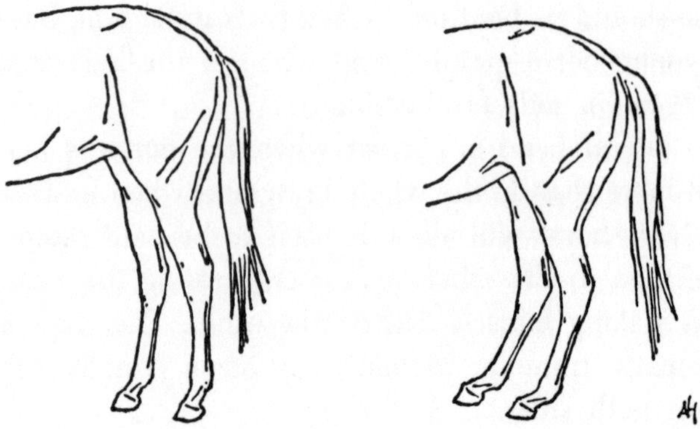

LEFT: *straight hocks* RIGHT: *sickle hocks*

comfortable when his hind legs are not properly bent. When all three joints of the hind legs are equally bent they will develop the elasticity of springs and create the activity of the hind-quarters that is necessary for regular movements full of impulsion and brilliance. They will impart suppleness to all paces, which the rider will feel in the pleasant movements of his horse. One of the basic requirements of a dressage horse has then been fulfilled.

As the horse becomes more supple and the bending of the joints of the hind legs has developed, the proficiency and balance of the horse will be improved. This will be seen in the increased collection and the smoother contact with the bit. Although the importance of attention to detail is recognised, the rider must never allow himself to be so absorbed in any one factor that he forgets the whole. Progress must never be one-sided. Every factor must be reviewed to ensure level progress throughout the whole training, just as the painter steps back from his easel when working on details to review his entire painting.

Before starting a contest the athlete will give special attention to loosening and suppling up his muscles and joints. In the same way the rider must supple up his horse by correct bending exercises before demanding more difficult ones. This is even more important with a horse as he may become tense when hampered by his rider's weight. These tensions should not be overlooked if suppleness, proficiency, balance, and even stamina are not to be adversely influenced. Moreover, tension may be the cause of physical damage, for a sharp movement of the horse, if not properly absorbed, may cause contusions. During the entire training suppling up before the beginning of proper work must be carried out with great care.

That is why bending—not overbending—is so important.

11. *Aids*

The principles of training would be incomplete if they did not include the means of communication between horse and rider.

If success is to be obtained the highest standard of understanding must be reached between the two living creatures concerned. This is as true for the commanding partner, the rider, as it is for the executing one, the horse. The rider must be a psychologist in order to understand, from the smallest signs, the behaviour of his horse and act accordingly. To be successful he must have the same qualities as a good teacher and know how to make himself understood by the pupil entrusted to his care.

At all times riding masters have tried to compile a means of communication between horse and rider—instructions, as it were, from the director to the executing partner. In the oldest book on riding in existence, Xenophon writes about aids and punishments. To these two mediums for the education of the horse another might be added, namely, rewards, which could even be placed before punishments. In his book (1623) Pluvinel stated that "the art of riding is based on reward and punishment."

These three factors are the elements of communication between horse and rider, and being the language between the two, they must be clear and simple. As the child is taught single words before full sentences, so must the horse gradually learn what is demanded from him by the different aids.

Equestrian language has coined the word "aids" to give it

a deeper meaning than orders. The rider should aid his horse to understand him; this means that the horse should never be afraid of the aids and that the rider has sufficient patience to be sure his horse understands what is demanded of him. The rider must have an exact understanding of his aids and their effect, and must make use of them intelligently; he must not allow himself to be influenced by his feelings. To follow this policy must be the constant aim of every good and successful rider.

There is a close relationship between aids, punishments, and rewards. Correctly and justly applied they will prove their value as a means of education and will complement each other in the course of training. The actions of aids and punishments may overlap because every aid can be increased to the degree of punishment. Therefore, the different aids should first be carefully considered before resorting to punishment, always remembering that reward is of greater importance than punishment. The rider must have not only a thorough knowledge of the means at his disposal, but also be able to decide at what moment and to what measure they should be applied. The number of aids is limited, but they can be applied in a great number of different combinations. The aids are addressed to the following senses of the horse: sight, hearing, and responsiveness to touch. Sight plays the smallest part. Its main role is to convert the horse's natural fear of strange objects or of human beings into confidence.

Hearing is of greater importance. The hearing of the horse is extremely well developed and far more receptive to any variation of sound than is generally assumed. The old riding masters made use of this fact and employed certain melodies for different exercises. These methods do not appear to have been of great value for otherwise they would have been made more use of in modern times. The fact remains that the horse will react well to the tone of voice. A smooth and quiet tone will tend to calm him and will be accepted as a reward, whereas rough words will convey a threat or even a punishment. The click of the tongue or the sound of the riding whip may be used as a stimulation, as may also the crack or the sound of the lash of the long whip being dropped on the ground.

The greatest number of aids are addressed to the horse's responsiveness to touch, to such an extent that in the fully trained school horse it must be the only means of conveying the rider's will. For this reason it is most important to preserve and develop the sensitiveness of the horse's mouth, and to cultivate and make use of the reactions of the horse's body to the legs of the rider. The distribution of the weight will also influence the movements of the horse, so that the upper part of the rider's body plays an important part in giving the aids.

The aids are thus divided into those which can be heard and those which a horse feels, with the latter divided into visible and invisible aids. The ultimate objective of training must be to guide the horse with invisible aids. Two creatures, the one who thinks and the other who executes the thought, must be fused together. This is the ideal of classical riding. For this reason the dressage tests demanded at the Olympic Games must be ridden without a whip and without the use of the voice. In spite of this, few riders today are sufficiently expert in the art of classical riding to perform the movements with invisible aids. Rather, they may often be seen presenting their horses while working with hands and legs and swinging their bodies.

The aids as a whole may be classified as follows:

Pushing aids: leg aids, weight aids, click of the tongue, spurs, riding whip and long whip.

Stopping aids: rein aids, back and weight aids.

Preventing aids: leg aids, unilateral action of the reins.

The degree of the aids must depend on the sensitiveness of the horse as well as the phase of his training. An aid strong enough to obtain the required effect with a lazy or inattentive horse could be looked upon as a punishment with a more sensitive one.

The aids may be subdivided according to the degree of their application: refined, increased, and strong. The co-ordination of the different aids must never be overlooked. Strong aids should rarely, if ever, be applied to green horses; with a thick-skinned or unresponsive horse they should come into action only for a short while and must be replaced as soon as possible by increasing aids. The increasing aids will begin with a light application and gradually be increased, without roughness, until the horse reacts. This is the first step towards the refined aids to which the horse must react upon the slightest application. This is the path to the invisible aids.

As a sculptor would first shape his future work of art from a rough stone with swift and strong blows of the chisel and, as it progresses, work on the details with ever more delicate strokes in order to produce the finished article in all its beauty, so must the aids of the rider become more and more refined as the training proceeds. The rider must always remember this and be careful not to be carried away by impatience or temper and destroy with rough aids what he has built up in his previous work. Following the parable of the sculptor it would be the same as if, by a careless or coarse stroke of his chisel, he destroyed his otherwise satisfactorily emerging work.

Progress is the essence of training. The rider's legs from the thigh downwards must be in touch with the horse's body. The lower legs on the girth or immediately behind it will make the horse's hind legs step more under his body and make him go forward with energy. The effect of the legs must become more and more refined in the course of training. With a green horse this aid will at first be a short and distinct action of the lower leg. When the horse has responded, the rider's legs will remain in touch with the horse's sides in the normal position in accordance with the correct seat. There is nothing worse for training than legs that are continually kicking the horse's sides; in the end, the more the legs worked the less would be the response. It is equally wrong to maintain a strong pressure on the horse's sides, as this would only tire the rider and make the horse unresponsive to the legs. The pressure of the rider's legs must be decreased the moment the horse has responded to his demands.

When the leg is correctly applied, the heels should be low and the muscles of the calf tightened, so that the horse, with correctly rounded body, will receive the stimulation to go briskly forward from the application of the rider's thighs, knees, and calves. In the course of training, the aids of the legs must become refined to such an extent that the horse will react to the rider's simply pressing more firmly into the stirrup.

Both legs applied on the girth will push the horse forward; the single leg applied behind the girth will have either a preventing effect that will stop the hindquarters deviating to that side or falling out, or, if the pressure is increased, will make the horse yield with the hindquarters to the opposite side. One leg pushing forward on the girth and the other pushing sideways behind the girth will make the horse go forward and sideways, that is to say perform lateral work.

The pushing aids can be supported by the aids of the rider's back. The back aids are of much more importance than is often supposed. If the upper part of the body is taken slightly behind the vertical line, while the rider remains firmly in the saddle, the horse will go forward. Wonders can be achieved if the body is inclined backward when the legs are applied and at the same time the reins are given, especially with a young horse that will not approach a certain object. These visible back aids must be used only at the beginning of training; the well-trained horse should go forward when the rider sits deeper into the saddle.

When the weight of the body is transferred into the direction of the lateral movement, it will support the effect of the outside leg because the horse will try to step under the centre of gravity of the rider. A man carrying another on his shoulder will step to the left side and not to the right if the burden leans to the left.

For the school horse it will be an aid if the rider sits a little more firmly on the seat bone in the direction of the movement. On the other hand, the rider should be warned against twisting his body as many do when trying to teach a new exercise to a horse. Aids of this kind are incorrect. Why should a horse be taught by aids that would later have to be replaced by others? These aids are unsightly, whereas rider and horse should always be a pleasure to look at.

As has already been mentioned, horses have a good sense of hearing. For this reason the click of the tongue will assist the other pushing aids to make them go forward, but the rider must be careful not to make too much use of this aid as the horse would soon become accustomed to it and cease to respond, as happens with a too active leg. This is one of the greatest dangers to success in training. Also, the rider must be careful that the click of his tongue is heard by his horse only and not by others present.

The spur should be used only in an advanced stage of training, and only when required to reinforce the pushing aids. The use of the spur is the last resort and, as with other things in life, the last resort should be reserved for emergencies. The spur should touch the horse's side with an increased pressure of the leg and the application should be discontinued the moment the aid has obtained the required result. The spur should never be used sharply as an aid, because it would then no longer be an aid but a punishment.

The rider must take great care not to make too much use of his spurs. There would be the danger of the horse becoming unresponsive and the rider would lose his last resort. Jerky movements, nervousness, and twisting of the tail are often the result of incorrect use of the spur.

The riding whip is another pushing aid; it can be used with young horses and when making greater demands with advanced horses. The use of the whip begins with just touching the horse's body and increases to a light tap but should never degenerate into a hard blow. The whip should be used just behind the rider's leg, but with very young horses it may be used on the shoulder. It is used behind the girth to support the sideways pushing aid, or to teach respect for the preventive leg. The rider should avoid touching the hindquarters with the whip, especially with young horses, as this may lead to kicking.

The use of the long whip demands very carefully considered action. It may be used by the instructor or an experienced man to support the rider's legs, in order to help him with a young horse, or with the more difficult exercises. Experience is necessary because, when using the long whip, the difference between aid and punishment is very indistinct. The horse should never be afraid of the whip, as it would then be of no use as an aid. It should give the horse energy and make him move more briskly, but should never make him jump away in fear. Generally it would be sufficient to show the whip to the horse in order to make him go forward or sideways. If the trainer wants to push his horse forward he must take a position more towards the hindquarters than the shoulders, but, if his object is to push the horse sideways, his position must be more towards the shoulder. If showing the whip to the horse does not obtain the required result, the point of the whip may be raised and dropped on the ground in the direction of the horse. Finally, this aid may be further increased by lightly touching the horse with the lash on the spot where the leg aids should be applied. The long whip should never be applied to the legs or quarters of the horse; this would only irritate him, cause unlevel steps, and make him kick.

The use of the long whip is of value only when it is used in conjunction with the rider's pushing aids. As the obedience of the horse to the aids increases so must the assistance of the whip be withheld until, finally, it is discontinued. When the horse has responded to the use of the whip, he should be shown it or even caressed with the handle and made much of in order to prevent him from becoming afraid of it.

All aids must take into consideration the sensitiveness, the temperament, and the degree of training of the horse. The horse must never be frightened or surprised by the aids.

The aids of the reins are the counterpart to the above-mentioned aids: they control the forward urge of the horse. By carefully adjusted co-operation with the pushing aids, they improve the carriage, collection, and raising of the forehand and thus assist the physical training of the horse. The rein aids also direct the horse into the direction demanded by his rider. They should be applied in short actions and never revert to pulling or jabbing. The pressure of the bit on the bars should be gradually increased and then gradually decreased, but not given suddenly.

The above-mentioned aids consist of taking and giving, the latter being of the greater importance. The action of the reins will consist of repeated short actions in order to allow them to pass through the body and not to be held up, as it were, by the horse stiffening because the taking aids are too prolonged. With young horses the whole arm of the rider must be employed to give the aids, but the ideal action of the reins with a fully trained horse will be brought about by the rider simply turning his hands without moving his arms, elbows, or shoulders. To be able to give the aids by simply turning the hands is the ultimate aim of training and can be achieved only by long and systematic work. A well-trained horse will immediately respond to a rider just closing his hand as if squeezing water out of a sponge.

The taking, yielding, and holding aids will be distinguished by their effects. The taking action of the rein will make the horse follow with his head and neck and turn in the direction of the applied rein. The action should be as short as possible in order to prevent the horse from becoming dull and unresponsive. As soon as the horse answers, the aid will be changed to a yielding one. If, with a young horse, the first action with the reins does not lead to success the reins should yield and the action be repeated until success is obtained. The action of the reins must never degenerate into a steady pull; this would lead to a tug-of-war between horse and rider, and the horse, having the greater power, would be the victor. The action of the reins should never be applied from a loose rein, as this would lead to a jerk.

The unilateral action of the rein will make the horse turn and, with the support of the other rein, will influence the hind leg on that side, thus reinforcing the sideways pushing aids of the rider to prevent the quarters from flying out. The action of the inside rein supports the rider's inside leg and prevents the hindquarters from falling in, whereas the action of the outside rein will influence and reinforce the outside leg behind the girth, which will prevent the quarters from falling out. This outside rein will define the degree of the position of the horse's head, the lateral bend of the body, and the size of the turn. If the outside rein is not applied the horse will not execute a turn but follow the action of the inside rein by bending only his neck.

When riding on the track in an arena, the side nearest to the wall is known as the outside and the other side the inside, but when inside the arena away from the wall, the side towards which the horse is bent is known as the inside and the other the outside. The rein is named according to the direction to which the horse is being ridden or to the side to which he is turning, for instance when turning to the left he is on the left rein and vice versa.

The rein aids will be effective only when used in co-operation with the back aids of the rider. With the support of the rider's braced back the action of the reins will decrease the tempo and increase collection. Rein aids alone, without the assistance of the back aids, would merely make the horse lie on the bit or even get out of control.

When the rider's back is braced, the action of the reins on the horse's mouth is transferred through the hands, shoulders, and spine of the rider to the muscles of the horse's back and hindquarters. The important role of the rider's body is to co-ordinate rein and leg aids; therefore, the rider's seat must be independent and well balanced. If this is not so, the incorrect position of the body may falsify the effect of the aids. If the rider leans forward while his seat remains in the saddle he will drive the horse's forelegs into the ground and prevent the hind legs from coming under the body.

With a straight horse, the action of one rein will have a checking effect on the hind leg of the same side. The action of both reins will, therefore, make the horse reduce his speed.

The co-ordination of all aids, especially of the pushing and stopping aids, is of the utmost importance. Experience has taught that the rider should never push more with his legs than he can control with his reins, or hold with his hands more than he can absorb with his legs and seat. This gives the individual measure of the degree of the aids. Most riders will have an inclination to hold more with the reins than they can control with their legs; therefore, the rider must always work from rear to front to ensure that the horse does not take too firm a contact with the bit.

At the Spanish Riding School the *Unilateral Half-halt* is considered to be of great importance with horses that take an uneven contact with the bit or are stiff on one side. The rein on which the horse does not accept the contact is firmly applied, and the increased position of the horse's head to this side is corrected by short actions of the rein on the opposite side, making the head and neck straight. These short actions must be supported by the rider's legs pushing forward and the half-halts must be repeated until the contact is equal on both sides. The regular forward movement must not be interrupted by this aid.

As with all principles of the art of riding, the aids, to be successful, must be correctly co-ordinated. Special attention should be paid to applying them always in the same manner in order not to confuse the horse.

The horse clings to his habits more than any other living creature. He will notice the least change in his surroundings or in the arena. Sometimes he will not feel at ease in a strange arena and his attention will be distracted by other horses working near him. This would show itself in inattention to his rider. The aids will help the rider to hold the attention of his horse both physically and mentally in spite of what is going on around him, so that he will concentrate entirely on his work. Sometimes he will be induced by boredom to cause difficulties by shying or bucking without any cause, just to enjoy himself. This should not be allowed. Once more it must be impressed upon the rider that the pushing aids are of greater importance than the restraining aids. The range of aids that the rider has at his disposal will make him realise this fact. The whole line of conduct, including the aids, upon which the art of riding is based may be summed up in a simple sentence: "Riding forward is the essence of correct training."

12. *Punishments*

Throughout the centuries, the punishment of the horse has been one of the most controversial aspects of the art of riding. The ancient Greeks tried to understand the mentality of their horses and to educate them with kindness. Xenophon, in 400 B.C., wrote: "Young horses should be trained in such a way that they not only love their riders, but look forward to the time they are with them." Contrary to this attitude, the riding masters of the Middle Ages employed very rough methods. Thinking that punishment proved the best means of education, they did not even try to make their horses submit by normal treatment. The aim of their training was the subjection of the horse. In order to make them obey, the horses were subjected to every sort of punishment, and it was no concern to the trainers how many horses were spoiled or broken down in the course of training. The cruel bits and other instruments of torture employed in those days and exhibited in museums are proof of this fact.

Pluvinel, at the beginning of the seventeenth century, was the first riding master to oppose these methods, and he started a campaign against his contemporaries, especially against de la Broue—a campaign which at first seemed to be fruitless. But after his death, these more humane methods were accepted and prepared the ground for the instruction of Guérinière. Anyone today reading de la Broue's advice on how to treat a horse that ran away would find his hair standing on end. And yet contemporaries placed de la Broue's methods far above those of Pluvinel. Luckily for the reputation of the art of riding, Pluvinel and Guérinière had many followers who influenced teaching throughout the years that followed. This not only saved the art of riding, but proved of great benefit to the horse.

With the general decline of culture in this century, which has influenced the art of riding, punishment of the horse has crept back into the system of training. There are riders today who attribute greater importance to punishment than to the correctness of the aids. Some of the exhibitions that may be witnessed in public are horrifying and make one wonder to what extent such scenes occur in private. Without doubt any punishment is wrong if the knowledgeable onlooker is unable to understand for what reason the punishment is administered. And in such a case how should the horse know why he is punished?

The rider with high ambitions and little knowledge will be more inclined to revert to punishment than will the more experienced rider. He will try to obtain by force what he cannot achieve by the correct use of the aids as taught by the classical school.

This is not to say that when dealing with a difficult horse the required standard can always be achieved without punishment. But for the welfare of the horse and the honour of equitation, punishment should be restricted to what is necessary for education. The value of punishment should never be over-rated and employed as a substitute for correct aids.

Before administering punishment the thinking rider should ask himself three questions:

(1) Is punishment necessary? If there is any doubt it is better to postpone it than to be unjust.
(2) What kind of punishment is appropriate and to what degree should it be applied?
(3) When should punishment be applied?

With reference to (1), before administering punishment the rider must be sure that the horse is disobedient and not that he has misunderstood or been unable to follow his rider's command. This decision is most important. To punish a horse when he has not understood a command or is unable to carry it out would shake his confidence in his rider and interfere with his progress in training. Moreover, unjust punishment or punishment which is not understood may lead to opposition. If the horse becomes aware of his strength he will measure his power against that of his rider, a situation to be avoided at all costs. On no account must a horse be punished if he is afraid, as then the fear of punishment would be added to the fear of the object that frightened him.

6 Young horse on the longe

7 Correct position of a school horse on the left rein

8 Extended trot

9 Shoulder-in

(2) The rider must have an exact knowledge of the temperament and sensitiveness of his horse. He must also take into consideration the horse's intelligence and the degree of training he has reached. Only when he has considered these points can he decide the appropriate punishment. It will be necessary to apply more severe punishment to dull and lazy horses than to those that are temperamental or overeager. With the latter an increased aid may even suffice as a punishment. Sufficient punishment to meet the purpose will improve the training, whereas punishment that is too rough or ill controlled will do the reverse.

(3) With children and horses the punishment must immediately follow the disobedience or its effect will be lost. Neither will understand why he is being punished in the evening if the fault was committed in the morning. If the rider is unable to administer punishment immediately he should not do it at all. No punishment is better than a punishment that is unjust or not understood. If a rider has been unseated by a bucking horse, there is no point in punishing his horse when he has scrambled back into the saddle and regained his stirrups. Unless the punishment is immediate the horse will not realise what it is for.

A selection of punishments is at the disposal of the rider and he must choose the one that is most suitable. If the horse refuses to go forward the rider has the choice of legs, spurs, riding whip, or long whip. If he refuses to reduce his speed a jerk of the reins may be required, but the top limit punishment must be used only when the others have failed.

As mentioned above, aids can be increased until they reach the degree of punishment. This applies especially to the leg aids. If the horse does not respond to a light pressure of the leg, the pressure must be increased until finally the spur is used. Care must be taken when using the spur that the rider does not take his legs away from the horse's sides, as then a sudden movement of the horse on feeling the spur might cause the rider to lose his seat and he would find himself in a position in which he would be unable to benefit by the success obtained by the spur. The punishment would lose its effect and the horse would be the victor.

As a punishment the spurs should be applied with a short action behind the girth, the rider maintaining the same position as when applying his legs firmly. The spur should not be used too far behind the girth as this might induce the horse to kick or buck. If he kicks against the spurs, they must immediately be applied again in the same spot. This must be repeated until the horse accepts punishment without opposition. Horses treated in this manner will, after a short while, no longer react against the spur. When using the spur the rider must consider its sharpness and the sensitiveness of his horse. He should never use spurs with such force that they draw blood, and their application should cease the moment the horse has responded. The foregoing remark applies to all punishment, and to a great extent to all aids. The rider must never forget that the spur, whether used as a punishment or as an aid, is a last resort.

It is not easy to distinguish between the use of the riding whip as aid or as punishment. A light tap will be considered as an aid, whereas a sharp stroke will imply punishment. When used as a punishment, the whip should generally be applied on the spot on which the aids are used, that is to say, immediately behind the girth; on rare occasions it may be used on the shoulder, but never on the neck or head.

In cases of particular insubordination the rider should take the reins firmly in his left hand and deal an energetic blow behind the girth with the whip in his right hand. This represents the highest degree of punishment and should be administered only on rare occasions when the behaviour of the horse justifies it, otherwise the horse would become frightened or cease to respect it. This type of punishment is best not applied in public. When necessary, however, it is more effective to administer one good blow than repeated, less severe strokes.

The application of the long whip is similar to that of the riding whip. The trainer should use it only on rare occasions as a means of punishment. If the horse, instead of going forward upon the use of the whip, insists on stopping or tries to kick against his trainer, the moment has come when the long whip must be used as a punishment in order to make the horse respect it as an aid. He should be dealt a few sharp strokes with the end of the lash until he stops kicking and goes forward. Once more, the use of the long whip as a punishment must be reserved for an emergency because, even more than spurs, the long whip is a last resort. Its use is the declaration of war, and the trainer should begin this fight only if he is sure of victory. Once he has started the fight he must carry it through to a successful end.

The whip should never be used on the forehand, neck, or head, and should not be applied to the hindquarters from above downwards as this would be likely to provoke kicking. The horse should be punished with the end of the lash in an upward direction. After punishment, steps should be taken to restore the horse's confidence. The trainer should approach the horse with the whip behind his back, speak to him, caress him, show him the whip, and finally stroke him with the handle. He should step back a few steps and encourage the horse to come to him. In this manner the horse will not lose his confidence in the whip. A horse that is frightened of the whip and tries to run away from it proves that the whip has been used in an incorrect manner.

Another punishment that should rarely, if ever, be used is a jerk with the reins. If the horse fails to respond to any giving and taking action of the reins or to an energetic half-halt, or if he lies on the reins with all his weight, or tries to run away, he may then be given a sharp unilateral action on one rein. But there is a danger that this conduct may disturb his contact with the bit and have a bad effect on the hind legs.

One of the milder punishments with an intelligent horse is to repeat the exercise until it is finally successful. Repeated halts will be the best punishment for the horse that tries to run away from the rider's aids. Remember, though, that these halts, if executed too sharply, would be harmful, especially if employed with young horses.

The rein-back is another useful punishment, but it must not be prolonged, as it would create pain in the hind legs and cause evasions from the horse. Even speaking sharply may serve as a punishment with some horses. In all cases it is most important that punishments be brought to an end the moment success has been achieved.

Punishment followed by reward will increase the confidence of the horse. It is hardly necessary to state that punishment must never be administered from temper or because the rider is in a bad humour. The rider should never forget that horses have long memories and are easily frightened. Every effort must be made to keep their confidence. As Xenophon said: "Punishment should never be given in anger because action committed in anger will later be regretted." Nearly 2400 years later the directions for Cavalry of the Austrian Army read: "Punishment must never be administered in anger."

The rider must always show himself superior to the horse in mental and physical self-control. Submission to his will should not be sought by force but by his superior intelligence.

13. *Rewards*

In most books on riding, punishments are discussed in much more detail than rewards. Grisone, in his *Instructions on Riding,* states that the horse would look upon it as a reward when his rider stopped punishment.

The rider has many different rewards at his disposal, from patting to giving sugar or other delicacies. There are many ways to gain the horse's confidence and regard in order to make him take pleasure in his work. The thinking rider will soon find out that his horse is not only grateful for any reward but will be stimulated to satisfy his rider.

If reward is to be of any value it must immediately follow the exercise. Unfortunately there are many riders who are quick to punish but forget about rewards and take the good performance of their partner for granted. The simplest way for the rider to show his appreciation is by patting or speaking with a soothing voice. Patting does not mean slapping the horse with the open hand to make as much noise as possible, which is often done to impress the onlookers; the horse's neck should be caressed fondly and delicately.

After a successful exercise, it is effective to walk for a while on a loose rein. The horse will soon accept this gesture from the rider—a break from the work—as a reward, and try to merit a repetition. It is interesting to note that Xenophon specified as a reward that the rider should, there and then, dismount and lead his horse back to the stable, not ride him back. Food or sugar after a successful exercise is another way of showing appreciation, provided it is given immediately.

This section on rewards should not be concluded without underlining that the reward selected should be appropriate to the character of the horse. Sensitive and affectionate horses will be satisfied with a caress, but more materialistic ones will prefer sugar or titbits.

From the manner in which rewards and punishments are administered, interesting conclusions can be drawn as to the character and mind of the rider.

CHAPTER III

THE TRAINING OF THE HORSE

The rider starting to train a young, green horse must have a definite idea of what he requires from his horse and the method by which he proposes to achieve it. The greater his knowledge and experience, the more quickly he will obtain success. But the thoroughness of the training should never be sacrificed to the temptation to gain results too quickly. Above all the rider must be warned against trying to hold too rigidly to a pattern and should give priority to individual education. Only then will he be able to perceive the many fine characteristics that will reveal to him the latent talent of his horse and that will help him to obtain the best results from his training in the easiest manner. Throughout the entire training the rider must develop his horse's mental and physical proficiency so that he will not only obey but also want to obey to the limit of his powers.

The first condition is absolute confidence of the horse in his rider who, by systematic work, must develop the abilities of his horse and make him supple and obedient. This is the basis of the entire training. As with children, so with horses, defects in conformation can be overcome by intelligent gymnastic training. The Spanish Riding School with its systematic and appropriate method of training might be considered an Academy of Equitation.

The rider must understand his horse both physically and mentally and base his training on the horse's natural abilities. By treating the horse as an individual he will get the best out of him without destroying his character. Furthermore he will be able to overcome faults in conformation and temperament, though the former will be easier to correct than the latter.

Horses that show greater intelligence are generally more sensitive and must be treated with greater care. Well-bred horses will not tolerate rough or unjust treatment, as they have a quicker understanding than those that are not so well bred and will object to unreasonable demands.

The first impression that the horse receives from man will lay the foundation of the later relationship. It can be stated that the majority of so-called vicious horses are not born vicious, but have become so by wrong treatment. Certain families have a reputation for being difficult. They may be high in courage and more difficult to handle than others, but is it not possible that because of their reputation the trainer approaches them with apprehension and by his subconscious attitude irritates them and converts their high courage into viciousness?

In most cases insubordination is caused by the horse's fear of his rider, by the fact that he does not understand what is required of him or is unable to execute an exercise for which he is not prepared.

With his first contact the rider must try to obtain the complete confidence of his horse, to make him understand what is required of him. His demands must be so clear that he is sure they are understood; only then can he expect obedience and be able to develop his horse physically by correct training.

The young horse will not get his first impressions from his rider but from the treatment by his groom. The importance of correct care in the stable cannot be emphasised too strongly with both the young horse and the fully trained one. Rough or unreasonable treatment may have a bad effect on the training, especially with shy or well-bred horses. Even with horses in an advanced state of training the efforts of the best rider may be adversely affected by bad treatment in the stable. If the highest standards are to be achieved the horse must be happy in the stable. Constant observation of the horse both in the stable and in the arena will help the rider to decide, when difficulties occur, whether the demands on the horse have been made too soon, or whether the cause is disobedience. As horses are for the most part good-natured, insubordination may more often be caused by overwork or pain than by disobedience. The amount of work to be given may be governed by the rule that the horse should return to his stable as fresh as when he left it. If he stands tired and dejected in his stable for hours after work it will be a warning that his rider should not overlook.

Before commencing work with a young horse the rider must remind himself that, besides being faithful to his habits, the horse has an extremely good memory. He will, therefore, try to anticipate the rider's aids if, from laziness or thoughtlessness, the exercises are performed on the same spot and in the same order. Xenophon has warned us against this, pointing out that the horse will no longer wait for the rider's commands, but having reached a certain point will perform the exercise of his own free will.

1. *The Young Horse in the First Phase of Training*

The training of the young horse begins in the stable when he is introduced to the new way of life and made familiar with saddle and bridle. Great care must be exercised the first time the bit is put in the horse's mouth. The trainer should talk softly to the horse to prevent him from being frightened, which might create difficulties later on. Much use should be made of the voice; whereas it is a mistake to shout at the horse, both trainer and groom will give him confidence by speaking softly. The saddle should be fitted while the horse is in the stable and he should be made accustomed to the feel of the girths. These should be placed sufficiently forward so that they are on the true ribs and to start with should be fastened only loosely, just enough to hold the saddle in place. If the girths are too tight they may cause uneasiness and the horse may blow himself out, rear up, or even throw himself down when he feels their pressure. At this stage every effort should be made to avoid a fight as it is so important that the horse should not realise his power and be encouraged to dispute the will of the rider.

Before starting the proper training the rider should have a

picture of the background of his horse and what he has done so far. The treatment would differ for a horse coming straight from the stud farm and for one that has already done some work.

The young Lipizzaner comes to the Spanish Riding School in his fourth year. He is a horse that matures late and only becomes fully developed in his seventh year; this must be taken into consideration in his training.

Because of the high demands to be made on these horses every effort is made to ensure that their health and soundness do not suffer. As a human being will age prematurely if worked too hard as a child, so will the useful life of a horse be curtailed if worked too hard when he is young.

The Lipizzaners remain at grass for the first three years of their life before being brought to the Spanish Riding School. In former times they were longed at the Stud Farm and broken to work in the carriage. This system did not prove successful as they showed an inclination to adopt bad habits and create difficulties with their tongues.

For the first eight to ten days after arriving at the School, in order to accustom him to his surroundings and the new ways of life, the horse is led in hand, at first without a saddle and later with a saddle with loose girths. When the horse has settled, longeing will begin. The first object of training is to make the horse familiar with his new and unaccustomed work. If this work begins under the rider he should not forget the youthfulness and inexperience of his horse and show leniency to his faults, overlooking playful bucking which is an expression of youthful gaiety to which the horse is entitled. On no account should the horse be punished, but the rider must make every effort not to be thrown off.

If the rider has sufficient experience—but only then—the early work will be made much easier by correct longeing.

WORK ON THE LONGE

The object of the work on the longe is to gain the horse's confidence, make him bow to the rider's will, teach him to balance himself without a rider, and increase his proficiency.

With the establishment of confidence, the foundation of obedience is laid. At the same time the horse will begin to learn the language of the aids.

Correct longeing is an art. It does not just mean making the horse run round in a circle; this would be no more than the task for an inexperienced person. A short definition of the term longeing must, therefore, be given before describing the work.

Longeing may be used for three different purposes:

(1) Exercising the horse.
(2) Training the rider.
(3) Training the young horse.

(1) This is useful when for some reason the horse cannot be ridden, or to supple him up and get rid of any stiffness before starting proper work. Side reins must be used and should be just long enough to help prevent the horse from running away, but he must not be allowed to go lazily round, dragging his feet. The object is to make the horse go on the circle with regular steps and free from any tension. Longeing may be compared to the loosening exercises of an athlete, and the trot is the best pace for this type of longeing.

(2) Will be used to train the rider how to sit on his horse and how to guide him. In order to obtain a correct seat, the side reins must be shorter as the horse must now go in a cadenced trot and canter as well as in different tempos. The demands will be increased as the rider gains progress. It would be of little value to try to train the rider on a lazy horse with bad action. On such a horse he would never develop a strong seat which is essential for an accomplished rider. When the rider's seat is sufficiently strong he will take up the reins and be taught how to guide his horse. The long whip will now be used only to help the leg aids of the rider.

(3) This use must be explained in detail as it is the most important of the three and many faults can be committed which will be responsible for difficulties in the later training. The trainer cannot be warned too often against longeing his horse

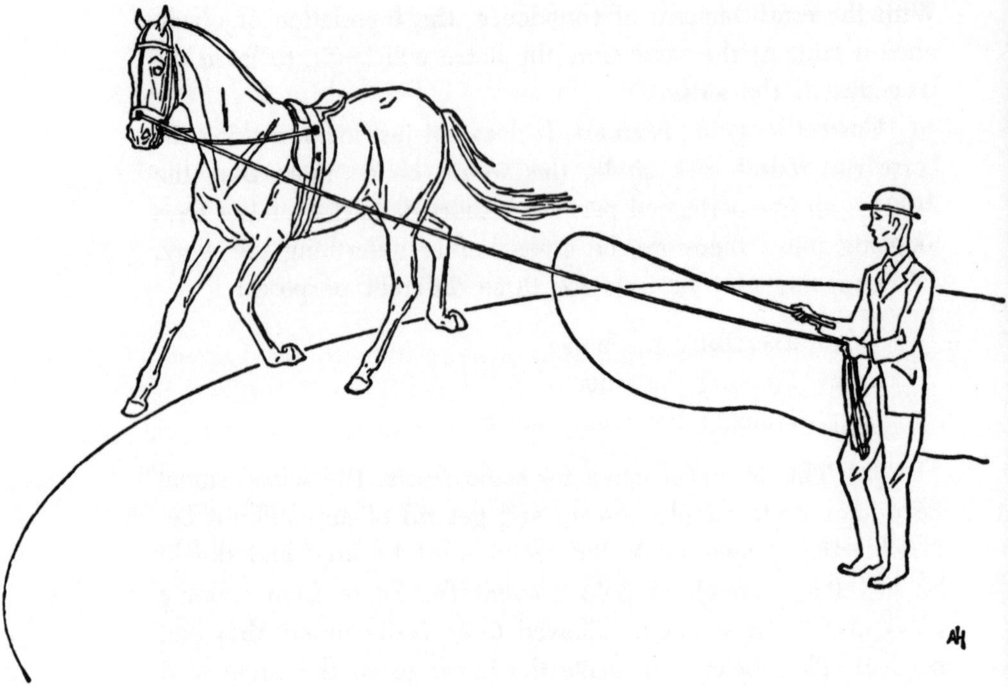

Work on the longe

on too small a circle as this has little value in training and may be the cause of physical damage.

It is on the longe that the foundation of obedience is laid and the horse becomes accustomed to being guided by having constantly to follow the turn required by the action of the longe.

The horse should be brought into the riding arena with a snaffle bridle and cavesson and a saddle with loose girths and without stirrups. The cavesson should be fitted in such a way that the noseband lies below the cheekbones and on the nose-bone, but not on the gristle below it. If fitted like this it will not interfere with the breathing of the horse by making the effect of the longe too severe. On the other hand, the cavesson must not be fitted so loosely that it could rub the horse by sliding backward and forward on the nose. The chin strap should be fitted underneath the snaffle and must not be too tight; the horse should be able to open his mouth wide enough to accept titbits. The throat latch is fastened on to the cheekpiece at the height of the horse's eye.

The girth should be sufficiently tight to prevent the saddle from slipping. After a while the girths should be tightened as required for riding. With a young horse the saddle is likely to slip forward, and it should be immediately adjusted to the proper place.

The side reins should be attached either to the longeing surcingle, which goes over the saddle, or to the front girth strap. This will prevent the saddle from being pulled forward, which could happen if the reins were put round the girth. To start with the side reins should be so long that they have no effect on the horse's mouth. For the first lesson on the longe two men will be required, one to hold the longe and the other the long whip. Later both these duties can be performed by the trainer.

The young horse will be led into the centre of the arena where he is to be longed. The trainer will very quietly fasten the longe into the centre ring of the cavesson and buckle the side reins as explained above. The assistant with the long whip will hold it in his left hand and, with his right hand, lead the horse on a circle to the left. Experience has taught that the horse will understand work on the longe quicker on this rein. The trainer will hold the longe in the hand on the side to which the horse is working and the slack of the longe in the other. When the services of the assistant are dispensed with, he will hold the longe and the slack in one hand, the whip in the other.

The centre of the circle which the horse describes must be the trainer's inside leg—the left leg if the horse is on the left rein. The trainer must pivot round this leg in such a way that a line drawn through his shoulders will be parallel to the longe.

After the horse has been led on the longe for some time, the assistant with the whip will slowly come into the centre walking beside the longe. He should stand close to the trainer and take the whip in the hand which is nearer to the horse, in this case the right hand. If the horse stops or tries to follow him towards the centre, he quietly leads him on the circle again. On no account should the assistant try to push the horse out with the whip. The horse will soon understand and go willingly on the longe. The exercise should begin at the walk, but if the horse breaks into a trot, the trainer should allow him to continue at this pace for a short time before taking him back into the walk. Much use should be made of the voice in order to calm the young horse and gain his confidence.

When the horse moves quietly round on the left rein, the same work will be performed on the right rein. This may prove more difficult to begin with, not only because the horse goes more easily on the left rein, but also because the assistant is usually able to use his whip better with his right hand. The trainer must never be carried away and punish his horse if he does not at once go as easily on this rein.

From the beginning, care must be taken that the horse is not overworked; he should be introduced only gradually to this unaccustomed effort. The circle on which he is longed should be as large as possible and he should not go for too long on the same rein. The period of work must be determined by the constitution and mentality of the horse. If he is obstreperous and does not settle he should be worked until he is obedient, but the trainer must not mistake fear for gaiety; it would be wrong to work a horse that tried to rush off from fear in order to settle him down, for on the next occasion this fear would be added to the fear of extra work.

During the first lessons it will be sufficient to longe the horse at the trot for two or three minutes and after a short rest the exercise can be repeated. Worked in this manner the horse will not become overtired and will not lose the briskness of his paces.

In this phase the horse must be made accustomed to the long whip. He must not be afraid of it so that later it can be used as an aid. The trainer should show him the whip while talking to him and caressing him. He should touch the horse's body with the handle of the whip and pass it gently over the hindquarters; the horse should not kick or show any sign of fear.

The long whip is a pushing aid and should not be used on the hindquarters but applied to the same spot as the rider's legs would be. The lash should never hurt the horse but should be allowed to fall by its own weight. In most cases it will be sufficient if the assistant drops the lash on the ground behind the horse or makes a quick step towards him. The whip should never be used on the head; apart from the risk of injuring the horse's eye, this could make him whip-shy, possibly for the remainder of his life.

If the horse tries to come into the centre of the circle, the assistant should point the whip towards him so that the tip touches his nose. In most cases this will make him remain on the longe. A horse is on the longe when he takes an even contact on the longe line which allows the trainer to regulate the size of the circle.

As already explained, the circle should be as large as possible. This will make it easier for the horse which up to now, while out at grass, has been accustomed to moving only on straight lines and will be likely to resent being asked to go on a smaller circle.

For the first few days on the longe the *side reins* should be so long that there is practically no contact. The trainer should be content if the horse moves calmly around on the circle. When this result has been obtained, the side reins should be shortened gradually until the horse can take a light contact. The neck must never be compressed in an unnatural way by too short side reins for this would have a bad effect on the horse's action.

When shortening the side reins, the horse must be kept moving forward at the walk while the assistant first shortens the inside rein and then the outside one. If this method is adopted there will be less chance of the horse, at the first feel of the reins, standing up on his hind legs and falling over backward.

Both side reins should be of the same length. On very rare

occasions the inside rein may be shorter but never the outside one. The shortened inside rein, added to the weight of the longe rein, will make the horse carry his head too much to the inside and the quarters will swing out. If the horse has a tendency to fight against the rein and carry his head too high the side reins should be fastened on the lowest "D" of the surcingle and, if this is not low enough, through the girth. With horses that carry their heads too low the side reins must be fastened higher. As a general rule with young horses the side reins should not be fastened too low as it may lead to resistance and encourage them to stand on their hind legs.

The side reins should be fastened into the rings of the snaffle above the reins. The horse should seek contact with a long neck and a lowered head which will help him to arch his back. He should not be allowed to raise his head and neck too high, which would cause him to drop his back.

The final length of the side reins should be such that the horse can adopt the position of head and neck required by a fully trained horse. This position may be obtained only after months of training on the longe by gradually shortening the side reins. In exceptional cases the correct length of the side reins will be obtained by lengthening instead of shortening them. This will be the case with horses that are inclined to rush off when on the longe. Then shorter side reins are employed to get the horse under better control at the beginning of training. They will gradually be lengthened to the correct length as the trainer obtains the tempo he requires.

As already mentioned, the most careful attention should be paid to the fact that when the horse is on the longe the contact must be light and elastic. The horse in his later training should take the same contact on the rein that he learned to take on the longe. Therefore, if the longe is to play its proper part in training the contact must be correct, neither slack nor too tight. As the long whip acts as a substitute for the leg aids, so the longe should play the same part for the rein aids.

The horse should never lie on the longe, which would make it difficult to hold him on the circle; nor should the size of the circle be decreased by the horse losing contact with the longe. If the horse leans to the outside the trainer should try to keep him on the circle by repeated short actions of the hand and not by a steady pull. If the horse falls into the circle he should be pushed out again by the trainer pointing the long whip in the direction of the horse's nose.

When the horse takes a correct contact with the longe the trainer can begin more advanced work. By vibrating the longe he will be able to reduce the tempo; if the horse begins to rush off he will be calmed down by these vibrations or circular actions of the longe against the movement and by the use of the voice.

The tone of voice, as we have noted, is important as horses have good hearing and will react to the pitch. A young horse that is being difficult will often be brought to reason by being shouted at. The horse's good hearing helps in yet another way, for if the trainer always uses the same word and tone for changing speed or halting, the horse will soon answer to the command.

If the horse overbends, the trainer will again use a circular action of the longe but in this case it will be the same direction as the movement while pushing the horse forward with the whip. The assistant, if there is one, will stand more towards the hindquarters. To start with the trainer should not interfere as long as the horse goes in a regular tempo and does not rush off. If the horse strikes off into a canter he should not be checked immediately, but the speed should gradually be decreased. If, on the other hand, he holds back when being asked to trot and breaks into a canter, the trainer should let him continue in the canter until he breaks into a trot.

The position is of little importance at this stage. The horse must first find his balance on the circle and learn to become obedient; he will also be strengthened by the work. When contact has been achieved by gradually shortening the side reins, the time has come to demand a correct position, which should be slightly to the inside. This position can be demanded by an appropriate action of the longe which consists of taking and giving at the same time as the whip pushes the horse forward.

This work must not begin too soon or the horse may try to avoid the discomfort of the position by throwing his hindquarters out, whereby he would evade the lateral bend, a fault difficult to correct on the longe. If the horse is pushed forward too soon, he may again, by throwing the hindquarters out, avoid the discomfort of stepping under the body with his hind legs and thus improving the longitudinal bend.

Another fault may appear if, in trying to obtain a more lively action (especially with a Lipizzaner), the trainer pushes the horse forward too energetically; the result will be that the horse will go faster by taking quicker steps instead of longer ones and will lose his rhythm. In this case it is better not to try to obtain more cadenced steps at the risk of encouraging a faulty movement that would have a bad influence on the trot.

When the horse takes a quiet contact on both the longe and the bit and has adopted the correct position, the trainer may demand *changes of tempo* from the horse which will increase his suppleness. Breaking into a trot and back again into a walk is a good exercise to increase his mental and physical powers. From the walk he must be pushed forward into a trot with the whip and at the same time taken forward with the longe. The same aids should be employed when increasing the tempo in order to lengthen the horse's strides.

Besides the pushing aid (the whip) and the stopping aids (the longe), much use must be made of the voice. The horse will understand the commands of the voice more quickly than any other aids and the trainer should use the media the horse can best understand. When the horse has understood this work and the aids, he is ready to be more collected by the pushing and holding aids and made to use his muscles more energetically.

At this stage the trainer may demand the *canter*, if the horse has not already produced it on his own. For the strike-off into the canter the horse should be drawn slightly into the circle by the longe, and when he is being made to go back onto the circle, he should be pushed forward with the whip pointing to the girth, which will make him strike off and do so with the correct leg leading. Bringing the horse into the circle and reducing its size will create more collection, which is the best preparation for the canter; by giving with the longe and again increasing the size of the circle, it will give more freedom to the inside leg and facilitate correct transition into the canter. The action of the longe has a restraining effect on the inside leg, which will have to take a shorter stride than that of the outside to enable the horse to go on the smaller circle. If the longe is not given, the inside leg will not have sufficient freedom to allow the horse to strike off. This is the reason why young horses will often canter on the wrong lead on the longe, in spite of the fact that it is less comfortable, because the trainer has not made it easier for them in the manner described above. If the horse drops back from the canter into the trot, the strike-off must be repeated calmly until he has achieved sufficient balance to remain in the canter.

The canter may now be made more brilliant by shortening the tempo and making the hind legs step more under the body. To do this the trainer makes the horse raise his forelegs more by a short action of the longe at the moment when the forelegs leave the ground. At the same time the horse must be pushed forward with the whip to maintain the movement. This is a typical example of the co-ordination of the aids.

At the end of each lesson the horse should be allowed to walk quietly for a while, the trainer making sure that it is a correct walk. He will then bring the horse into the centre of the circle by shortening the longe rein and calling the horse to him, the assistant remaining behind the horse. When the horse comes up to the trainer he should be made much of and the side reins and longe unfastened before he is taken back to the stable. The trainer and assistant ought to be particular always about details to set an example of correct methods: the longe must not be twisted, for instance, and the long whip should be held in such a way that it can come into action as a pushing aid at any moment.

The duration of training on the longe must depend on the conformation of the horse. Experience has shown that the longer the period of training on the longe, the greater will be the trainer's influence on the horse. The Lipizzaner stallions are longed for two or three months before work under the saddle begins.

The horse will be *mounted for the first time* before work on the longe is brought to an end. The horse must never be allowed to become conscious of his power and the possibility of defence, so every effort must be made to prevent him from throwing his rider. Once a young horse has succeeded in getting rid of his rider, he will always be liable to try to do the same thing again. On the other hand, rough methods should never be used to hasten the process of mounting; horses treated in this manner would always tend to be difficult to mount and try to throw their riders.

The horse should be made accustomed to the weight of the rider in the following manner. The rider slaps the saddle with the flat of his hand to prevent the horse being disturbed by noise coming from this area. He then places one hand on the pommel and the other on the cantle and is given a leg up, but remains for a short while with both legs on the same side. When the horse stays quiet without showing signs of fear, the rider may swing his leg over the horse's back and let himself down gently into the saddle. The horse must stand still, and the trainer should stand in front of him and hold the longe in such a manner that he will not make the horse afraid. Short actions of the longe should be made only if the horse moves. The trainer should calm the horse by speaking to him and patting his neck while the assistant with the whip stands behind the right hind leg of the horse to prevent him from creeping backwards. When the rider is mounting for the first time the horse should be given oats or titbits to occupy him. It would be a sign to be on the alert if the horse stops taking food and becomes tense. He may try to rear up or buck through fear of the unaccustomed weight. When the rider has succeeded in mounting the horse while standing still, the same procedure should be repeated at the walk.

When the young horse has learned to carry the rider quietly at the halt and at the walk, he must become accustomed to being mounted in the correct way. An assistant should hold the horse with his right hand on the cheekpiece of the bridle and press the right stirrup down when the rider puts his weight on the left stirrup. This is to prevent the saddle from slipping. Before mounting, both rider and assistant at a given signal should press down on the stirrups to accustom the horse to the weight. When the horse has become used to the weight on his back the rider will take up the reins and ride for some time on the longe before going around the arena.

Walk and a little trot with constant halts will accustom the horse to the rider's weight and teach him to be obedient. By soft actions of the longe the trainer should support the action of the reins until the horse follows the action of the reins alone; at the same time he will urge the horse forward in combination with the leg aids of the rider. Thus the habit of obedience to the rider's aids will best be achieved.

The practice of keeping the horse on the longe for the first lessons with the rider on his back will help control the horse, prevent him from playing up, and reduce the risk of accidents.

Work on the longe as described above will never be a waste of time. Horses three or four years old are not fully developed and if they are to stand up to the work required from them later, they must be worked slowly and with great care at this stage. If this early work were to be done under the rider, it could hardly be more than exercise and little would be learned. Whereas a horse longed by an expert will be made familiar with the aids, will learn obedience and balance, and will become stronger, with the result that when he is mounted he will be able to make better progress. For this reason the preparatory work on the longe is important for every riding horse.

UNDER THE RIDER

When the young horse has been prepared by work on the longe and has become familiar with his rider, it will be time to begin riding through the whole arena.

At first the horse will have difficulty in going straight

alongside the wall and may begin to sway. The reason is that he has found his balance on the circle by the systematic work on the longe, but not being accustomed to going straight he finds it more difficult. Another reason is the herding instinct which is in every horse—he will try to join his comrades in other parts of the school, and this the rider should avoid. As the rider's aids are not yet sufficiently effective, he will find it difficult to keep the horse straight. But these are only teething troubles and to be expected.

When breaking several horses at the same time it will be an advantage to have an assistant to lead the horses by the inside cheekpiece during the first lessons and have the horses go closely one behind the other. The distances between them can then be increased gradually until the horses are equally spread over the whole arena. They will then no longer follow their herding instincts but submit to the guidance of their riders. If the horses have been correctly worked on the longe this result should be obtained in a few days. If a horse comes to a halt and the rider cannot push him forward an assistant should lead him on quietly, but on no account drive him forward with the whip.

In these first days the rider should be content to make the horse go willingly along the wall; there should be no turns and the corners should be very round. When changing the rein the rider should change through the diagonal at a walk to begin with and be careful not to meet another horse on the way.

During work on the longe under the rider the long whip has reinforced the pushing aids of the rider's legs; now it will be necessary to reinforce these aids by touching the horse lightly on the shoulder with the riding whip. In the later training the whip should be applied immediately behind the rider's leg in the vicinity of the girth. When applying the whip great care must be taken not to interfere with the horse's mouth as this would not only annul the effects of the aid, but also irritate and confuse the horse.

At first the horse must be worked at walk and trot only.

As when on the longe, every period of trot must be followed by one at the walk to prevent the horse from getting tired; otherwise it would not be possible to preserve the liveliness of the paces and prevent the horse from dragging his feet. It is of great importance at this stage to decide on the correct amount of work to be given at each lesson. If too much is demanded the muscles and joints of the horse will be overtired and will not only create a bad influence on the paces but will also lead to resistance.

Accordingly it is necessary that the work of young horses always be carefully supervised. The best way is to take them in a group under the supervision of an experienced trainer. Young riders will be better suited for the first lessons of a horse than older ones. Apart from the fact that in all probability they will be lighter, they are likely to make less demands on their mounts. Experienced riders might, from sheer boredom, try to demand more from a young horse than his muscular development is capable of. Moreover, the young rider would be given the opportunity to gain experience in breaking a horse.

The instructor responsible for the training at this stage must thoroughly understand the physical and mental abilities and the temperament of each horse. This will enable him to build up his work correctly and gradually increase the demands, which will depend on the proficiency nature has given to each horse. Individual treatment will have the best results. Weak horses should be worked for shorter periods than stronger and more high-spirited ones; the former will be liable to drag their feet and forge. The instructor must not overlook the possibility that even horses that appear strong may have physical weaknesses. Any demand that exceeded their powers would give them a dislike for their work and shake their confidence in their riders.

Absolute confidence between horse and rider is the basis of successful training, and this confidence must be established from the beginning. Observing the horse after dismounting and in the stable will improve the relationship between horse and rider and enable the latter to draw conclusions from the behaviour of the horse as to the correct measure of work he should be given.

It is part of the individual training that horses with an inclination to hang back should be ridden forward more briskly and those inclined to rush off should be ridden more quietly and in a slower tempo. A regular tempo is important with all horses and more especially with a school horse.

Throughout the whole training of the horse, including the first phase, the trot plays the most important role in the work. It is better qualified than any other pace to make the young horse supple and flexible, to teach obedience, and to make the paces more rhythmic and regular.

In this stage the *rising trot* should be employed and the rider should ride on the outside diagonal, that is to say, he should rise from the saddle when the inside hind leg and the outside foreleg come off the ground and return to the saddle when the same diagonal returns to the ground. When breaking into a trot, the rider should sit in the saddle until the transition has been made and in the same way he should sit for the last few strides before the transition to the walk.

During the first lessons of riding around the arena the reins should be as long as possible without losing connection with the mouth. The term long rein should not be misunderstood. It does not mean that the horse is ridden on a loose rein or goes in an uncontrolled manner, as this could lead to a strained tendon, or have a bad influence on the carriage of the horse and his mental and physical development. Added to which the progress obtained by the work on the longe would be lost. The rider should recognise the difference between the long and the loose rein.

Only the unilateral rein aid should be employed at this stage when taking the horse through the well-rounded corners or executing turns when they are absolutely necessary. The inside rein only should be used without holding the outside rein. When the horse has become familiar with the new work, the *correct contact* can be taught. Any position of the horse's head and neck is correct at this stage as long as it enables the horse to take a quiet contact, carry the rider's weight willingly, and go forward with impulsion. Also in this stage of training a lower position of the head and neck, without being overbent, will meet the rider's demands better than having head and neck raised prematurely. This will be especially true with horses that have a weak back, which is the case with most young horses. By a lower position of the head and neck it will be easier for the horse to arch his back, step under the body with his hind legs, and carry the rider. Incorrect raising of the head will render difficult the correct activity of the hind legs even with horses with good conformation and will detract from impulsion and the beauty of the paces. Any position which has been obtained by sacrificing the purity of the paces is incorrect and a proof of ignorance in the principles of the art of riding.

At the beginning of training the horse will try to avoid the pressure of the bit; he will either lie on it or get above it, that is, by raising his head he will not accept the pressure on the bars of his mouth, or he will avoid the action of the reins by getting behind the bit. Horses that have sensitive mouths or that have been roughly treated will try to avoid the pressure of the bit by getting behind it or getting above it. Horses with weak backs and nervous temperaments will get above the bit, which will cause them to drop their backs. The rider must make every effort to regain the confidence of the horse in his bit. For some time the rider may allow a firmer contact, but on no account should the training be continued before any faults in contact have been eliminated. Improvement of contact will follow the progress in the rest of the training.

It must be remembered that a unilateral action of the rein aid without holding the other rein would only turn the head and neck of the horse to that side and influence the diagonal hind leg. It will, therefore, be seen that the use of the inside rein alone would influence the hindquarters, whereas, with the same action when the outside rein is held, the whole side of the horse would be influenced and especially the hind leg on the same side, thus compressing the horse on this side. As mentioned before, young horses should be guided by the unilateral aid to begin with in order not to confuse them, but as soon as they have become accustomed to this new work, it is essential for the future training that they should always be guided with both reins, especially in turns.

After a short period at the trot, the horse should be allowed to walk in order to rest; he should walk on a very long, or even loose rein, but the rider should maintain a lively walk. Premature collection at the walk is a great danger to the success of future training, as the horse may lose impulsion and adopt the habit of an uneven walk. The importance of making a young horse walk out must never be lost sight of; he must never be allowed to walk in a lazy fashion even when being given a rest.

At times, after the excitement of more intensive work, the horse when given a loose rein will hurry away with irregular steps. Should this happen with a school horse, it would point to faults in the basic training; with a young horse, he must not be pushed forward or it would lead to an unlevel walk. The rider must try to calm his horse down; he should sit a little more forward while keeping contact with his legs, should give and take with the reins and keep on repeating the action until the horse settles and walks calmly with unhurried steps on a long rein. When this happens the pushing aids may again be carefully applied in order to make the horse lengthen his stride.

To keep the horses' attention in the school it is a good exercise to let them walk towards each other and then turn away just before they meet. Turns and large circles should now be performed at the walk and the horse frequently brought to a halt before continuing the exercise. When coming to a halt, it is important that the horse should stand still on all four legs, and the length of these halts should be gradually increased to teach the horse to stand still quietly under the rider's weight. Even in this stage of training the horse must be made to stand still after the rider has mounted until he has been given the order to move on. There is nothing more trying, besides being a bad influence in the training, than to have a horse fidget about after the rider has mounted. It goes without saying that the duration of the halt after mounting a young horse must be only gradually increased. The best way to teach a horse to stand still is to bring him to a halt after work, standing firmly on all four legs, and to make him stand for a few moments before the rider dismounts. The horse will then consider dismounting as a reward and grow accustomed to standing still while waiting for the dismount.

When the horse goes willingly forward and allows himself to be ridden alongside the wall and through the corners, the moment has arrived when the rider can begin to *make him straight*. With all young horses and often with insufficiently trained older horses, the hind feet do not follow the tracks made by the forefeet but come away to the side; in other words, the horse is crooked.

Horses are narrower through the shoulders than they are through the hips. If the outer side of the body is parallel to the wall, the hindquarters are carried further into the arena than the forelegs. Also, by pushing his shoulder against the wall the horse can evade the guidance of the rider and cannot be turned so easily. On the other hand, which is a matter of greater consequence, he will be able to avoid, by this crookedness, the bending of the joints of the hind legs, thus escaping the gymnastic training of the hindquarters that is so necessary for balance and physical training.

With a straight horse the spine must be parallel to the wall, that is, the distance from the outside shoulder to the wall must be greater than that of the outside hip. This indicates the way to straighten the horse: the forelegs must be brought in front of the hind legs, which means that the shoulders of the horse must be taken away from the wall so that the hind feet will step into or in front of the corresponding footprints of the forefeet. Only when the horse is straight, when the hind feet follow the forefeet, will it be possible to bend the three joints of the hind legs to make them carry a greater proportion of the weight and thus obtain balance.

Both reins must be employed to take the horse away from the wall, while both legs push him forward. The action of the reins without the corresponding use of the legs would make the horse reduce his speed and the exercise would have no effect, for the horse can only be straightened if the speed is maintained during this correction. The rider must not try to bring the forehand in with the inside rein without holding the outside rein, as this would lead only to an increased position of the head and neck to the inside, not to a straightened horse.

If the horse leans to the wall with his shoulder and consequently evades the inside rein, the exercise *from the wall to the wall* will be of great benefit at this stage of training. When the horse has passed through the corner after the short side, he should be taken on a straight line to the centre of the school where his position is changed and he is taken back on a straight line to the wall from which he started, sufficiently far from the next corner so that he can pass through it without discomfort. This exercise will increase the horse's obedience and prevent leaning to the wall becoming a habit.

The first step in preparing the young horse to become a school horse is to develop the hindquarters so that their carrying power exceeds their pushing power. If the hind leg of the horse is to carry the same weight as the foreleg of the corresponding diagonal, it must be placed in the hoofprint made by the foreleg, which is below the centre of gravity, at the exact moment that the other diagonal leaves the ground. The horse can only develop good paces, in full balance, when the hind legs track up to the forelegs. Horses with normal conformation will find little difficulty in doing this, but a horse with a weak or lowered back or with weak hindquarters will have much greater difficulty in bringing the hind legs under the body. This fact must be taken into consideration when training and the work must be made easier for such horses.

As already explained, it is of great advantage when breaking in young horses to allow them to seek the contact with a lowered head and, from contact obtained in this manner, to proceed gradually to a correct position. This is still more important for horses with weak backs or weak hindquarters and the rider must not make the mistake of trying to raise the head and neck prematurely, for this would later make correct work

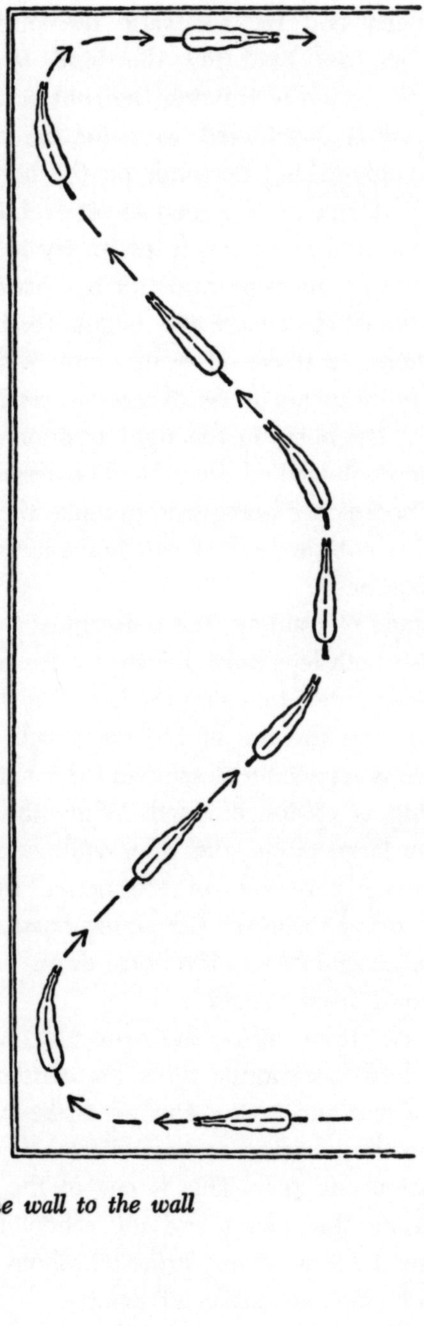

Exercise from the wall to the wall

more difficult. A horse that raises his head and neck more than his conformation or degree of training warrants will increase his speed and try to evade the pushing aids of his rider when he tries to bring the hind legs further under the body. In this stage of training the conformation of the horse must be constantly considered, even for the simplest exercises, in order to avoid making demands on the horse that he is not able to execute. It may be too soon as yet even to think of raising the horse's head and neck, much less to try to force it.

When work at the walk and trot has been established, but not before, *work at the canter* may begin. To start with the rider will ask the horse to strike off from a trot, which will be easier for him, and he must make use of the corners or the large circle which will put the horse in the right position to select the correct leg (commonly called "lead"). The corner into the short side of the school is the best place to make the first attempt because if it does not succeed, it can immediately be tried again at the next corner.

In this stage of training, the horse must be pushed forward at the trot with both legs until, helped by the turn in the corner, he breaks into a canter; touching the horse on the inside shoulder with the whip and the use of the voice will reinforce the leg aids. The voice is especially recommended for it will be available when the whip is no longer used. When the canter has been started on the large circle, the rider will then "go large," that is, use the wide perimeter of the arena, as cantering on a circle would be too tiring for the young horse. The canter must be brought to an end before the horse drops back into a trot on his own account from fatigue.

If the horse strikes off on the wrong leg (or lead) the rider should allow him to continue for a few strides before bringing him back to a trot and trying another strike-off. On no account must he bring the horse to an immediate halt, which would result in confusion and fear. This is one of the many differences between training the young and the school horse. The latter, as a punishment for a wrong strike-off, should be stopped immediately and made to strike off again.

If the horse when asked for a canter instead dashes off into a fast trot, he must not be allowed to strike off from this pace; he must be slowed down and calmed before being asked again.

The rider must be careful that the canter is practised equally on both reins or leads, as at this pace the inside and outside legs do not work evenly. The necessity of cantering equally on both leads must be underlined, as some riders are inclined to work more on the lead on which the horse finds the canter easier. This development of one side more than the other would create difficulties in the course of training. The further training now will improve balance and proficiency, increase obedience and attention to the rider.

The balance of the horse is best reflected in the regularity of the tempo and the rhythm of the steps, but while these qualities must be expected in the action of the horse at this phase, they should only be practised for short periods if perfection is expected later. To obtain a regular tempo, horses must be worked individually, but in all cases riding forward must be the main concern. This should not be misunderstood: riding forward does not mean rushing off with hurried, unlevel steps, but gaining ground to the front with ever lengthening strides in an even and regular tempo.

Lazy horses must be stimulated by legs and whip in order to create this forward urge, but the rider must distinguish between laziness and weakness. With the latter, shorter periods of work should be allowed in order not to discourage the horse by demanding too much. It cannot be repeated too often that one of the greatest faults a rider can commit is to demand more from his horse than is justified by his physical and mental condition.

A horse whose steps are naturally hasty should not be dealt with in the same way as a lazy one. Pushing him forward would destroy his paces completely. The rider should try to calm him down and help him to find his balance, and only then, by carefully applied pushing aids, should he try to obtain longer strides.

The rhythm of the steps will be the result of increasing proficiency and will be fully established only with a school horse.

The rider must remember, throughout this first phase of training, that he must not expect a perfection which can only be achieved with a fully trained school horse, just as the ballet dancer reaches perfection only after years of hard work.

The work with the young horse is now more or less completed. The object of this stage has been to gain the horse's confidence, to make him obedient, develop and strengthen his muscles, and improve his suppleness, efficiency, and stamina. The most visible result of this stage should be that the horse has learned to go straight and forward.

If the rider adheres conscientiously to these principles he will not depart from one of the chief aims of dressage, which is to obtain clear and pure paces. The object of correct dressage is not to teach the horse to perform the exercises of the High School in the collected paces at the expense of the elementary paces. The classical school, on the contrary, demands that as well as teaching the difficult exercises, the natural paces of the horse not only should be preserved but should also be improved by the fact that the horse has been strengthened by gymnastics. Therefore, if during the course of training the natural paces are not improved, it would be proof that the training was incorrect.

It must also be remembered that faults that have been allowed to become established during the early training, even though they come from freshness, will become a habit. If it is difficult for a human being to give up bad habits, how much more so it must be for a horse! Those faults that have not been clearly eliminated at this stage will appear again and again even when the standard of High School is reached, and especially when more difficult exercises are demanded. This underlines the necessity of a thorough basic training, a well-invested capital which will pay good dividends.

The training of the Lipizzaner stallions in the first stage is the same as that laid down by H. E. von Holbein for the first stage of training for the High School, that is, riding the horse on straight lines without collection in a natural position which he calls "forward riding." This stage of training will be of benefit to every riding horse and constitutes, as it were, the first step

10 Collected canter

11 Half pass to the right

12 Pirouette to the left

13 Halt

on the ladder that leads to the art of riding as set forth by Guérinière.

Another obvious benefit that will be derived from this phase of training is that by correct physical exercise the horse will become more beautiful in his movements and his appearance, just as the human body is made more beautiful by correct gymnastics.

Indeed, the proof of the correctness of training will be shown best by the increased beauty of the horse through the development of his muscles and the improvement in his carriage and movements. Over 2000 years ago Xenophon perceived that horses by correct training will become more beautiful but never less so. I would like to add that if a horse does not become better-looking in the course of his training, it will be a sign that the training is incorrect.

2. *The Young Horse in the Second Phase*

The training of the young Lipizzaner stallion in his first year is, as already explained, very slow and its principal object is the physical and mental development of the horse. In consideration of the late maturity of this particular breed it will not be up to the standards usually demanded from other breeds, so that the more serious work of training will not begin until the second year. As a general rule, after one year of training the young stallions will be ready for the second stage, but every horse must be considered individually. Those that have fallen behind in their development through sickness or immaturity should continue their work with the first-year horses.

Throughout the entire training of the horse the time taken should be governed by the constitution and the talents of the individual. Experience has taught us, however, that most of the young stallions will be equally up to the demands of the first and second part of training. Only in the further education of the horse will the time vary according to his physical and mental capabilities.

In the first year of training young and inexperienced riders may be used; they are even preferable as explained earlier in this chapter, but afterwards experienced riders with profound technical knowledge and physical abilities should be employed. This second stage of training is by far the most important one and demands the greatest dedication and consistency on the part of the rider. But this work will also be of great value to the rider himself, for a horseman who has never taken his horse through this stage of training will have difficulties in obtaining a thorough understanding of the art of more advanced horsemanship.

Because this phase is of such great importance for the training of a school horse, repetitions must be tolerated for the sake of thoroughness. As with the rider, so with the horse, only by repeated exercises can perfection be attained. By the same token a book of instruction can achieve its full value only if every detail is thoroughly discussed and clarified even at the risk of repetitiveness.

It is the rider who carries out the training of his horse. He must unceasingly control and observe him in order to be able to absorb and profit by every small sign of progress. A thinking rider will progress more quickly and easily than a rider who simply follows a rigid pattern. He will always have the experience of life before his eyes. There is no standing still: either he will go forward or he must go back. So with the training of the horse "resting means rusting." It is by his sense of feeling that the rider will recognise progress in the training. But this feeling needs to be constantly checked by an expert on the ground, for feelings are apt to mislead. Even an experienced rider may be taken in by a horse that has acquired a degree of suppleness and so can give a false feeling while committing errors which can be pointed out only by an observer on the ground. In this way faults may creep in that later on are difficult or even impossible to eliminate.

Feeling is as important to the good rider as hearing is to the musician. They will exist in various degrees of sensitiveness but both can be developed. When a rider registers a new feeling the instructor should explain the difference in the movements of the horse that has caused it. Although this difference in most cases is the result of a fault in the movement of the horse, it need not necessarily be so. Of all living creatures it is the horse that clings most to his faults, especially if they come from imperfections in his conformation. As with human beings, omissions in education when young will register throughout their whole lives, so faults that creep in now and have become habits will cause difficulties throughout the entire training and will be even more noticeable in the more advanced stages. Crookedness, irregularities in the mouth, and many other faults may be observed particularly in moments of nervousness, when the mental balance of the horse is disturbed.

The rider must realise that this early training may be of long duration. He will have to lay a sound foundation especially if it is his ambition to reach High School. The greater part of the training time, even as much as two thirds, may be required to consolidate this early conditioning. The rider will then have little difficulty in giving the last touches to his work of art. No time, be it ever so long, is lost in the consolidation of this basic training.

Just as the most perfectly made human being may appear as a puppet without a soul if not moving correctly and with grace, so a horse can only display his full beauty when able to move correctly with impulsion and suppleness. Correct movement is the cornerstone of the more serious work. It is no longer just a question of carrying his rider but of how correctly the horse moves in all his paces under his rider.

Weyrother said: "The first thing a horse must do is to move correctly." One could add: he must learn to move under his rider with elastic steps and a swinging back. Horse and rider should move as one body. A dancer must first obtain the highest degree of suppleness and balance before entering the sphere of ballet. But with a horse one has to overcome the added difficulty, namely, the weight of the rider to be carried in all movements and figures. Throughout the whole of this stage of training the fact that the correct movement is essential to all training must be kept continually before the rider's eye. The uninitiated will find it difficult to recognise progress in this stage, but the serious rider will feel it. A serious rider is one who will not think of adopting all sorts of tricks which would harm his four-legged pupil in order to astonish his spectators, but will recognise that his task lies solely in the education of his horse.

At the beginning of this stage of training it will, together with many other tasks, be an absolute necessity to make the horse take a *correct contact* with the bit and to improve his collection in an ever increasing measure. When teaching new exercises the rider must never lose sight of these two principles.

Every horse will accept the reins in a different way when they are applied by the rider. The contact itself will be uneven: on one side it will be firm; on the other side soft or even non-existent. In equestrian terms the horse makes himself stiff on one side and hollow on the other. At the same time the hind leg on the stiff side (that on which the contact is firm) will be less bent than the hind leg on the hollow side (that on which the contact is soft) which will move more to that side so the track of this hind foot will be outside that made by the corresponding forefoot. This accounts for the *crookedness* of the horse. Nearly every horse tends to be crooked, but the degree will vary with the individual. It must be the rider's main object to overcome this fault and to make the contact with the bit equal on both sides of the horse's mouth. This object must be the rider's constant endeavour throughout the entire training. It is easier to overcome the crookedness in the young horse than it is in one that has not been made straight in his early training.

In order to obtain an even contact with the bit, the rider should take an even pressure on both sides of the horse's mouth and try to make the horse seek the contact with a lowered head. Only when this is achieved can a level effect be obtained with the reins. When the reins are taken up most horses will adopt more position to one side than to the other—generally, but not always, to the right. In this case the rider must now hold the right rein, that is to say the rein on the hollow side, and try by short actions of the left hand, like squeezing water out of a sponge, to give the horse the correct position. This may be described as a *unilateral half-halt* through the left side. On the other hand, if the head is too low, the object may be to raise the head, with the assistance of the seat and legs, but, at the same time, prevent the horse from poking his nose. The half-halt should be practised only when the horse is in motion. In the very early training it may be necessary to ask for a bend from the horse when he is standing still in order to make it clear to him what is required. Before and during the half-halt the horse must be pushed well forward with the seat and legs in order not to lose impulsion or allow the pace to slacken. If the horse does not react immediately to these short actions of the reins on the stiff side they must be repeated, but on no account should a steady pull be maintained. As soon as the horse answers by relaxing the muscles of the throat and a nodding of the head as if he were to say: "yes, I understand," the action of the rein on the stiff side and the pushing aid must immediately cease, and for a short time the rider will direct his horse with the rein of the hollow side only. For instance, when performing a half-halt through the left side the horse must be pushed forward with the seat and both legs—the left leg to ensure that the action of the rein does not cause the left hind leg to cease to step under the body, and the right leg to ensure that the horse does not carry his hindquarters to the outside, in this case to the right, in order to evade the discomfort caused by the demand of the rider. But the right rein, the rein of the hollow side, must stay in contact with the mouth. This is very important, as the horse must be taught to take a contact with this rein. It may even be a firmer contact for a time. If the rein of the hollow side is not held, the value of the exercise will be lost for the horse would be made to relax the contact on the stiff side and would not be made to accept the contact on the hollow side.

The proof that the half-halt has succeeded will be recognised by the fact that after the half-halt through the left side the horse will, having accepted the contact on the right side, maintain the position to the left. Then the unilateral action of the rein must cease, otherwise this wonderful aid would end up in a seesaw action of the reins, which is one of the greatest mistakes that the rider can make.

Not only in the present stage of training, but also in the

beginning of work in the more collected paces, it can happen that the horse will lie on both reins and the contact will become too firm. The horse then is not in balance and is too much on his forehand. This fault can have various origins, but for the most part it will be caused by the fact that the pushing aids are too strong and the horse gets out of control. In other words the pushing aids create more impulsion than the rider can accept through the reins. Changing the speed with an increased influence of the back and a frequent giving and taking action of the rein will be the best remedy. On no account should the rider try to raise his horse's head with both reins or attempt to relieve the pressure of the contact by a constant pull at the reins. In general the half-halt is employed to make the horse carry his head and neck lower; in this case the short action of the rein is done by a lower hand in the direction of the rider's opposite hip. If a higher position of head and neck is required the hand must be held higher and the action of the rein is made towards the rider's opposite breast.

Later in the training, horses that are inclined to make themselves hollow on the right side, for instance, should be worked with little position to the right. But on the left rein, on which they try to make themselves stiff, they should be ridden with a definite position to that side. This correction will be practised even with the High School horse but in this case the observer must not be able to perceive the half-halt. During the course of training the horse may reverse the hollow and the stiff side, which is always a good sign, but the rider must be able to recognise this and employ his aids in the opposite way.

The half-halt can be practised only if the horse follows the unilateral action of the rein by lowering his neck, but should he raise it and produce a bulge in the lower side of his neck he is not yet ready for this aid or else faults have crept in unrecognised during the first stage of training. There is but one remedy for this, namely, to go back to the early stage of training and teach the horse to seek the rein with a lowered neck. This is most important to ensure that the horse steps well under the body with his hind legs and swings his back.

Along with achieving a good contact with the bit the horse must be made straight, for only then will correct collection with all its advantages be possible.

As already explained in the first phase of training the *making straight* will be achieved by the forehand being brought in front of the hindquarters. It is easier to do this alongside the wall, which gives the horse the direction, than on a track away from the wall. As noted before, because the horse is narrower through the shoulders than through the hips there will always be a tendency for him to incline the forehand to the wall. The forehand of the horse must be taken from the wall with both reins in order to make the hind feet step into the tracks made by the forefeet. Only then will the horse be in balance. The pushing aids are responsible for maintaining the uninterrupted forward motion. It will be easier to take the forehand towards the side on which the horse is stiff, because on this side he accepts the rein. On the other side he will try to follow the action of the rein by bending his neck in order to spare himself the inconvenience of being straightened. In this way he will show his resistance to giving up a fault which has become a habit dear to him. The half-halt by the outside rein must teach him obedience and must make him carry the whole forehand in and not only the neck.

Only the straightened horse will enable the rider to carry out the thorough physical training which will be required if the highest standard is to be reached in the art of equitation. All serious books on riding stress this point: "Straighten your horse and ride him forward." I should like to amplify this sentence with: "Only when your horse is straight can he go forward with impulsion and harmony."

When the horse has been taken thus far in his training, it is time to concentrate to a greater degree on collection, but perfection can only be achieved later on.

Collection is produced by pushing the horse with seat and both legs up against the reins which are held equally in both hands. By driving the hind legs more under the body the horse will become shorter and his neck will be more beautifully shaped.

Without any further action on the part of the rider the horse will raise his forehand by lowering his hindquarters. In this way the necessary balance is achieved for an impressive pace; the activity of the hind legs will be stimulated; and the correctly arched back will be made to swing harmoniously. Success will be revealed to the rider in the pleasant way he will feel the back of his horse swinging rhythmically beneath his seat—what Xenophon described as a "divine sensation." The rider must have the feeling that he is part of his horse—this is the aim of the classical art of riding—and the onlooker will be captivated by the harmonious movements of horse and rider.

The brilliant trot depends on the suspension that the horse can produce. *Suspension* can only be achieved if the hindquarters produce a strong carrying and pushing force. The longer this moment of suspension lasts, the more beautiful and impressive will be the action of the horse. But the rider must beware of a false suspension in which the horse makes slow and tense steps. Then the fusing of horse and rider will not be possible.

Thus we may say that an elastic and impulsive pace depends on the suppleness and even more on the spring developed from the hindquarters. This can be much improved by the development of their muscular power. One of the main objects of training for every type of riding horse must be to strengthen the hindquarters, to give them suppleness and to make them carry the weight of horse and rider. In terms of mechanics the hindquarters are the motor which produces the movement and the place where the energy is stored. Just as with a mechanical vehicle, steering is only possible when the motor produces the movement, so with the horse the aids with the reins will only produce the required effects when the impulsion is developed from the hindquarters. One of the most important principles of horsemanship is that the horse must never be worked from front to rear but always from behind forward.

This principle must become an irrevocable rule with the young horse but even more in the advanced stages of training. The rider must beware of achieving an apparently good position mainly with the reins and neglecting impulsion and, above all, the action of the horse. An apparently correct position reached by incorrect methods will lead to disappointment and difficulties when the rider tries to obtain extension; either the horse will come off the bit and give up his contact with the reins or he will maintain his position and not gain sufficient ground to the front but make hasty steps without lengthening his strides. The rider, therefore, must check again and again, even in an advanced stage of training, to ensure that the horse goes sufficiently forward with long, even, and cadenced steps. Only if the collection and contact are reached by impulsive action will they last and continue throughout the most difficult exercises. Not only will the work of the horse from behind forward be best guaranteed by increasing the length of the stride but also the necessary impulsion will be secured for the later, advanced work in collection.

One must never forget how close the relationship is between balance, contact, and collection. Progress in training should always be obvious throughout the whole and not confined to one detail. While particular attention may have to be directed to one part, the combined effects on the whole training must never be lost sight of.

During the first stage of training the horse should have been worked in the rising trot. But now that he has been prepared by this work he can gradually be introduced to the *sitting trot*. To start with, the rider remains sitting very lightly in the saddle for short periods. Particular attention should be paid to preventing the horse from dropping his back and acquiring the habit of going with a hollow back. He must not lie on the reins or change his speed. Nor should he be induced by the change from the rising trot to the sitting trot either to increase or slacken the pace. If one of these faults creeps in, the rising trot must be resumed and the sitting trot tried only when the trot has become even again. If the young horse is strong enough, he will, in this way, soon become accustomed to the sitting trot. The proof of this will be when he shows no difference in action, impulsion, and position whether the rider is sitting or rising. The rider should begin the sitting trot on the large circle and later alternate the exercise by "going large" around the arena. As a rule the sitting trot will be employed on the circle but an exception can be made in this stage of training. It is an excellent exercise to change from the sitting trot to the rising trot.

In further training the rider will nearly always employ the sitting trot because it offers him a better opportunity to influence his horse and to shape him accordingly; but should the horse, in the course of this work, show signs of losing impulsion, as may happen with young horses, and show a resistance to going forward, it is then necessary to activate the impulsion by riding forward in a lively rising trot. This will be especially necessary with horses inclined to get behind the bit—a bad habit frequently found in the Lipizzaners. On the other hand horses that lie on the bit can be brought to a correct contact by collected work at the sitting trot.

In this phase of training a considerable amount of time must be given to *work on the large circle.* The young horse has already had the experience of performing a continuous turn in this exercise on the longe. The bend in the spine must always correspond to the arc of the circle and the degree of the bend will be regulated by the size of the circle. Thus the rider is able to determine the exact aids to be employed. The inside rein must hold the horse on the track and give him the position while the outside rein defines the size of the arc as well as the degree of the position. By the influence of this outside rein on the hind leg of the horse on the same side, the rider's outside leg, which must be employed behind the girth, is helped to prevent the hindquarters from swinging out and at the same time to maintain the bend of the horse's body, so that it conforms with the arc of the circle.

The inside leg on the girth will make the horse go forward and increase the bend of the inside hind leg which has to carry a greater proportion of the weight. At the same time this inside leg must prevent the hindquarters from falling in and the horse from becoming crooked. On the large circle the horse will try, by crookedness, to avoid the inconvenience of bending the inside hind leg. Thus it is the rider's inside leg that ensures that the body of the horse will be bent according to the circle, and this is

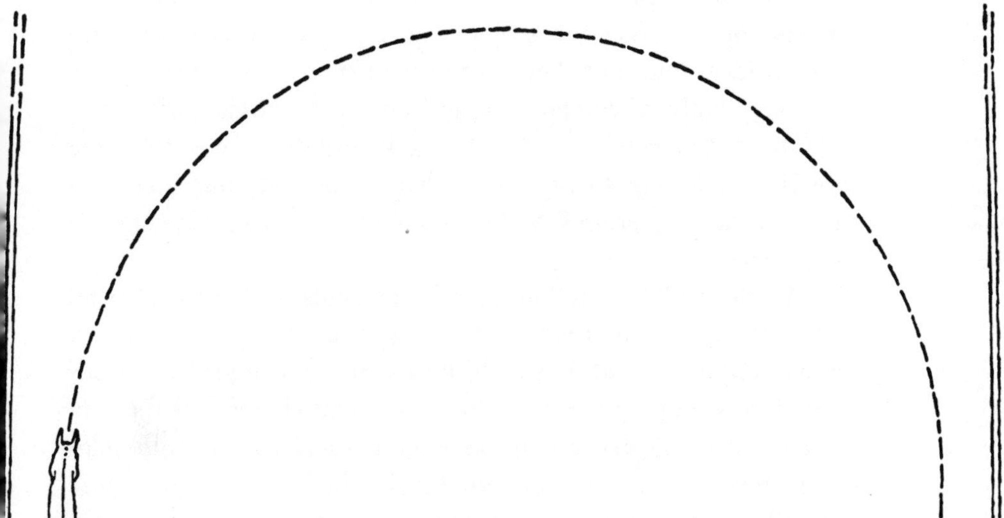

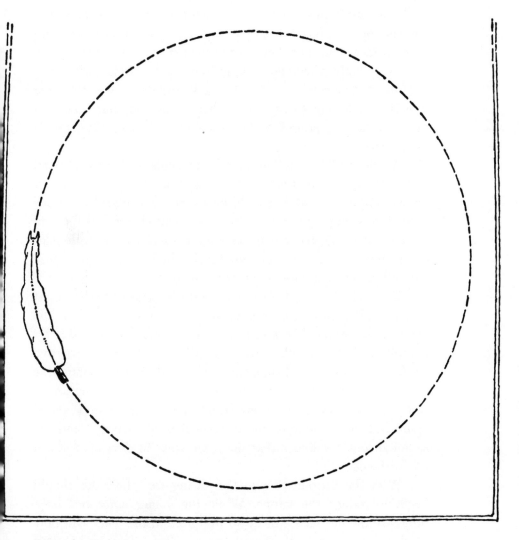

Large circle

the reason why this leg is so important. It is more important in a turn than the aid of the inside rein. When employing the inside rein the rider must take great care to support it with the outside rein in order to prevent the neck from being more bent than the whole body, which would interfere with the development of the action.

The rider will now ensure that these exercises on the large

circle are performed in a correct manner. The horse must not increase or decrease the size of the circle in accordance with his own ideas and must keep the correct speed demanded by the rider, especially when "going large" out of the circle and returning into it. As a rule horses try to slacken the pace when coming into the circle and to hasten it when going out. But now it is time for these exercises to be executed with accuracy and an even tempo.

As the work on the large circle demands an increased bend and is, therefore, an effort to the horse, it must not be continued for too long at a time. It should be interrupted often by periods of walk or going on a straight line. Frequent changes of the rein must be made so that equal influence is exercised on both sides of the horse to prevent one-sidedness, which later might cause difficulties when greater demands are made.

The following fault, when working on a large circle, must be guarded against. It occurs when the circle is bounded by the walls of the arena. The horse, in order to make work easier for himself, will try to follow the side of the wall for one or two strides and, as it were, lean against it instead of just touching the track at the point where the circle meets the sides of the arena. Not only will the circle be imperfect and become a many-sided figure but the training of the horse will be interrupted and the instantaneous obedience that the rider seeks to develop will not be furthered.

With the introduction to the sitting trot the rider should begin to reduce the tempo. While the young horse has been ridden in the ordinary trot up to the present, the work will now be done mostly in a shortened tempo. The difference between the various tempos—the ordinary trot, the collected trot, the extended trot—does not lie in the acceleration or the reduction of the pace, but exclusively in the lengthening of the stride or the elevation of the steps while maintaining the rhythm. This rule cannot be impressed too often or too strongly on the rider because it is so important to realise that this is the goal we are trying to reach throughout our training.

The horse must put his feet forward in an even and cadenced sequence. In the *collected trot* he will gain less ground to the front but will step with more elevation; in the extended trot he will increase the length of his stride and, therefore, stretch his legs more. The rider must take care that in the collected trot the horse does not lose his impulsion and that the activity of the steps is maintained, a rhythmic and regular tempo kept. As the correctly executed collected trot is a considerable strain on the horse, it should be practised only for short periods and brought to an end before the horse shows signs of fatigue, otherwise the brilliancy of the steps will be lost. Should impulsion be lost, the rider must seek to regain it by increasing the speed to the ordinary trot. This will stimulate the hindquarters and bring them more under the body, and in this way the collected trot will be recaptured.

In order to make the young horse understand the collected trot better, the rider should use the *working trot,* which is between the ordinary trot and the collected trot, but this kind of trot should be regarded merely as a stepping-stone. By frequent changes of speed the horse will acquire more activity in his steps. He will become accustomed to responding to the pressure of the rider's legs by immediately going forward and to decreasing the pace as a result of the action of the reins supported by the back of the rider. Thus he should gradually learn to concentrate on his rider and react immediately to the lightest of aids. This is the language between horse and rider which appears to be so mysterious to the onlooker.

At the same time the horse will acquire a greater suppleness and proficiency, but this work can only be done individually. Horses with an inclination to hurry or make hasty steps, either from overeagerness or nervousness, must be worked for longer periods in the same tempo in order to calm them down. On the other hand, lazy or dull horses should be woken up and taught to be attentive by frequent transitions from the collected trot and vice versa. While recognising these advantages of the frequent *changes of the tempo,* the rider should give the horse the opportunity of longer periods at the same tempo. These longer periods are especially valuable when the rider thinks the horse is showing signs of anticipating the changes of tempo. Should this be allowed to become a habit the horse will later on find difficulty in keeping a regular tempo—a fault in the basic training which the horse would make the rider pay for as he approaches the realms of High School.

If these changes of tempo are correctly executed the rider will reap the benefit of improvement in the contact, impulsion, obedience, and the action of the rein going through the body. This improvement will give him the opportunity to check the action especially when asking for collection, and it will prove the relationship between exercise and result. The *work in trot* remains the foundation of the training of the young horse as well as of the school horse whose abilities must be preserved at the highest level. In short, it plays a most important part in the entire training of the horse.

It is the trot that is best suited for obtaining and preserving impulsion. At the same time it improves suppleness and develops obedience, for the rider can influence his horse better in the trot than in the walk where the natural impulsion is lacking, or in the canter where the horse can easily become tense. In the trot the rider has the best opportunity to control the regularity and the rhythm of the steps. The sensitive rider will immediately notice any irregularity in the pace and will change his work accordingly. The regularity of the tempo is the essence of training as it reflects the balance that the horse has acquired. One of the main objects of dressage is to make the horse find his balance which not only improves his movements but also brings about the correct contact with the reins. The rider must never lose sight of the fact that his work is only justified when it not only preserves the movements given to the horse by nature but even improves them. This most important principle cannot be underlined too often. By obtaining the correct balance the rider will avoid wearing out the forelegs of his horse prematurely, and this is why it is so important to obtain it in every kind of horse. Only the degree of balance will distinguish the High School horse from those required for everyday purposes.

The moment has now come for executing simple turns correctly and the rider should pass through the corners with the same exactness as practised on the large circle. Other simple turns such as crossing the arena from one long side to the other should not be practised unduly. When "going large" from the circle the rider must take great care to preserve the bend of all the joints of the hind legs and to ensure that these legs continue to step well under the body in order to prevent the horse from losing collection. It may not be possible to achieve this with the young horse, but this work can be much improved by correctly *passing through the corners*. Every corner of the arena offers the rider the opportunity for the same influence on his horse as when working on the large circle.

So far the horse has been allowed to pass through the more or less rounded corners, but now he must be taken through them correctly and made to describe an arc as directed by his rider.

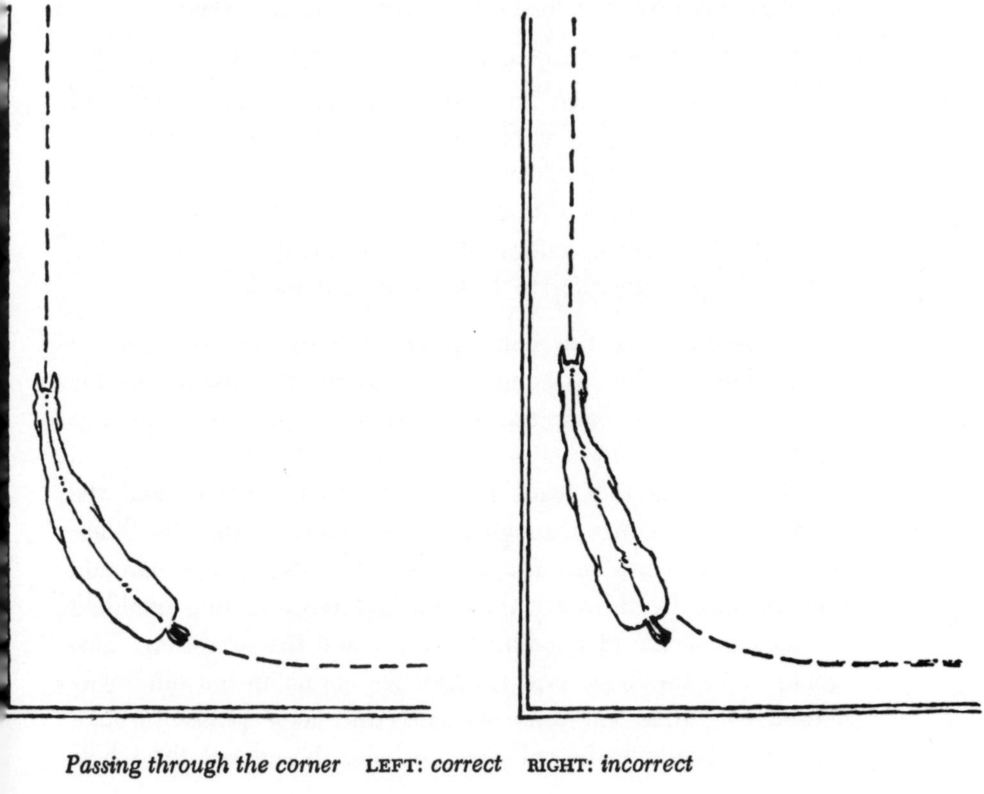

Passing through the corner LEFT: *correct* RIGHT: *incorrect*

To perform a correct corner, the horse should execute a turn of a quarter of a circle, the diameter of which does not exceed six yards. The body of the horse should be bent in such a way that his spine corresponds to this arc. To begin with, the rider should be warned against trying to ride the corners in too small an arc, as the horse would then lose his balance and, consequently, the regularity of his steps. The correct tempo must be maintained, that is, the speed must be neither increased nor decreased, and he must not lean into the arc with his body. The hind feet should follow exactly in the tracks of the forefeet and the hindquarters neither fall out nor fall in.

A corner correctly passed will serve as a test of the physical training of the horse and is closely related to the progress of training. To insist that the corners are properly ridden is not fussiness but an important part in the physical training of the horse.

This exercise will lead to the following progress:

(1) The horse's bend will be increased (a) longitudinally, assisted by the increased bend in the three joints of the hindquarters; (b) laterally; (c) the horse will move with more proficiency.
(2) The obedience to the rider's aids will be increased.
(3) The exact execution of the movement helps to combat any inclination to laziness or bad habits.

From the way the horse passes through the corners the expert will be able to come to important conclusions on the correctness of the basic training and the degree of obedience reached.

The outside rein leads the horse into the corner and the inside rein takes him through it. It is important that the hindquarters do not fall out. Young horses will often try to maintain their balance by throwing their quarters out and thus avoiding the inconvenience of bending the body and the inside leg. This would make the horse pass through the corner in the same way a tram car turns. The more correctly the horse passes through the corner the more he will have to bend throughout the whole body and in all the joints of his hind legs, and the more difficult will be the exercise.

For this reason the rider should not attempt to make the corner too small at first. It is better to ride a large corner correctly than a small one incorrectly with a loss of rhythm. Another fault that frequently occurs is that the horse is led into the corner with the outside rein and shows a tendency to adopt the wrong position to the outside. The young horse, in order to make things easier for himself, will try to shift his weight towards the inside shoulder. In this case the correction is by a half-halt on the inside rein in an upward direction in order to take the weight off that shoulder by raising the forehand.

The rider's inside leg is of great importance, because it not only has to push the horse forward and prevent the hindquarters from falling in—a fault equally as bad as falling out—but it also has to bend the horse round itself through his whole length and thus maintain a correct position. The rider must be careful when passing through a corner neither to remain behind the motion with the upper part of his body nor to lean forward in the saddle. He should sit slightly to the inside and not allow the weight of his body to be drawn to the outside by the action of his outside leg.

As soon as the horse has passed the corner he must be straightened by the outside rein in order to enable him to go along the wall without swaying.

In this stage of training the work at the trot is again interrupted by periods at the walk. But now the transition must be made by a definite *change to the walk* and no longer by the trot being allowed gradually to fade away as with the young horse. Frequent changes of tempo will be the best preparation for such a change to the walk. When increasing the speed the rider pushes the horse forward with both legs but only gives sufficiently with the reins to enable the horse to make longer strides without losing his position and collection. When shortening the tempo the horse is again pushed forward with both legs and by repeated short actions of the reins, the so-called half-halts, and by bracing the back, the horse is made to take shorter steps.

Therefore the rule is that with any half- or full-halt—this rule may sound paradoxical—the rider first pushes forward and then reduces the speed; only by the combination of the aids of the legs and the hands will the collection be preserved during the transition. At the same time this makes the horse go through the transition with the hind legs placed well under the body.

At first it will be the action of the reins that brings about the transition but later it is done by the bracing of the back. When changing to the walk the horse will be pushed forward with both legs, in the same way as when reducing the speed at the trot, and brought to the walk by repeated actions of the reins together with a braced back. It is most important that the horse should not lie on the rein or shift his weight onto the forehand. The result that the rider seeks is a smooth and fluent transition to the walk by merely bracing his back and maintaining the contact with both legs. Immediately after the transition to the walk the rider's legs must ensure that the horse moves forward in an appropriate degree of collection and does not falter or move with lazy steps.

When transitions to the walk are practised without the necessary aids of legs and back, various faults are likely to appear. The horse will come off the bit and drop his back, so that the hind legs cannot step sufficiently under the body. This will also be the case when the horse lies on the reins. Horses with an inclination to get behind the bit will anticipate the aids and produce a rough transition. If this should be the case the rider must demand a transition at the moment when the horse least expects it. The horse will perform the most correct transition to the walk when the rider succeeds in bringing it about through the rein of the hollow side together with a braced back.

Long periods at the collected walk should not be practised at this stage. Only through systematic physical training in the trot and the maintenance of full impulsion will the collected walk drop like ripe fruit into the lap of the rider. From long experience at the Spanish Riding School the walk is employed only as a reward and as a rest, and then it should be only on the long rein. The work at the collected walk will not be intensified until the end of the training of the horse. Only movements calculated to increase impulsion will be employed and now the canter will be included.

Up to this point the *canter* has been employed more or less to exercise the horse, but now correct work in the canter must begin. The rider will no longer be content to push the horse forward until he breaks into a canter, but will now demand a *correct strike-off*. This exercise offers further opportunity for the physical training of the horse.

The outside leg placed passively behind the girth gives the signal for the canter and prevents the horse from carrying his hindquarters to the outside, while the inside leg, pushing forward on the girth, makes the horse strike off. At the same time the rider must sit a little more firmly on his inside seat bone. With the transition to the canter the rider must be careful not to allow his inside leg to slide forward as so often happens, thus diminishing the value of the aid in this pace. The inside rein must place the horse in the right position and, with the support of the inside leg, prevent the hindquarters from falling in, which would cause a crooked strike-off, a serious fault not to be allowed even with the young horse. Should the horse try to lie on the inside rein or to make himself stiff, the rider must execute a short half-halt with the inside rein in co-operation with the aids for the strike-off. This will make the horse strike off in the correct position and prevent him from rushing off.

To begin with, the work in the canter should be practised mainly on the large circle, which gives the horse the best preparation for this higher pace. At first the rider should ask for the strike-off from the trot, but the speed of the trot must not be increased or decreased, nor must the horse be allowed to fall into a hasty canter. This will be possible only when the horse is sufficiently relaxed and in physical and mental balance. Not just in the canter but throughout all stages of training it is of the utmost importance that the horse be completely relaxed before the commencement of any exercise. Whereas in the first year of training it was sufficient that the horse carry his rider in walk, trot, or canter, it is now important *how* he moves under his rider in the various paces.

Every athlete and every dancer loosens up his muscles before starting to work. How much more important this is with the horse, which in all his movements and actions must not only bend to the will of another living creature but also carry him. As the sculptor's clay must be soft before he starts to mould it, so must the horse be relaxed both in body and mind before he is ready to be trained by his rider.

Many riders think that the best method of *relaxing* their horses is by a long ride in a rising trot. It is very doubtful whether this has any beneficial effect. An athlete will not be relaxed by a run of several miles, but merely tire himself. Both horse and rider need all their powers in order to meet the demands made upon them. So the best method of relaxing before starting serious work should be carefully considered and suitable to the particular situation. Young horses or horses that have been confined to the stables will come out over-fresh. The best method of calming them down is a short steady trot with the reins as long as possible. At the same time it will also help to gain the animal's confidence and to improve the standard of work if the rider speaks to him with a soothing voice. It would be absolutely wrong to try to relax the horse by a long and forced trot. Horses that are highly strung would get even more excited and, ignoring any fatigue, instead of becoming relaxed would become more tense. Besides which, this method is unlikely to make them forget their own ideas and to submit themselves to the will of their riders. Fresh horses will look for any excuse to buck or shy in order to make difficulties. *Tenseness and shying* are closely related, for a horse that is not relaxed will be more inclined to shy and the tenseness will be increased by shying.

When a horse, especially a young one, shies the rider must proceed with great care in order not to lose the animal's confidence. When approaching the object of the horse's fear the rider should not tighten the reins, as so many novice riders do, as this will draw the horse's attention to the object and suggest to him the idea of shying and make him more tense. The best way to overcome the fear in the horse and to further his obedience is to approach and pass the object with an almost loose rein. In an especially difficult case it may be best to show the horse the object and let him approach it slowly and sniff at it, at the same time caressing him. The rider will never achieve success by becoming impatient and administering punishment. This would only increase the horse's fear and the rider would have difficulty in recapturing the physical and mental relaxation required for successful training. It is a well-known fact that sense cannot be obtained from an excited horse any more than it can be from an excited child.

While the best way to relax the horse and loosen his muscles is by a steady shortened trot, the rider sitting with the reins as long as possible, this exercise will be effective only if the horse trots with short and relaxed steps. Should he begin to drag his hindquarters out of laziness, the rider should insist on increased action of the hindquarters by riding energetically forward, though he must not cause tension by overdoing this. After a short period at the increased pace, he should return to the shortened steps until the horse executes them in a completely relaxed manner and gives himself up to the will of his rider. However, it is not so simple to achieve these short relaxing steps, which are necessary to improve balance, because the horse will always prefer the walk to the strenuous shortened trot.

The steps of this relaxing trot should be as short as possible. Their chief object is to maintain an even tempo and a regular light contact with long reins. If the horse moves in this way he must arch and swing his back with rhythm. This attitude should be maintained when riding circles and turns and when making transitions to the walk and again to the trot. Then the relaxed horse will go forward with energetic steps upon the increased influence of the rider's legs and will strike off into a canter smoothly and without increasing the contact or changing the rhythm.

The horse will achieve his most beautiful form only after he has been liberated from all stiffness by this loosening work; he will go forward full of impulsion, moving in perfect balance without increasing the contact on the bit. This will be possible only when the rider is able to sit in such a way that he does not disturb the movements of the horse. In short, he must have an independent seat.

During the whole training of the horse the basic elements of relaxation, impulsion, going straight forward, and collection must be established. The only difference between the young horse and the school horse is how long it will take before these basic elements can be established so that the work demanded can be carried out. What will take months to establish with a young horse will require only minutes with the school horse.

In practising the canter on the large circle, the rider must take particular care that the transitions from trot to canter are soft and smooth, nor must he forget to change rein or direction and thus the lead frequently. These repeated exercises will improve the suppleness and the balance of the horse and, above all, the activity of the hindquarters so that there will be increased impulsion. Furthermore, the horse will learn to react to the lightest application of the aids, which will be a proof of his complete obedience. These frequent changes will keep him on the alert and force him to concentrate on the will of his rider, instead of playing the fool out of sheer boredom. Boredom is, in fact, the greatest enemy of success. As soon as the rider notices that the horse shows signs of anticipating his aids by striking off into the canter, or going back into the trot on his own initiative, he must immediately change the order of his work.

The time has now come to ask for the *collected canter.* The tempo must be shortened gradually by half-halts. In this exercise it is important to remember that the shortening must not be brought about by a slackening of the speed but by decreasing the length of the bounds. When teaching the collected canter, the rider has to be content at first with a lesser collection and the work must be for short periods, otherwise the activity of the hindquarters will be lost. The collected canter is even more difficult for the horse than the collected trot. The horse should become shorter throughout his whole body and the spring, as it were, should be more tightly compressed. He should move forward with regular bounds which are more elevated and gain less ground to the front. Much impulsion is needed for this exercise and this is obtained by repeated increases in the tempo. The hindquarters must jump well under the body in order to prevent the contact with the mouth from becoming firmer as the collection is increased. The braced back of the rider absorbs the impulsion created by the repeated aids of the seat and legs applied as for the strike-off.

In the beginning many faults may appear: the horse will slacken the movement and drag his hind legs without force; he will become longer in his whole body and his movements will be slovenly; the canter will became four-time instead of three. This latter fault will be recognised by the onlooker through the fact that the horse will appear to hobble along, and the rider will feel it through the harder movement of the back muscles of his horse. The rider can avoid this fault by ensuring that the impulsion is kept up by increasing the tempo. Again the rider must take plenty of time in order to reach this goal and should not make the mistake of trying to force progress at the expense of correctness.

When training his horse, the rider must repeat over and over again: "I have time." It takes time—a great deal of it—for a horse to develop and to understand what is required of him. Nowadays, when everyone seems to strive for quick success, this cannot be repeated too often. The need for time cannot be refuted by false successes which only go to prove the opposite. For even if it is possible to train a horse up to High School at the age of eight years, at the age of ten years the so-called dressage horse would be completely worn out and useless. The principles of the classical art of riding cannot be undermined by a singular phenomenon. On the contrary, such a display merely proves that personal vanity and the desire to show off will in no way contribute to the development of the art. If the time of training is ruthlessly reduced it will lead only to a general lowering of the standard, to a caricature of the various movements, and to premature wearing out of the horse. Nature cannot be violated.

Of course, taking time does not mean doing nothing. All training must be marked by progress and never be at a standstill. Continuous progress in training is of decisive importance up to the highest degree of dressage. Along the way the serious rider will have an unmistakable sign of progress in that the attentive and impartial observer will notice that the horse has become more beautiful.

The inclination of every horse to be more or less crooked will be more visible in the canter, especially in the strike-off. On the large circle this crookedness will be less noticeable because the horse is bent in his whole body according to the size of the circle. But the inclination to strike off into a crooked canter can be noticed by the fact that the hindquarters are brought more in, or the shoulder allowed to fall more out, than is required by the arc of the circle. This fault will be still more noticeable when striking off on a straight line, and even more so on a line away from the wall. It must, therefore, be eliminated in this stage of training. This can be done by pushing forward forcefully with the inside leg on the girth, which will prevent the hindquarters from falling in, while the shoulder is prevented from falling out by the inside rein, supported by the outside rein, whose duty will be to keep the horse straight and prevent too much bend of the neck to the inside.

When the young horse has made progress in these various exercises on the large circle, the same must be practised throughout the whole arena. The rider should, however, alternate short periods of canter with periods of collected trot, and not yet attempt a correct collected canter but a working tempo, which is a somewhat more collected ordinary canter, in order to make this unaccustomed and still difficult work easier for the horse. It may happen that young horses that are able to become more compressed (collected) when cantering on the large circle will become longer when taken on a straight line and sometimes even crooked and unable to maintain the same canter, going too high in front and losing collection. The reason for this is that the rider can apply the pushing and holding aids more effectively on the large circle than on a straight line, and this is the secret of why the horse can be shaped more easily on the circle and why this work is of such great importance.

Before "going large" the speed of the collected canter must be increased to that of the working canter while still on the large circle. Should the rider increase the speed when changing from the circle to the straight line, the horse will acquire the habit of making this increase in pace every time when going out of the circle. This would mean the very opposite of what is required. One of the most important principles of training is that in making any change of direction the horse should go from the curve into the straight line without change of tempo.

The corner should be more or less rounded according to the tempo and the stage of training, but it must be the rider, not the horse, who decides the size of the turn. The rider should, however, be alive to the fact that it is far more difficult for the horse to execute a correct turn at the canter than it is at the trot and that he can only gradually be introduced to this work. At this stage of training it is not the size of the turn that matters but the fact that the horse is correctly bent and maintains a regular rhythm without leaning into the turn. There is no value in riding a small corner if the horse loses the rhythm of his movement. Again the rider cannot expect too much at this stage: perfection can be obtained only as the result of systematic training.

The canter, alternated on the circle and on the straight line and with frequent changes of tempo, will gradually lead to the collected canter on the straight line and throughout the turn. The balance of the horse will decide the correctness of the collected canter. Whenever difficulties appear they can best be eliminated by periods of work on the large circle.

On the straight line the rider must be careful that his pupil does not contract the habit of making a crooked strike-off. At this stage of training every effort should be made to eliminate this fault, for it can seriously interfere with later training. Crookedness of the horse ought to be the nightmare of every honest rider. It appears mainly when changing the tempo in the canter, when increasing and even more when decreasing the speed, and still more when the rider, absorbed in his work, gives insufficient thought to this habit. Horses will immediately take advantage of any inattention on the part of the rider, which is why riding, probably more than any other sport, entirely absorbs the mental and physical abilities.

When the young horse has learned to go correctly through the corners, then the time has arrived to increase the demands by the performance of *simple turns.* So far the horse has been taken along the wall, and the turns in the corners have been controlled on the outside by the right angle formed by the two walls. Riding along the walls and away from them may be compared to writing with lines and without them. As a child is first taught writing with the help of lines, so should the young horse be helped to move straight by going along the wall, especially until his balance is established. In a simple turn, either from the long or the short side to the opposite wall, the outside rein supported by the outside leg is responsible after the change of direction for the horse going absolutely straight across the school to the opposite side. This outside aid supplies the assistance formerly given by the wall; otherwise the action is exactly the same as when riding through the corner.

At the outset in these exercises the following faults are likely to appear in the trot and still more in the canter: the hindquarters will fall out in the turn, or they will turn too much to the inside, or the horse will fall into the turn with his inside shoulder. As a consequence he will no longer be able to go straight across the school to the other side. The remedy is the same as when riding through the corners. The rider must be careful that the horse does not begin to sway by coming off the straight line to either side when no longer guided by the wall. If this fault appears obvious, the best exercise is frequent turns parallel to the long side and a few yards away from it. Practice will make perfect. Once more this attention to detail in the fundamental training will be of great help later in correctly carrying out more difficult exercises.

Another point that the rider must be particularly careful

about is that the horse go absolutely straight up to three yards before reaching the other side and then be directed by the rider into the new direction. In most cases the horse will try to anticipate the approach to the wall. He will try to do this because he wants to make the work easier for himself. This anticipation may be observed in all training up to the standards of High School. In this particular case the horse will try to execute a larger turn in order to avoid the increased bend demanded by the correct turn, or he will try to come away from the straight line by swinging out in the opposite direction before coming to the turn; in other words, before a right turn he will swing to the left.

The above points are very important, as they may be the cause of many faults. The rider must never neglect finding out the cause of every defect, nor should he forget that every exercise demanded of the horse is supposed to contribute to the perfection of balance and cannot be too correctly executed.

If the rider continues the circular movement he has begun on the turn it will lead into a *volte or small circle*. The volte is of the same importance to the advanced training as the large circle was to the young horse. Correctly executed, it is not only an excellent exercise, but also the key to the suppleness and balance of the dressage horse, and above all to the action of the reins going through the body.

This is the reason why the volte plays such an important part in the training at the Spanish Riding School, and the reason why some students there had to practise these voltes for weeks on end because, in spite of their previous equestrian experience, they were not able to execute them correctly. *A volte is a circle of six yards diameter and on no account is it an oval or a many-sided figure.* Dressage riders should remember this fact and realise what an important instrument they have for the education of their horses in the correct riding of small circles.

To make it easier for the horse the rider will first practise these circles in the corners of the school, where the walls will give him support and guide him in the first part of the circle. The rider has then only to continue the second half to complete the circle. The horse is led into the circle by the inside rein and bent around the rider's inside leg at the girth. This leg is also responsible for maintaining the forward motion and the regular rhythm. The outside rein defines the size of the circle and the degree of the position; it helps the outside leg—passive behind the girth—to bend the horse around the inside leg and to prevent the hindquarters from falling out.

The rider must sit upright on both seat bones and not allow the body to lean into the circle or his seat to slide to the outside. Leaning into the circle would make the horse incline his body inwards, thus ignoring one of the axioms of classical riding, namely that the legs of the horse when performing a circle must always be vertical to the ground. If the seat of the rider is allowed to slide to the outside it will encourage the hindquarters of the horse to fall out and the symmetry of the circle will be lost. In general, horses will execute circles more precisely on the stiff side—the side on which the horse accepts the rein—than on the hollow side. If the horse tries to throw himself onto the inside shoulder the rider must check this fault by raising the forehand through a half-halt made in an upward direction with the inside rein. On the hollow side the horse will try to take too much position to the inside, thus bending the neck more than the rest of the body. The inside rein will then be away from the side of the neck and the circle will become oval or many-sided because the horse will allow the shoulder to fall out of the volte.

This is one more proof of how closely cause and effect are interlaced. The effect will be easily recognised, but the cause must be discovered so that the fault may be attacked at the root. This is the motif that directs the line to be followed throughout the whole training. The rider will not eliminate faults by repeating exercises unsuccessfully executed, but only by going back to the basic training. On the other hand every exercise correctly performed will not only be good for the training but also a test of the stage the horse has reached.

With a rider who has little experience, the preparation for the volte will commence with the large circle. The large circle must be gradually decreased by means of a spiral to a circle slightly larger than a volte (eight to ten yards diameter). This gives the rider the opportunity to accustom his horse gradually to the small circle. The inside rein leads the horse into the circle and the outside rein is responsible for the correct position and the gradually decreased size of the circle. The important duty of the inside leg on the girth is to maintain the motion and to bend the horse correctly, while the outside leg, supported by the rein on the same side, prevents the hindquarters from falling out and the inward bend from being lost. The horse should not be asked to perform these smaller circles more than two or three times before he is taken back to the large circle with the outside rein by way of spirals. The inside rein maintains the correct position to the inside and the legs play the same part as when diminishing the circle.

The position and bending, especially of the inside hind leg, are gradually increased when reducing the size of the circle, thus demanding a greater effort, but when enlarging again the effort will be decreased.

In the course of further training the horse can be made to perform a smaller circle within the large circle by executing a small circle from a determined point—usually where the circle touches the short side of the school—and then passing through the centre of the circle to end where the exercise began. Again it is important to perform this exercise correctly because only then will it be of any value. Unless continual changes of rein are practised during these exercises, the strain on the inner and outer sides of the horse will not be equally proportioned.

The *change within the circle* can now be practised. The rider leads his horse in a small half circle which ends at the centre of the large circle; when this point is reached the position is changed and the rider performs a small half circle on the other rein, finishing it at the point on the circumference exactly opposite to the point where the first half circle commenced. The changing of the rein in the centre has the following advantages: it increases the suppleness and the attention of the horse; and it ensures obedience and prevents the horse from

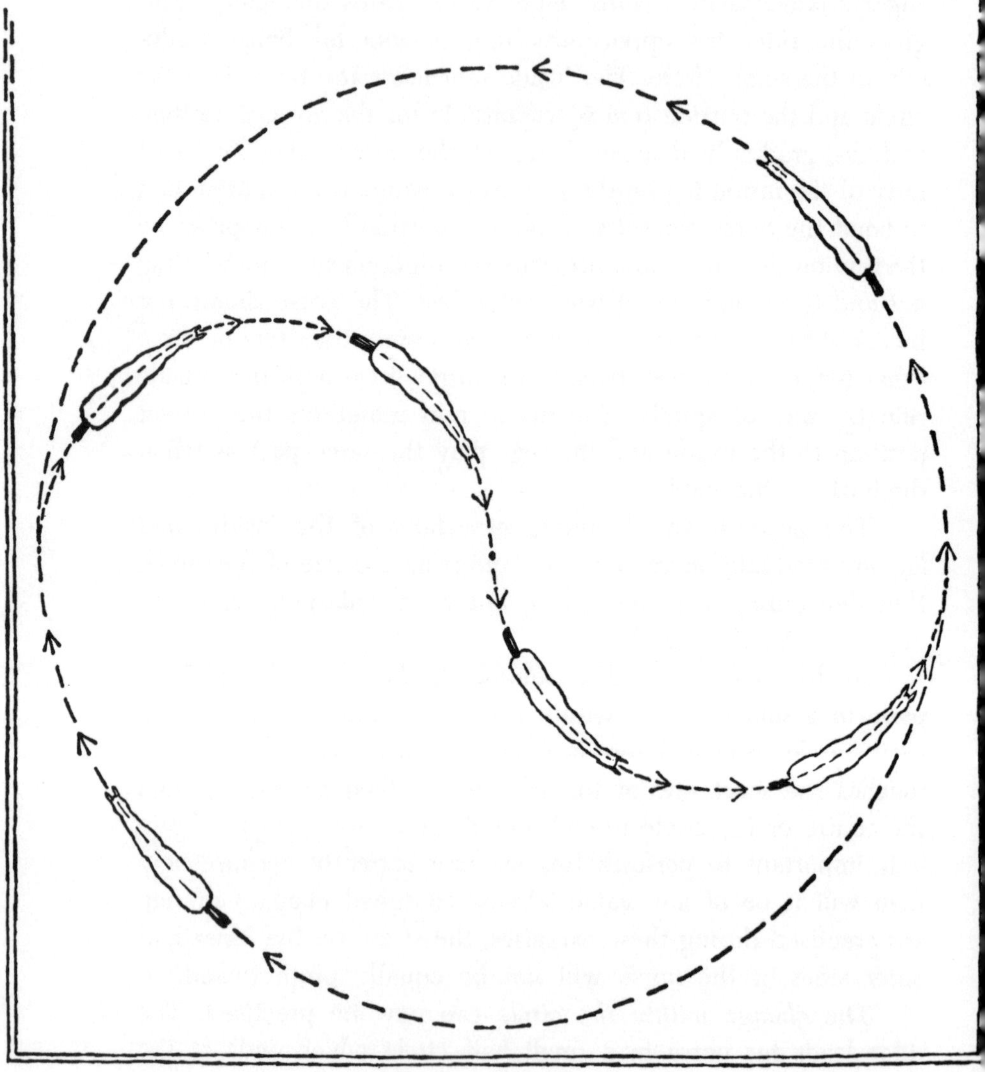

Change within the circle

anticipating. The aids remain the same as already explained, the rider merely reversing the aids when passing through the centre of the circle. The rider must be sure that the horse does not fall with his weight into either of the half circles. The remedy would be the same as that employed in the riding of turns and small

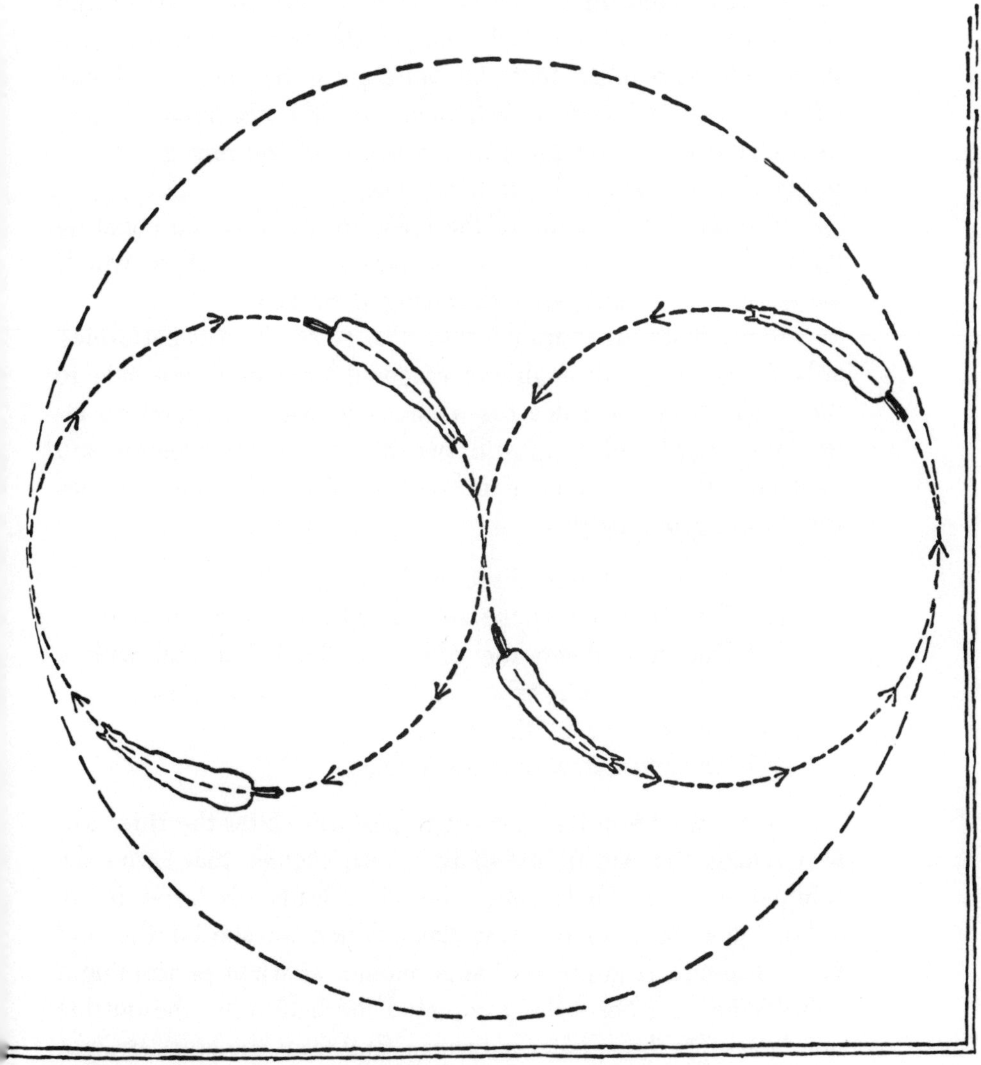

Figure of eight within the circle

circles. This exercise can be continued until it becomes a *figure of eight within the circle.*

The correct performance of a volte within a large circle will be more difficult than the performance of a volte in the corner. Therefore the correct order in which these exercises must be practised is as follows: smaller concentric circle within the large circle; volte in the corner; volte in the large circle; and finally volte at any required point of the arena. It is most important to remember that the volte must be round and end exactly where it began. It will then meet the necessary requirements and be another proof of the action of the rein going correctly through the body of the horse.

The physical training of the horse must always be equal on both sides and not greater on the easier side, a fault to which many riders succumb, thus deceiving themselves.

In the first year of training the *change of rein* was performed only by changing through the diagonal from one long side to the other. Now the rider has a choice of various exercises; alternately employed they will benefit the whole training and especially the perfection of obedience. The following exercises can now be practised:

(1) Change of rein through the diagonal.
(2) The turn across the school with a change of rein.
(3) The turn down the centre of the half-school with a change of rein when reaching the opposite side.
(4) The change of the circle.
(5) The change within the circle.

When the horse has learned to perform voltes the rider can also change the rein by a *half volte and change*, that is, on the completion of the half volte, the rider leads his horse in an oblique line back to the side from which he started the half volte. The aids begin in the same manner as when performing a volte. When the horse has completed the half volte, the outside rein interrupts the circular movement and leads the horse straight on an oblique line back to the wall; at the same time the passive effect of the outside leg behind the girth must cease in order to make the horse straight. Both legs now make the horse return to the wall on a straight line, the outside rein becomes the inside rein, and the other aids come into action as the position demands. The fluent forward movement must not be interrupted.

Half voltes with changes of direction and voltes, practised

14 Passage

15 Extended trot

16 Piaffe

17 Piaffe

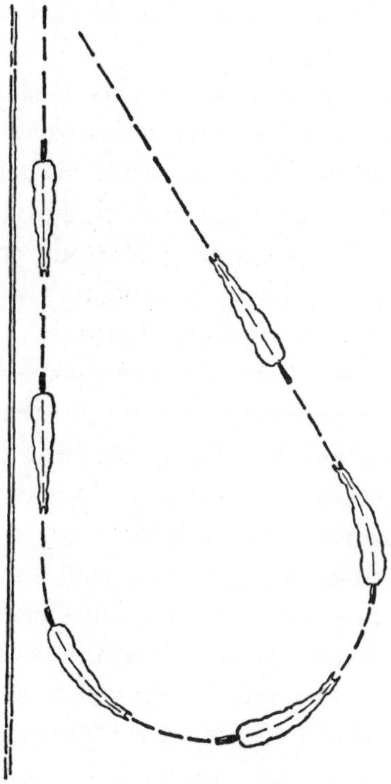

Half volte and change

with intelligence, are excellent exercises to improve and control the action of the rein going through the body. Changing the rein at the canter, however, must be reserved for a later stage of training.

As has been repeatedly underlined, the individual training of every horse is preferable to any rigid pattern; that is why the training of the second stage does not mean that the rider must follow any particular order with the various exercises. It is the duty of the thinking rider to find the correct order, and he must know exactly the effect and object of these exercises. He must also recognise the strong and the weak points of his horse. It is, therefore, not surprising that from de la Guérinière (1733) via Weyrother (1814) up to von Holbein (1898) the emphasis is always placed on the "thinking rider."

Holbein in his *Directives* stresses the fact that every intelligent rider must be able to explain why and at what moment he demands the various exercises from his horse. He will make use of his strong points in order to eliminate his weak points, and thus make learning easier for his pupil while saving much time for himself. He must not just make use of the strong points and forget about the weak ones, a fault so easily contracted by the vanity in every human being. He must also have an exact knowledge of the physical conformation of his horse and understand his temperament. It is a well-known fact that faults in conformation can be overcome more easily than faults in temperament. The rider will be able to recognise the latter only if he succeeds in penetrating the mind of his pupil. A good rider, in short, must be a good psychologist.

It is also a well-known fact that well-bred horses "full of temperament" will present themselves more beautifully and with more brilliancy than common horses which are lacking in breeding and spirit. The latter will execute their exercises willingly; they will not be inclined to play up, but, rather, will give the impression of dullness. Their performance will be uninspiring and without glamour. It goes without saying that these different types will need different treatment in their training.

The more lively a horse is the more obedient he must be before he gives himself up to the effort demanded by his rider. Only by obedience will it be possible to calm the exuberance of his temperament. This type of horse will, by the beauty of his movements, give a wonderful impression of controlled energy. On the other hand there will be greater problems in the course of his training. For this reason it is necessary to keep highly intelligent horses fully occupied physically and mentally so that they do not get bored by monotonous work and acquire bad habits, which will make difficulties for their riders and divert them from their proper work. With horses that are more temperamental it is of great importance to calm them down and develop a mental obedience. This is not an easy matter but the consequent work will make the horse surrender himself happily. Willing submission, together with the qualities given by nature to these horses, will result in an outstanding work of art. The rider must hold himself under strict control and not be led astray by impatience to some action that in a few moments could undo all he has achieved through months of patient work. It is advisable to select particularly calm riders as trainers for excitable horses in order to restore the balance.

Common horses without temperament must be woken up out of their lethargy by work full of variations and surprises. Obedience will be no problem with this type of horse, but the rider must endeavour to make him livelier in all his movements, which even then may not be very impressive. It will be an advantage to provide riders with great energy for this type of horse. In fact, the success of training can always be decisively influenced by the selection of the right riders for the right horses. An over-energetic rider on a highly strung horse may lead to disastrous results; similarly, a phlegmatic rider with a lazy horse will soon be lost in sleepy, indifferent movements. It can also happen that a rider takes an aversion to some particular horse and vice versa. Better progress can often be obtained by exchanging horses and riders.

Having made progress in balance and become more confirmed in contact with the bit, in collection and obedience, the young horse will now be ready for *lateral work.* This work will also contribute to the improvement in the above-mentioned requirements and especially increase to the highest degree the horse's obedience to the aids of the rider.

The term "lateral work" includes all those movements in which the horse not only steps forward but also sideways. These movements are not performed by young horses at liberty and should be taught only after appropriate progress has been made in the physical training of the horse. The physical training, however, will in turn be considerably improved by these exercises. Once again we can see the relationship between practice and result.

For centuries equestrian art has recognised the following lateral exercises enumerated here, but not necessarily according to their degree of importance or their age:

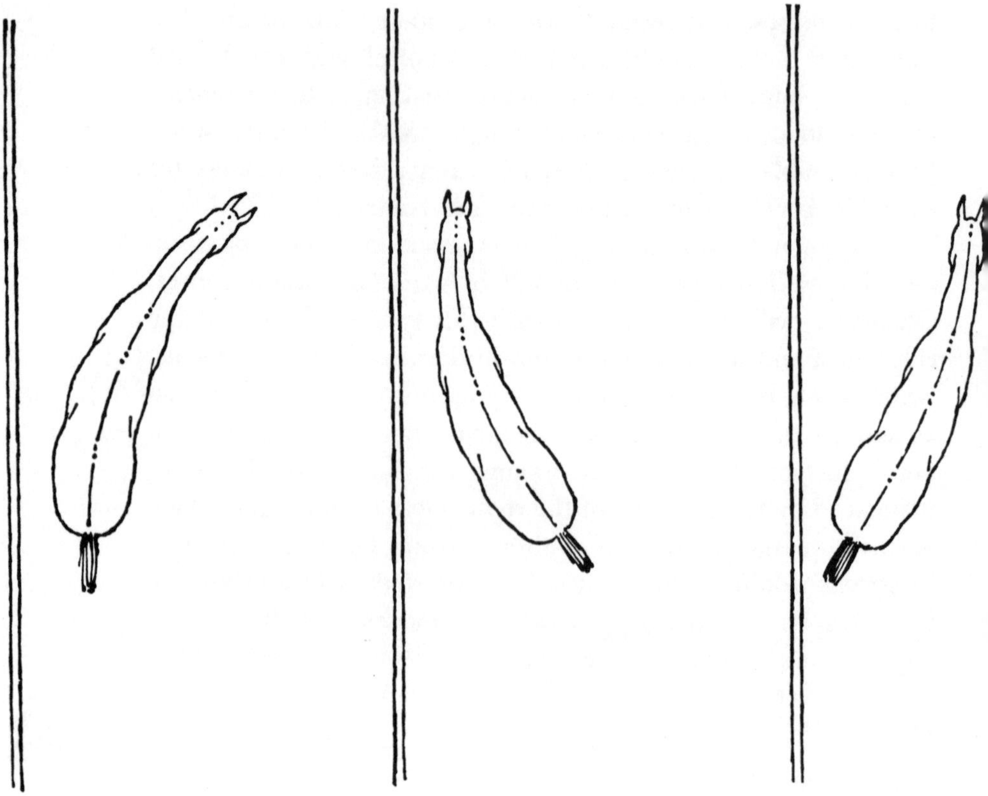

Lateral work LEFT: *shoulder-in* CENTRE: *travers or hindquarters-in* RIGHT: *renvers or tail to the wall*

(1) Shoulder-in
(2) Travers, quarters-in, head to the wall
(3) Renvers, quarters-out, tail to the wall
(4) Half pass
(5) Full travers, full pass

The renvers and half pass can be executed in all three paces, whereas the shoulder-in and travers can be executed only in the walk or trot and the full travers only from the halt.

As a preparation for lateral work the exercise known as *yielding to the leg* may be practised in order to make the horse understand the effect of the rider's legs pushing sideways. But the importance of yielding to the leg must not be over-rated; it should be used only to teach the young horse to understand the rider's leg aids. Unfortunately in recent years the contrary is often the case when practising equitation. This auxiliary aid has taken too great a part in the German instruction for cavalry. The Spanish Riding School has always used this yielding to the leg only to a limited degree, recognising its original purpose.

At first the young horse must learn to understand the yielding to the leg when at a standstill. He must stand still with his weight equally balanced on all four legs; then the action of the rider's leg behind the girth, for instance the right leg supported by the rein on the same side, will make the horse give way to the pressure of this leg and move his quarters to the left. This practice can be continued until the hindquarters make a turn round the forehand, thus executing a turn on the forehand. On no account should this turn on the forehand be considered part of the classical exercises but should be recognised as an auxiliary practice to teach the horse to move away from the leg. This exercise should not be demanded in a dressage test.

Yielding to the leg will be made easier for the horse by giving his head more position to the opposite side, that is to say, when yielding to the left, the position should be more to the right.

When the young horse has learned in this manner to answer to the pressure of the rider's leg by stepping to the side, the yielding to the leg should be practised only when in motion in order to consolidate the understanding of these aids. At the Spanish Riding School it is practised in the walk only and disapproved of at the trot. It seems illogical that the horse should be taught to go sideways and forward with exactly the opposite position to that which will later be demanded of him in the half pass.

As soon as the young horse is obedient to the sideways pushing action of the rider's leg, the rider may start to practise correct lateral work.

Without doubt the most important exercise on two tracks is the shoulder-in. It is not only the backbone of the training for all other lateral work, but also of the utmost importance in making the young horse straight.

In the *shoulder-in* the forehand of the horse is brought in about half a yard, thus describing a separate track parallel to the original track on which the hind legs must continue. The inside foreleg will step over that of the outside, whereas the inside hind leg will move more in the direction of the centre of gravity of the horse. This will make the hind legs carry a greater proportion of the weight, thus relieving the shoulders and allowing the forelegs to step forward more freely. In ancient riding instructions we find frequent references to the fact that it was de la Guérinière who invented the shoulder-in, and in his *Ecole de Cavalerie* he describes this exercise and gives exact diagrams of the hoofprints of the horse.

According to these diagrams the shoulder must be taken in to such a degree that the inside fore and hind legs step over and in front of those of the outside, thus describing four tracks. (The rider must be careful that the outside hind leg does not fall out and thus prevent the correct bend of the body.) This is the method to which the Spanish Riding School remains faithful.

Nowadays there are different opinions as to the degree of the angle which the horse forms to the wall in the shoulder-in. In opposition to de la Guérinière's theory it is maintained that the forehand should be taken in to such a degree that the inside hind leg follows exactly in the track of the outside foreleg, thus making a single track, so that three instead of four hoofprints appear. This interpretation generally leads to a sort of outline of a shoulder-in, and the inside foreleg does not cross sufficiently over the outside one. In this case the purpose of the exercise—the bending of the three joints of the hind legs, the freer movements of the shoulders, the improvement of the contact with the bit, and the increase of suppleness and obedience—will not be achieved.

Neither can the bending of the three joints of the hind legs—the chief object of this exercise—be achieved by the horse adopting an exaggerated position, because then the horse, instead of bringing the shoulder-in, will allow the hindquarters to fall out and exercise a kind of yielding to the leg, and yielding to the leg will never lead to a correct bending of the hind legs.

When judging the shoulder-in the expert should never allow himself to be involved in controversy as to which of the two doctrines is the correct one, but he should look to see whether the exercise is executed in the same manner on both reins. If, however, the horse has little position on one rein and as much as de la Guérinière demands on the other, then neither of the two versions is adhered to but the exercise is presented just as the horse thinks fit, which is wrong and useless. A horse will always take his shoulder-in better on the rein of the side on which he accepts the bit and try to avoid the discomfort of the exercise by overbending his neck on the other, the hollow, side.

At the Spanish Riding School, the young stallion is taught the shoulder-in as well as most of the other lateral work at the trot. The reason is that for all lateral work impulsion is most important and the trot provides more impulsion than the walk.

It is of great advantage to make the young horse familiar with the shoulder-in on the large circle providing that he moves on the large circle in steady contact with the bit, is correctly bent, and executes a brisk collected trot, for lateral work can be practised successfully only in this tempo.

The shoulder is taken into the circle with the inside rein, while the outside rein must prevent the horse from bending his neck too much. The inside rein maintains the position and the outside rein defines the degree of the position and leads the horse in the desired direction. The rider's inside leg, with a deep knee, is applied on the girth and maintains the inside bend of the horse's body evenly from head to tail. It also causes the inside foreleg to step over that of the outside and the inside hind leg to step well under the body. The object of the outside leg behind the girth is to prevent the hindquarters from falling out, and to maintain the fluent forward movement. The speed should never be allowed to slacken when practising shoulder-in, which is so often the case, nor should it be increased with hasty steps as many horses have the inclination to do. Only when the horse is able to maintain an even tempo on the single track as well as in the shoulder-in will this exercise be perfected.

The rider's weight must be shifted on the inside seat bone. The movement of the horse must not cause him to slide towards the outside and collapse his inside hip. In the shoulder-in, contrary to other lateral work and other exercises, the position of the horse is not in the direction of his movement; he does not look in the direction to which he is going.

As with any new exercise a few steps in shoulder-in will be sufficient to start with. The horse will then be ridden forward on a single track as a reward and in order to gain new impulsion for the repetition of the exercise. As soon as the young horse responds to the rider's aids at the shoulder-in, it is advisable to practise this exercise along the wall. In spite of all the advantages that can be obtained from performing it on the large circle, it has the effect of encouraging the hindquarters to fall out.

Again, along the wall a few steps of shoulder-in will be sufficient in this stage of training before obtaining fresh impulsion by riding briskly forward. It is of great advantage to begin this lateral exercise directly after passing through a corner. The horse is led into the corner as if he were going to execute a small circle. As soon as the forehand has begun the arc of the circle and moved half a yard away from the wall, the pressure of the inside leg is increased and the outside rein takes the horse in shoulder-in along the wall.

When practising lateral work the rider should never overlook the fact that these exercises consist of a forward and sideways movement of the horse. There is no difficulty in determining the sideways movement which is clearly distinguishable. It is most important, however, to keep the forward movement continually under control. The rider must always be certain that the horse, obedient to the aids, moves sufficiently forward. Therefore, it will be of great value to interrupt this exercise occasionally by a small circle on a single track.

The inside rein leads the horse into the circle and is supported by the inside leg pushing forward on the girth. The outside rein gives just enough to enable the horse to leave the wall

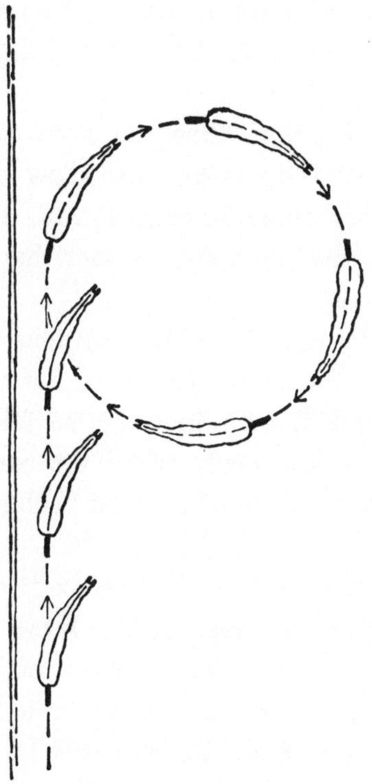

Transition from shoulder-in into a volte

and begin the circle. This transition into the circle is not only a test but also a very effective means of maintaining the necessary impulsion for the shoulder-in after completing the circle. It will also increase the obedience to the rider's legs. Another very good exercise to control the natural impulsion as well as obedience is to interrupt this lateral movement by going forward on a single track, that is, by going forward on a diagonal line to the opposite wall, thus following the direction of the horse's head.

When the horse has obtained sufficient proficiency and is able to move forward and sideways without altering his regular tempo, then, but never before, can the shoulder-in be practised in longer periods and demanded through the corners and, finally, away from the wall. The horse must execute lateral work joyfully and be completely relaxed, free from any tension or constraint, and maintain his position, that is, the angle of his body to the wall, without faltering until his rider brings the exercise to an end.

When this is the case, then the horse has perfected this important exercise. But the rider must allow time to reach perfection and in the beginning be content with little progress. It is preferable to make this concession rather than lose the general line of training.

It is the shoulder that the horse must take in while the hindquarters remain on the track. He must not take the shoulder halfway in and allow the hindquarters to fall halfway out, as can so often be seen especially when the exercise is executed away from the wall. A position obtained in this manner is wrong and of no value.

The degree of the position must be maintained from the beginning to the end of the exercise. The horse should not be allowed to take his shoulder slowly back to the wall, which tends to happen when a longer period of shoulder-in is demanded, as a horse will always try to make things easier for himself. Furthermore, the rider must not be deceived when the horse bends his neck more and takes the shoulder in less. It is up to the rider always to be aware of these probable faults.

Riding through the corners in shoulder-in will increase obedience and skill and furnish a precise measure for the degree of balance the horse has achieved. When passing through a corner the distance covered by the shoulders is decreased while that of the hindquarters is increased. For this reason the forehand is given a half-halt with both reins before reaching the corner. The action of the inside rein will be of greater importance, for it gives the position to the horse and holds the shoulder-in. The inside leg on the girth bends the horse's body inwards and pushes the hindquarters through the corner.

Once more let it be remembered that the shoulder-in improves the bending of all three joints of the hind legs and makes them carry a greater proportion of the weight. This bending improves the suppleness and the activity of the hind legs, and

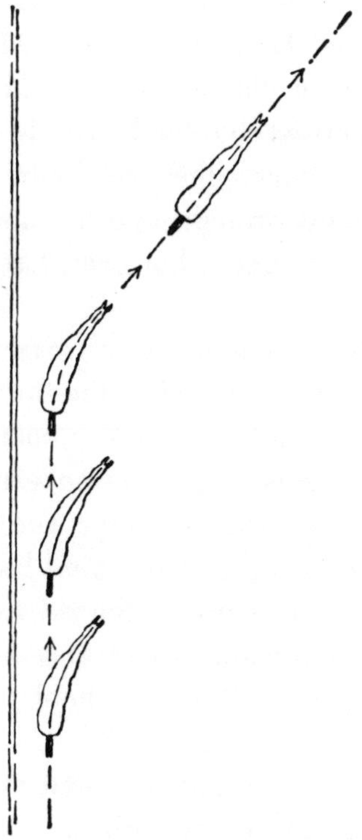

End of shoulder-in by going forward on a single track in the direction of the horse's head

gives more freedom to the shoulders, which improves the paces and favours a lighter contact with the bit.

All this makes the shoulder-in a valuable auxiliary in obtaining a more expressive extended trot. From a brisk energetic shoulder-in, place the horse straight alongside the wall and immediately ask him to go forward in extended trot. Or discontinue the sideways movement of shoulder-in by sending the horse in the extended trot diagonally to the opposite wall on a single track, thus following the direction of the position of the horse's head. In both these exercises it will be found that the steps in the extended trot will be longer and more energetic.

A straight strike-off into the canter is also much improved by the shoulder-in. Moreover, it will prove of value with horses that have an unlevel trot or those inclined to strike off into the canter on their own volition. Even a fully trained horse will derive much benefit from the shoulder-in and it will be found an excellent remedy for many difficulties. The old masters were well aware of this and practised the shoulder-in in the canter with the so called "plié-gallop" which they no doubt found an excellent means to make the horse straight and to improve the activity of the hindquarters. This exercise, however, has not been practised in recent years.

Travers (*Quarters-in*) is a lateral exercise which is rarely practised and very seldom applied at the Spanish Riding School. As most horses have a tendency to go crooked, why should this inclination be further encouraged by an exercise in which the hindquarters are taken in from the wall? The possible advantages to be obtained in the bending of the hind legs, improved lateral bending, or increased obedience to the rider's leg aids are so far outweighed by the disadvantages of this movement that it is employed at the Spanish Riding School only in exceptional circumstances.

To perform the travers the forehand must be held on the track with both reins but mainly with the outside one supported by the inside rein and the outside leg; the inside leg on the girth pushes the horse forward and ensures the correct position of the head as well as the lateral bend of the body. The outside leg applied behind the girth makes the horse take his quarters away from the wall and the outside hind leg steps over and in front of the inside one. It must be understood that even a travers with very little position is by no means identical to a crooked horse, as in this exercise, when correctly performed, the lateral bend is regular from head to tail. This explains the advantages of this exercise, i.e., increased activity of the hindquarters and improvement in suppleness.

Some horses have a strong inclination to be crooked on one side and to make themselves stiff on the other and resist any position. This makes it difficult to execute certain exercises such as a correct half pass to the stiff side. In this case it is of great advantage to practise shoulder-in on the crooked side—the hollow one—to straighten the horse by preventing an excessive bend to the hollow side, and hindquarters-in on the stiff side to obtain the correct bend on this side, make the horse more obedient to the rider's outside leg, and carry the quarters more to the stiff side.

For slow and heavy horses quick changes from shoulder-in to hindquarters-in and vice versa will be of great benefit. As a result of the increased suppleness, dexterity, and obedience to the rider's legs, all transition in tempo or pace demanded immediately following this exercise will be done more fluently.

At the Spanish Riding School, in addition to the shoulder-in, the *renvers* plays an important part in the training of the young stallions as well as in the training of the School horses. The renvers offers the same advantages as the travers and hardly any of the disadvantages.

Renvers might be described as inverted travers, for now the hindquarters remain on the track whereas the forehand is taken in just as in shoulder-in except that the horse is bent to the outside looking in the direction to which he is moving. Literally expressed renvers can be described as "hindquarters-out." Guérinière named this exercise "croupe au mur." Renvers is more difficult than travers or even than shoulder-in. For this reason the rider should demand only a few steps to commence with and mainly concentrate on the regular fluent movement of the horse.

In the renvers the forehand must be taken from the wall. The outside rein must then be lightly applied in order to maintain the position of the horse's head to this side. To begin with the rider should be content with less position than in the other lateral exercises but care must be taken that the lateral bend of the horse, to the outside in this exercise, is distinctly noticeable and, by pushing his horse forward, he maintains the regularity of the tempo. Seat and both legs will be the pushing aids. The outside leg on the girth plays the greater part in pushing and is responsible for the lateral bend and the position to the outside. The inside leg behind the girth makes the horse step sideways. Should this leg be applied too far behind the girth, or with a raised heel, the sideways pushing effect would be lost. If the horse does not follow the rider's commands by stepping sideways, a short and energetic aid from the leg will give better results than a leg taken too far back. The rider should sit on his outside seat bone, that is to say, in the direction of the movement.

In the renvers on the right rein the rider demands a moderate position of the horse's head with the left rein, at the same time pushing forward with his legs. It is around the left leg that the bend of the horse's body to the left will be brought about. The rider's weight is to a greater extent on his left seat bone and the right shoulder must conform to the movement. The right leg behind the girth is responsible for the bend to the left and the lateral movement.

As a rule, at the Spanish Riding School the renvers is begun after a *passade* to make things easier for the horse. A passade is a very small turn in a half volte, the hindquarters describing a smaller circle than the forehand. Executed in the walk or the canter it would be a preparation for the half pirouette.

During the passade and afterwards the horse continues to walk or to canter in the same rhythm as was employed on the straight line. The correct passade is an excellent exercise to improve suppleness and mobility. It is first taught on the large circle. The inside rein leads the horse into the turn, the outside rein with slightly firmer contact defines the degree of the position and supports the outside leg pushing sideways behind the girth which must, also, prevent the hindquarters from falling out. The inside leg maintains the fluency of the movement and makes the horse go forward. It is preferable to execute a larger passade to begin with because it is easier for the horse to maintain the movement. If it is too small the hindquarters will be apt to lose the rhythm or even come to a standstill. The passade may be performed in a corner of the arena or on the long side.

In a *passade and renvers,* as this exercise is called in the Spanish Riding School, the horse will not be led into the new direction on a single track, as is usual after a passade, but taken into the renvers by the outside rein which does not allow the forehand to reach the wall, thus producing the position required for the renvers. The aids for the renvers will then be applied.

With the same aids the horse can be taken from the shoulder-

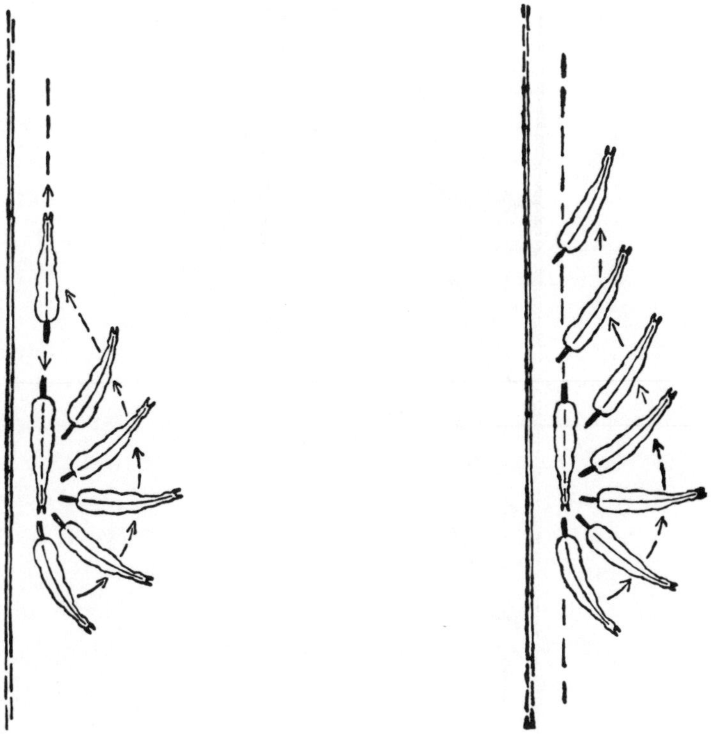

LEFT: *passade* RIGHT: *passade and renvers*

in into a passade and renvers. In this case the inside leg already applied firmly on the girth will prevent the horse from falling into the passade or the movement from coming to an end.

By changing the aids the shoulder-in may be converted into a renvers while still maintaining the same direction. The lateral angle remains unaltered but the position of the horse's head and bend is reversed. If in shoulder-in the position and bend were to the left side, for the renvers the horse changes his position and bend to the right side without, however, altering the lateral angle and the regular tempo. The rider must change his aids accordingly. This exercise is of great benefit in obtaining immediate and accurate response to the aids.

The renvers can also be started after a half pass. Before reaching the wall at the end of a half pass across the arena, the horse is taken into the renvers instead of continuing on a single

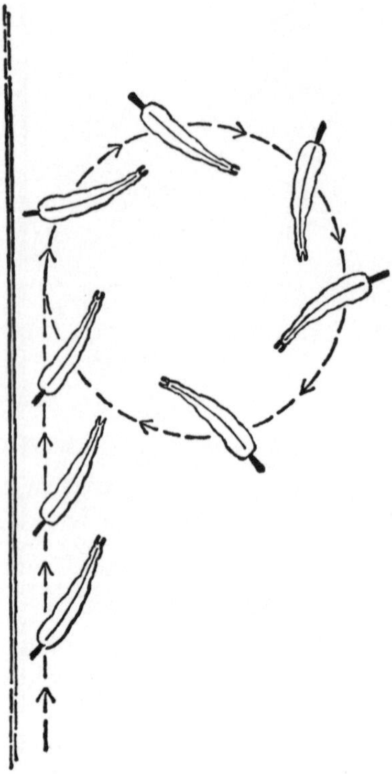

Renvers-volte

track. The forehand is checked before reaching the wall with what, up to now, has been the outside rein, while the hindquarters are pushed against the wall with the hitherto outside leg.

Another exercise beneficial to the physical development of the horse is the *renvers-volte.* From the renvers alongside the wall the horse is taken into the renvers-volte in which the position is to the outside. The forehand follows a smaller circle and the hindquarters a larger one. The rider must sit to the outside and take his inside shoulder a little back in order to be able to hold the hindquarters to the outside with his inside leg. This is a very good, if somewhat strenuous exercise, in which it is most important to maintain the lightness and the regularity of the horse's steps. The rider should maintain this liveliness by his pushing aids without allowing the horse to lose the rhythm of the movement.

The forward and sideways movement, which is the foundation of all lateral work, is best demonstrated by the *half pass.* In the half pass the horse moves on an oblique line with his body parallel to the wall. The outside fore and hind legs step over and in front of those of the inside, but the forehand must clearly show a tendency to precede the hindquarters. The position of the head and bend of the horse's body must conform to the direction of the movement.

The half pass may be executed on very short lines—in a half volte and half pass; on longer lines—in a half pass from the centre line; or on very long lines—in a half pass from one long side of the arena to the other.

The best way to teach a half pass to a young horse is to begin with *a half volte and half pass.* The inside rein supported by the rider's inside leg on the girth takes the horse into the half volte; the outside rein defines the position of the head and the bend of the horse's body and, together with the outside leg applied behind the girth, prevents the hindquarters from falling out. The most important aid is given by the rider's inside leg which pushes the horse forward and is responsible for the correct bend. At the end of the half volte the circular movement is interrupted by the outside rein supported by the rider's inside leg; the horse is then led back with both reins in an oblique line to the wall from which he started, as in a simple half volte and change, except that now the outside leg behind the girth, supported by the outside rein, makes the horse step sideways while the inside leg maintains the impulsion and ensures that the horse goes forward. The position of the head should be such that the neck is not more bent than the whole body. An exaggerated position of the head, as is so often seen, would hinder the free and elastic movement of the horse's legs, thus taking away the brilliancy of the half pass.

In all lateral work, with the exception of the shoulder-in, the rider's weight is shifted into the direction of the movement as already explained in the section on Aids (aids of weight). This is why in the half pass the inside leg must be pressed well down,

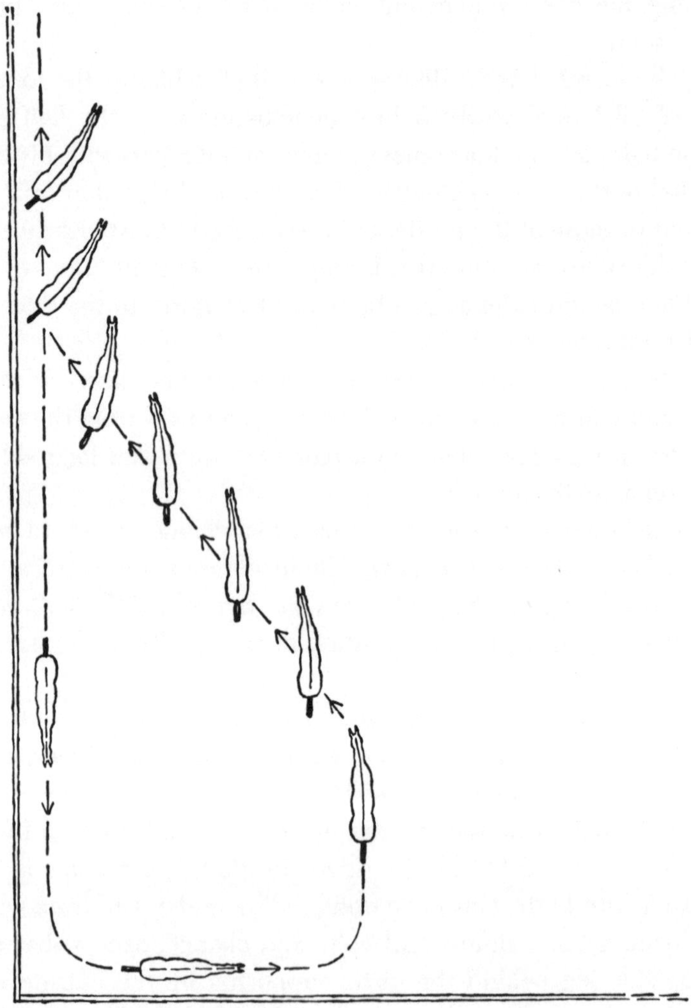

Half pass and renvers

making it appear longer, in order to prevent the seat and thus the weight of the rider from sliding to the outside, a fault that can easily occur in this type of movement. On arrival at the wall of the arena, the position is changed and the horse continues on a single track. For reasons already explained the trot is preferred for teaching these lateral exercises.

When the young horse is able to execute a half volte and half pass without difficulty—prefection can only be expected at a later stage—the exercise may be developed into a *half pass from the centre line*. The horse is taken from the short side on to the centre line with the aids for a simple turn, and after some three yards on the straight line is taken in the half pass towards the centre of the long side. These three yards straight down the centre are very important because they tend to prevent the horse—once familiar with this exercise—from falling into the lateral movement as soon as he has turned the corner, thus anticipating the rider's aids and developing faults resulting from anticipation. Here again, as with every exercise, it is the rider's will that must dominate the horse.

When the horse has been straightened on the centre line he is led by the inside rein into the direction of the middle of the long side. The rider's inside leg applied on the girth supports

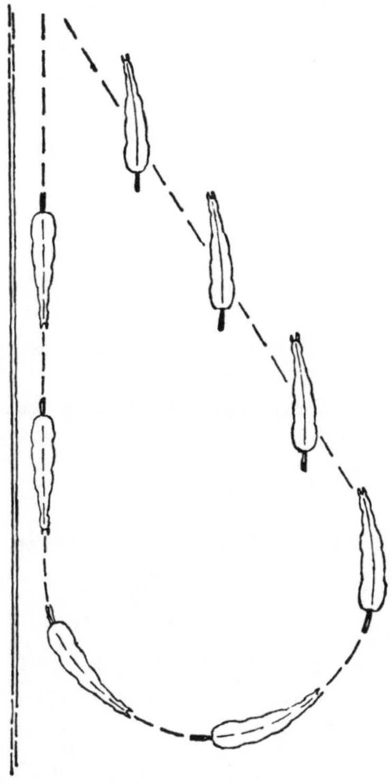

Half volte and half pass

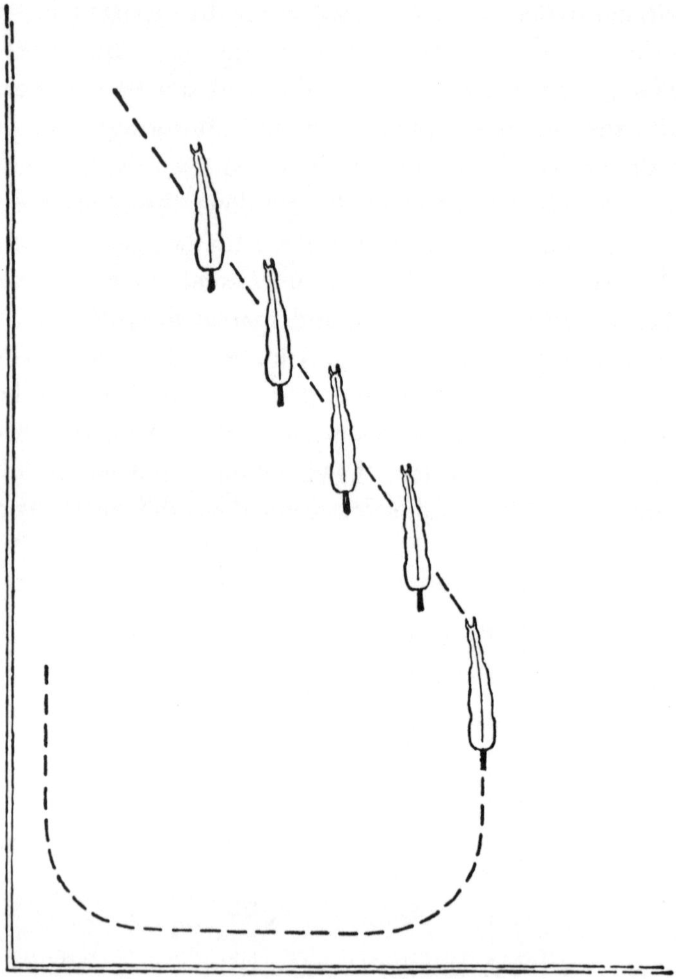

Half pass from the centre line

this rein, bends the horse's body to the inside and pushes him forward. Any falling in of the hindquarters must also be prevented by this leg, for, as already explained, it is the forehand which must always lead. The outside rein defines the degree of position and bend and helps the inside rein to maintain the direction of the movement, supported at the same time by the outside leg behind the girth pushing the horse sideways. The rider must carefully avoid any sideways pressure of this rein on the neck of the horse. When the horse has reached the side of the school, his position is changed in the same manner as with the half volte and change. The movement should continue smoothly.

When the horse has acquired enough dexterity to be able to execute a half pass on a short line without faltering or tension, the half pass may be practised from one long side of the arena to the other. Having passed through the corner leading to the long side, the horse is taken by the inside rein on an oblique line to the opposite wall. In the beginning the direction should be as oblique as possible in order to maintain the impulsion by the prevailing forward movement. The inside leg on the girth, together with the weight of the rider sitting in the direction of the movement, maintains the fluent forward motion. The outside leg behind the girth, supported by the outside rein, is responsible for the degree of the sideways movement and makes the outside fore and hind legs step over those of the inside. Once more, the body of the horse must be parallel to the wall with a distinct bend to the inside, that is to say, a bend towards the direction of the movement and with the forehand definitely leading.

In order to fulfil this important demand and, above all, in order to prevent a very serious fault, namely the hindquarters leading or falling in, it has been the practice at the Spanish Riding School for the past forty years to take the forehand so much forward when going away from the wall that the crossing of the outside legs is less distinctly visible and only just before reaching the opposite side to increase the sideways movement to such a degree that the horse's body is parallel to the wall when he reaches the track.

By this method the regular rhythm of the steps is ensured, which is preferable to a parallel position with irregular steps. This concession, made in the course of training, does not alter the rule that in a correct half pass the horse's body should be parallel to the wall.

In the half pass, as in any lateral movement, the tempo of the horse's steps must be regular and even; he should not lie on the rein but maintain the same contact with the bit as when on a straight line. If the contact is too firm the bend and suppleness will be lost and as a consequence the hind legs will not step sufficiently under the body.

In the half pass the rider insists that the horse move in the direction decided by him rather than follow his own inclination in order to make things easier for himself. This is of greater importance than might be supposed. The horse will execute the half pass more easily to one side than to the other, generally finding it easier on the hollow side, whereas, on the other—the stiff side—he will move less freely and with a different position. And he will often move more to the side on which he finds it easier than his rider demands, sliding to this side, as it were. But it is up to the rider to control the movement. In more advanced dressage tests, therefore, the judge should demand that the rider direct his horse to the exact spot indicated. To the expert judge, who performs the exercise in his own mind, as it were, the faults in training will be revealed. If, for instance, the half pass comes to an end a horse's length before the spot indicated in the test, the judge must look upon it not only as a careless way of riding but also as a bad performance of lateral work because the horse quite obviously anticipated his rider's will. The judge's opinion is not then dogmatic but an effort to improve the performance of the dressage rider and make him, as one well-known rider took pride in describing himself, a "professor of the track."

If the horse slides to the side in the half pass, thus allowing the sideways movement to overtake the forward one, the rider's inside leg must push the horse more forward in order to hold the hindquarters under control. This may demand more than the rider's leg is capable of and may not be the solution. It may be advisable to fall back on the method employed in the Spanish Riding School and give the horse a more oblique position, thus making him go more forward and prevent the hindquarters from leading.

It is a very good exercise and one that is a test for the degree of training reached to demand a half pass from the long side to the centre line, then to ride the horse straight forward for a few yards, and then to continue the interrupted half pass in the same direction, or back to the side from which the exercise started. This

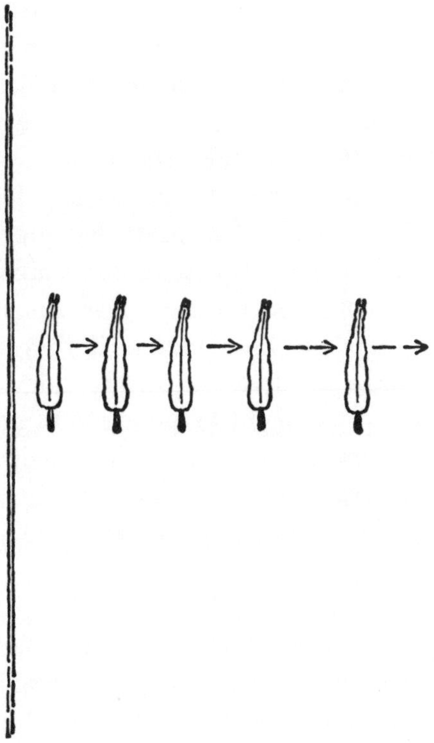

Full travers

will teach the horse to concentrate on his rider as he will never know in which direction the exercise is to be continued.

The *full travers* (*full pass*) is a movement in which the horse moves to the side only. This lateral exercise was introduced for military requirements in order to allow the riders to correct their distance between one another. In Austria it is demanded in the more difficult dressage tests.

It is rarely practised at the Spanish Riding School, but as most exercises can be traced back to military origin and as the Spanish Riding School has always made a point of keeping close contact with general equitation, every rider is required to have an exact understanding of the full travers.

In the full travers, which can only be executed from a standstill, the horse's outside legs step over those of the inside, the hoofmarks of the fore and hind legs making two parallel lines. The rider gives the aids as for the walk and in the precise moment when the feet are lifted from the ground, the inside rein takes the horse to the side to which the travers is to be executed, and which becomes the inner side. The outside rein prevents the forward movement and supports the outside leg as it pushes sideways behind the girth. The inside leg prevents the horse from creeping back and is responsible for maintaining the correct bend, thus making the forehand lead the movement, and this leg also controls the hindquarters if they should show a tendency to overtake the forehand in the sideways movement.

The full travers is brought to an end with a halt. The reins check the sideways movement and the horse halts. The action of the outside leg ceases, while the inside leg remains in contact in order to stop the sideways movement. The position of the horse is made straight.

The time has now arrived when the horse may be introduced to *spurs*. The actual moment will depend on the individual horse; with lazy horses it will be sooner; with excitable ones, later.

Practice in lateral work, the exact execution of the exercises, and the changing of pace and tempo will increase the balance, suppleness, and the action of the rein going through the horse's body, so that now he will be ready to learn the *halt*. So far halts have been practised only at the conclusion of the daily work or between working periods. A correct halt belongs to the more difficult exercises and needs appropriate preparation. Once more I emphasise the same important rule to be followed throughout the entire training: it is better to wait until the horse is ready for a correct halt than to allow a wrong performance to grow into a bad habit.

At first the halt should be practised from the collected trot. The horse should end the movement without making any steps at the walk—the movement must not die away into a halt—and the horse should stand straight, step well under the body with his hind legs, and carry his weight equally balanced on all four legs, fore and hind legs side by side. The horse should not lose contact with the bit nor lie on it, should concentrate on his rider, and be ready to move off at any moment in any demanded pace. Unfortunately halts are not practised with sufficient care nowadays, as most riders prefer the more spectacular movements to the simple basic training—an alarming sign of the general decline in equestrian art.

To produce the correct halt the horse must be pushed forward with both legs on the girth and held in a lively collected trot. The impulsion procured in this manner will then be absorbed by repeated short actions of the rein and the braced back of the rider in order to ensure that the hind legs step well under the body and to obtain a halt in the direct line of the movement. Experience has taught that if the action of the rein is too prolonged and too firm, it will have a restraining effect on the hind legs, thus making it difficult, or even impossible, for them to step well under the body. This is why horses that lie too much on the rein will get on to their forehand and lose the action of the hindquarters. On the other hand the expert will be able to relate a weak action of the hind legs to a too-firm contact with the bit.

The rider will obtain a near perfect halt if he succeeds in bringing it about mainly by bracing his back. The rein on the hollow side should remain applied with a slightly firmer contact supporting the action of the rider's back, while the rein on the stiff side, by repeated short actions, prevents an increased position of the horse's head to the hollow side, thus helping the movement to end correctly.

When the horse has come to a halt, the pressure of the legs and the action of the reins must cease. The rider sits straight and firmly in the saddle, his upper body neither leaning forward nor hanging back, and his legs remain applied to the horse's sides in order to be able to prevent the horse from creeping back. After the halt a light contact with the mouth will keep the horse on the alert and ready to continue any movement without having to be again collected.

If the halt is repeatedly exercised the horse will be inclined to anticipate it, drop into a walk, and execute the halt on the forehand. The rider should not, therefore, practise the halt on the same spot too often, and when he notices a certain faltering in the movement of the horse, he should practise a few changes of tempo.

From the halt the horse should move off directly into the pace the rider demands without making any steps at a lower pace. For the collected trot he must lift the diagonal legs in his first step, thus proving that he begins the movement from his hindquarters, which is an essential rule in classical equitation.

For the *move off into the trot,* the pressure of both the rider's legs on the girth is stronger than for the walk and the reins are given just enough to enable the horse to begin the movement without losing collection. The rider must sit more firmly in the saddle when demanding this pace; his body will then follow the movement of the horse without leaning forward or back. It is most important that the aids of the legs are not applied too suddenly, thus surprising the horse. The transition into the movement must be smooth and supple.

This transition into the correct pace may seem simple, but it is very difficult to execute correctly. On the other hand, it reveals the degree of physical training. Most horses will try to begin the movement on the forehand, sometimes even after a few steps at a lower pace. They will lose their collection and not be able to begin the trot immediately from the halt. It may often be seen that a horse will extend his neck when commencing the movement, thus becoming longer in his body and losing collection, which he recovers only when in motion. It cannot be underlined too often that the horse must begin the movement when in a state of collection. This collection may have to be produced by a unilateral half-halt on the stiff side at the same time pushing forward with a braced back, especially if the horse tries to bend in the wrong direction or drop the bit. Horses that lie on the rein, thus going on to the forehand when beginning the movement, should be given a half-halt with the rein on the stiff side in an upward direction at the moment of the transition, the rein of the hollow side being lightly applied.

If the horse finds difficulty in placing his feet side by side and carrying his weight equally on all four legs when coming to a halt, it will be helpful to demand the halt from a half pass at either the walk or the trot. The inside legs stepping sideways will thus be more easily placed in line with those of the outside.

In addition to the work already laid out, the *canter* should now be practised in order to further the physical training of the horse. This will include transitions into the canter from the trot both on a large circle and on a straight line. Work in the canter is the best way of enlivening the impulsion, but before practising the halt from the canter, the horse must be prepared by transitions from the trot and walk and vice versa. He must learn to pass from the canter into a walk without any steps at the trot. He should, therefore, be trained to execute an elastic, lively canter, the collection for which is mostly produced by the rider's braced back. When this stage has been reached the rider increases the aids of his legs, at the same time absorbing the impulsion produced by bracing his back. By repeated short actions of the reins, being careful to avoid a too-firm contact with the bit, he passes into a clear walk after five or six bounds at the canter, each one shorter than the previous one. To be correctly executed this transition must be smooth, with the hind legs placed well under the horse's body. The rider's legs must ensure that the horse proceed in an even regular walk. If, during these bounds of very collected canter, the horse, anticipating the rider's wishes, allows the movement to die down, the remedy is a few changes of tempo in order to secure the regular bounds in canter before the rider again demands a correct transition to the walk. From the walk the horse must strike off directly into the canter and not after a few hasty steps. Most important of all he must remain straight. A short shoulder-in will be found to be of great benefit in obtaining a straight strike-off.

The rider should begin to teach the *halt from the canter* only when the young horse is well advanced in his balance and able to maintain his position in the various movements with skill and obedience. Once more the point must be stressed that a halt is correct when done directly from the true canter without any false steps in between.

This halt is prepared in exactly the same way as the transition to the walk. In the collected canter the horse's hind legs are made to jump well under his body by the aids of the rider's legs. The rider's back, supported by repeated short actions of the reins, makes these bounds shorter and more elevated, gradually preventing them from gaining ground to the front and bringing the hind legs well under the centre of gravity. After five or six of these shortened bounds the action of the reins and the braced back of the rider are increased and the horse is brought to a halt. The horse must stand straight in the direction in which he was moving with his fore and hind legs placed side by side. The hindquarters must be slightly lowered by the well-bent three joints of the hind legs, and the forehand, with the correct position of the head, must be proudly erect, horse and rider looking like a statue. When the halt is completed in this manner the rider's legs cease their pressure but remain applied to prevent the horse from stepping back. The actions of the reins cease without losing contact. In this way the horse will stand motionless and collected, listening for his rider's next commands.

The best halt from the canter is obtained by the pushing aids of the rider absorbed by his braced back and opposed by the rein applied on the hollow side. Short actions of the rein on the stiff side applied at the same time prevent an increased bend in the horse's neck. The rein on the hollow side also helps to keep the horse straight by preventing him from bringing his quarters in on this side. The strike-off into the canter from the halt must be brought about without any intermediate steps in another pace; the first movement must be the bound of canter. This is a difficult exercise to execute correctly and will be successful only after a thorough training of the horse, as explained in this chapter. Indeed, correct halts from the canter will reveal a well-founded basic training of the horse.

When *striking off into the canter from the halt* the outside leg will be applied lightly behind the girth in order to announce the movement—lightly, because the horse must on no account be made to yield to the other side, thus making a crooked strike-off. The strike-off is demanded by the inside leg, supported by the rider sitting more firmly on the inside seat bone, while the reins are given just enough so that the horse can strike off without losing collection. As soon as the horse moves off, the normal canter aids will maintain an easy motion. Faults that occur when striking off into a canter are dealt with in the same manner as those when moving off from the halt into a trot. These exercises should be continually varied in order to prevent the horse from anticipating the rider's aids; for instance, halt from canter and strike-off into the trot, or halt from the trot and strike-off into the canter, etc. The thinking rider will devise many different combinations to hold the attention of his horse.

The time has now come when work in the *collected walk* may begin. The reins will no longer be given after the transition to the walk in order to let the horse rest, but the rider will try to maintain the same impulsion in the walk that has been achieved and established in the other paces by long and strenuous training. The horse must walk with brilliancy, not let his weight drop on to his forehand or drag his legs, especially his hind legs. On the contrary, he must show a pure collected walk, with even and cadenced steps, ready to change the tempo or movement at any moment according to his rider's demands. The rider must have that wonderful feeling of perfect control, so that he can execute any demands made upon him and not only those practised for a test. This must be the aim of training, and the thinking rider will invent tests that will prove to him how well and willingly the horse can execute them and how much he has benefited from his training.

In response to the rider's increased leg aids, with the corresponding giving of the reins, the horse must be able to go from the collected walk into the extended walk without any unlevel steps. He has to become slightly longer in his neck to enable him to lengthen his strides without losing contact with the bit. This will also enable him to find a smooth transition back into the collected walk. It must be emphasised that the extended walk should be ridden with contact and not on a loose rein, as is so often seen. Impulsion for the extended walk is produced by the activity of the hindquarters and the rider should not attempt to deceive by going on a loose rein.

The collected walk is the result of correct training. Frequent changes of speed, as exercised in the trot and canter, are not advised with the walk, as at this pace such changes are inclined to have a bad influence on the regularity of the strides.

Lateral work at the walk should be limited to what is necessary as a test of the training. Any horse that can show a correct walk and knows how to execute lateral work at the trot will have no difficulty in doing lateral work at the walk.

The *turn on the haunches* is the smallest turn that can be made; it corresponds to the half pirouette at the canter, must be taught at the walk, and should be executed only in this pace.

In the turn on the haunches the forehand describes a half circle around the hind legs. The inside hind leg turns on the spot in the rhythm of the movement and forms the centre of a half circle, while the outside leg performs a small circle around the inside one.

The turn on the haunches is wrong if the inside hind leg pivots without leaving the ground, or is only raised once or twice during the turn, thus losing the rhythm of the pace. It is a greater fault to pivot than it is for the hind legs to perform a small circle in the correct rhythm.

Those who maintain that the inside leg should pivot without leaving the ground are reminded that in equestrian art the horse must be either in the rhythm of the movement or at the halt. If he is in motion, the hind legs must conform to the movement of the forelegs in the pace that nature has given to the horse. As the turn on the haunches can only be practised in movement, the hind legs must turn in the correct sequence of steps at the walk, in the same way that the half pirouette is performed at the canter.

The inside rein leads the forehand into the turn; the inside leg on the girth maintains the correct position, ensures that the movements of the legs are not interrupted and, together with the outside leg, prevents the horse from stepping back, which would be a bad fault in this exercise. The outside rein, lightly applied, defines the degree of the position of the horse's head and prevents the horse from falling into the turn or from hastening the move-

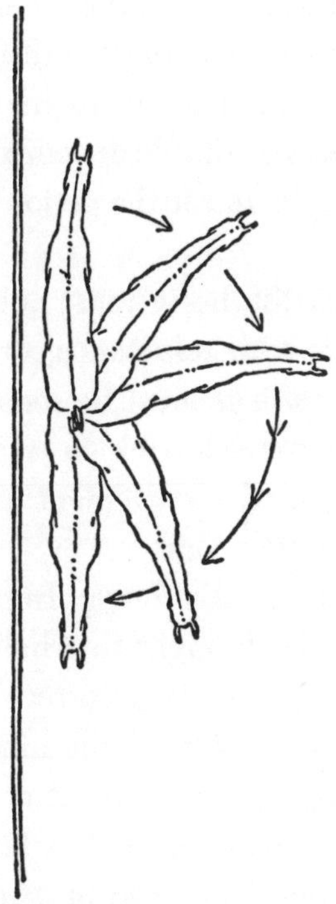

Turn on the haunches

ment. The outside leg, behind the girth, demands the turn around the inside leg and must push forward the moment the horse shows any sign of stepping back.

If the turn on the haunches is asked from the halt the horse must make the movement in the action of the walk and again come to a halt on the completion of the movement. From the walk, his position will be changed when he arrives on the other rein and the forward movement will be in the same pace and rhythm on a straight line.

In some dressage tests there is an exercise called the turn on the haunches at the trot or canter. In this case the horse is taken into a walk before the turn is made and as soon as the turn is completed, strikes off immediately into the trot or canter. This is an excellent exercise during the early preparation for the pirouette, and as a remedy if the horse is inclined to anticipate the movement.

If, by means of the above mentioned exercises, the horse has made sufficient progress in his ability and in the development of his joints and muscles, he is ready to be taught the *rein-back.* This can be the case only if the three joints of his hind legs have become sufficiently supple and if the action of the reins goes well through his body.

When reining back the horse must not oppose the action of the reins or move back with reluctance, dragging his feet along the ground. The diagonal legs must be seen to be lifted from the ground as a pair and moved back in a straight line, step by step, without faltering in the movement and without the hindquarters deviating to either side.

The rein-back will usually begin from the halt. After the rein-back the horse can be brought to a halt or be made to move off in any of the three paces. As a correct rein-back demands a strong bending of all three joints of the hind legs, the movement should not be practised for too long at a time. When teaching this exercise the rider must be content at first if the horse, on the action of the reins, steps back one or two paces.

Before reining back, the horse should stand correctly on all four legs; the rider then demands the walk with both legs on the girth, the reins being only slightly given. At the moment the horse is about to move, he will be made to step back by the increased action of the reins. The action of the rider's legs should be decreased at this moment, but not discontinued because this action must not only maintain the collection but also be increased if the horse shows signs of creeping back instead of stepping back. The rein-back will be the proof of the degree of the suppleness of the horse, of the action of the rein going through the body, and above all, of his obedience. It may also be used as a punishment for naughtiness or inattention. Above all, it will be proof of the correct bending of the joints of the hind legs, which will make the strike-off into the canter easier from a rein-back than from a halt. This exercise is correctly executed when the horse can strike off into the canter from the rein-back without any intermediate steps.

18 & 19 Passage

20 All four reins in one hand, riding on the curb only

21 & 22 Piaffe in hand

23 Levade in hand

The young horse has now reached the end of the second phase of his training.

The work he has so far done corresponds in general to the work of the remounts of the Austro-Hungarian Cavalry as laid down in *Riding Instructions to the Cavalry* mentioned by H. E. von Holbein, one of the sources, as we have seen, on which the method of training at the Spanish Riding School is based. At this school, however, more accuracy and impulsion are demanded from the horses in their second stage of training than is demanded from the Army horses.

The two phases of training that the horse must pass through cannot be measured by time, and they must be taken only as a general guide to the methodical proceedings to be followed. Individual work is always given preference to a set pattern, as long as it does not digress from the basic principles of classical riding.

But a programme based on classical rules, built on the knowledge and experience gained through the course of centuries by the great riding masters of the past, and arranged to fit into a certain sequence, will guarantee progress. Thus the young rider will be able to keep his goal before his eyes, will be provided with a programme by which he can obtain it, and will be prevented from getting lost in the maze of his own ideas which have not yet passed the test of time. Moreover, by following this method, faults that would be difficult to eradicate later in the training will be nipped in the bud.

Just as the work of a painter will be recognised by its individuality, so experienced riders will not all follow details in the same way and the results of their training will be influenced by their characters and physical abilities. But painter and rider have one thing in common. They both must have an exact conception of the work they wish to produce. Any method can be considered correct if it leads to success without offending the rules of classical horsemanship, because these are the rules that divide classical riding from the circus, rules in which all short cuts and tricks are eliminated.

The length of time required for the training, especially in

the second phase, will depend to a great extent on the knowledge of the trainer, on the constitution and abilities of the horse, but above all on his character and temperament as well as his intelligence. If a cavalry soldier can achieve the required results in two years, an expert rider should find no difficulty in doing the same, and with more accuracy and in greater detail. He should even achieve them in a shorter time. But the necessary time must always be allowed for the physical and mental development of the horse. The time thus spent will never fail to reap its reward. In the latter part of the second phase the emphasis on individual training should be increased. As with a human being, the more intelligent a pupil is, the more important it is to depart from a rigid pattern and practise more ingenuity in the training. In this way the riding will develop from ordinary work into art.

Nowadays the term "art" is bestowed too freely, a sign of the general deterioration of standards. It is as absurd to call the first years of training of the young horse Equestrian Art as it would be to put a novice class in that category. This over-rating gives rise to the question often heard: Why is riding called an art and not a sport?

The second phase of training is described by H. E. von Holbein as follows: "Riding the horse in all paces, turns and figures in collection and full balance is the so called 'Campaign School.' Only when by this training suppleness, impulsion, and skill have been obtained, accompanied by stamina, and when the intelligence has been developed, then, and only then can the rider proceed to art—the Haute Ecole." Indeed I agree that it is after this period of systematic and conscientious training that horse and rider will stand on the threshold of High School and be able to enter the sphere of art.

3. *The School Horse*

In the words of H. E. von Holbein, "The High School is unthinkable without a thorough training in the first two phases, especially the second phase, the Campaign School."

Actually, the three phases must be interwoven and all training based on this policy. This is the reason why the casual observer will notice the same exercises being performed in this phase as were practised in the second, with the following essential difference: so far perfection has been strived for, but now it will be demanded unflinchingly. Now it is no longer a question of the horse performing one or the other of the exercises, but of *how* he performs them.

The thinking rider should understand the influence of each exercise on the entire training and eradicate any fault the moment it appears as the training progresses. Profound knowledge and experience together with understanding and sympathy towards his four-legged partner will make the rider mature into a professor, and he will blossom out from an ordinary workman into an artist. As an artist he will be awed by the creations of nature, will honour the beauty of his horse in all his movements as a gift from Heaven, and despise any form of artifice. He will realise that nature can exist without art, but that art cannot exist without nature.

Now as before, the purity of the paces and their development will take priority. The rider can improve the paces of his horse by correct physical training, which will be the best proof of the standard of his work. On the other hand, the paces that nature has given to the horse will deteriorate under unintelligent riding and be proof of a poor standard. For this reason, even in this last phase of training the greatest importance is paid to the development of the paces.

The collected paces by their regularity, rhythm, and liveliness must be the image of controlled force. Impulsion must be seen in collection as well as in the immediate extension. The impulsion must be checked and improved constantly. If difficulties occur, the best remedy will be to ride the horse busily forward.

The technique of *breathing* plays an important part in the performance of the horse, in the same way that it does with a human being. This technique will be the result of methodical training and will increase the powers of endurance. Excited horses, which do not carry the weight of their riders correctly, will be sooner out of breath and unable to produce as good a performance as well-trained horses. Regular breathing will reveal to the observer a physically and mentally well-balanced horse stepping with regularity. High blowing is a sign of well-being.

The rider must keep his horse under continual observation in order to be able to draw conclusions from any symptoms, no matter how insignificant, which may give him ideas for his method of training. The success of individual schooling depends largely on this constant observation. This observation must begin in the first year of training and its importance will increase as the horse matures, while the origins and results of various faults and difficulties must be continually reviewed.

The *correct position of the saddle* will have to be checked as the horse develops, for a proper position of the saddle is of the greatest importance in obtaining balance. If the saddle tends to slide forward, the rider must immediately dismount and correct its position, always moving it from front to rear. After re-tightening the girth it will be advisable, especially with a highly strung horse, to move him back a few steps and forward again before mounting. This will ensure that there is no tension and will guard against the risk of the horse rearing up and coming over backward.

Still greater attention must be paid to *correct bitting*. On this will depend the correct contact with the mouth, which is the foundation on which the whole training is based. From the manner of contact, experts will be able to draw instructive conclusions on the training of the horse.

At the Spanish Riding School the *snaffle* is used for the entire training, because it offers the best means of obtaining a steady contact and ensuring a thorough physical training of the horse. It also helps to prevent the rider from trying to work his horse from front to rear which can so easily happen if the severer curb bridle is used.

It is of the utmost importance that the bit chosen fits correctly. Even then the horse may contract bad habits caused by faulty training. These must never be overlooked, for the sooner they are discovered and combatted the more easily they can be corrected. If they are allowed to become habits, they will be far more difficult to eliminate.

The horse must accept the bit with a closed mouth, his tongue lying quietly beneath the snaffle. Nervous horses are inclined to open their mouths, which is the beginning of a bad habit caused by paying insufficient attention to their riders. Tightening the noseband will usually keep the mouth quiet, but care must be taken that it is not made so tight that it interferes with the breathing. It should never be so tight that it prevents the horse from taking titbits from the hand.

Besides natural faults others will be liable to creep in during the course of training; for instance, cunning animals will soon learn that they can avoid a half-halt or a unilateral half-halt by opening the mouth. If the rider does not recognise this false reaction, the horse will learn to yield only with the jaw and not from the gullet.

The rider must strive to obtain a quiet and *moist mouth* which does not show the action of the reins. The moisture comes not so much from chewing the bit, as many people think, but from the action of the gland which produces the moisture when stimulated by the flexion of the gullet. The degree of moisture will vary with the individual and may be as much as a thick lather. A dry mouth is a bad sign and will be the result of the action of the rein not going through the body. The amount of moisture will not always be the same on both sides of the mouth, another proof that it depends on the contact. Sometimes there is more moisture on the stiff side, where the bit is likely to protrude more than on the hollow side because on the hollow side the horse will not take contact and bend his neck more on the action of the rein.

The rider should pay particular attention to any difficulty with the tongue. This will not always be connected with an open mouth, but will certainly be increased by it. For this reason the rider should always watch for any activity in his horse's mouth.

Difficulties with the tongue, either putting the tongue out or over the bit, are often caused by a bit that fits badly. Or they may originate from pains in the mouth which come from heavy hands of the rider. They may also be caused by pains in the hind legs or, with nervous horses, be a consequence of excitement. Troubles with the tongue must never be overlooked. They will become worse as the exercises grow more difficult. On the other hand they will act as a warning to the rider of faults in his training and give him the chance to correct them in time. To try to overcome these difficulties with a tongue strap will seldom succeed, although violence may have a temporary success. But as with other things in life, violence only provokes resistance.

In most cases the horse will put his tongue out—often through the fault of the rider—on the side on which he is stiff, or he will try to relieve himself from the action of the bit by putting it between the bar on this side and the bit. A repeated short action of the rein on the opposite side will be the best remedy. If this fault has not become too much of a habit the rider should have no difficulty in overcoming it in a short time. These actions of the reins must be accompanied by pushing sufficiently forward to ensure that the pace is not allowed to suffer. Sometimes, though, much time and patience may be needed to correct a fault with the tongue. A horse that presses his tongue against the front teeth may be cured by tightening the noseband. This is a difficult fault for an inexperienced rider to be aware of at once, but if not immediately corrected it may become difficult to cure.

Putting the tongue over the bit is one of the worst faults and is generally caused by incorrect and hurried training. The best cure is to go back to the early stage and teach the horse to take a correct contact. The rider may find it helpful to put the bit higher in the mouth and tighten the noseband. The snaffle should be placed as high as possible in the horse's mouth without creasing the corners of his lips, as this will make it more difficult for him to draw his tongue from under the bit. When this does happen, the rider must dismount and put it right.

It may be necessary to do this several times during the lesson when the horse first displays this fault.

Horses may develop great ingenuity in playing with their tongues. A horse can pull it back, put it over the bit, or hang it out. Nervous horses will be more inclined to have these difficulties, but they are generally the rider's fault. Dressage judges should severely mark down any faults with the tongue. They are proof of incorrect training, showing that the horse does not pay sufficient attention to his rider and does not take a correct contact with the bit, one of the main principles of training.

The fact that some horses, in spite of faults with their tongue, succeed in performing some spectacular exercise is no proof that these faults should be neglected. The rider must never lose sight of the principles of classical riding and allow himself to sink to the level of the circus.

Another fault that the rider may have to contend with is the *grinding of the horse's teeth.* There are different opinions about the degree of this fault. It may be caused by anger or by something that has nothing to do with temperament. If from anger, the horse will open his lips and lay his ears back; this is a serious fault as the horse will change his contact and pay no attention to his rider, with the result that his performance will suffer. On the other hand there will be horses that will grind their teeth with a closed mouth; their jaws will not appear to move and only a regular grinding will be heard, which conveys more an impression of well-being than of temper and the horses are attentive to their riders. It would be absurd to put these two types of grinding in the same category. The latter would be more a shortcoming than a fault and it would be inconsistent to admit the quality of the performance and penalise the grinding. Some of the horses of Oberbereiter Zrust—a famous rider well-known for the brilliant performance of his horses which were full of impulsion and harmony in their movements and easy to ride by any rider with a good seat—noticeably ground their teeth.

The rider will be able to obtain much information regarding temperament, intelligence, and the mood of his horse from the *movement of his ears.* If a horse flattens his ears, either from dislike or distrust, it will be advisable to approach him with care. Vicious horses will always flatten their ears when kicking or biting, but the rider should not over-rate the significance of this movement. A horse is an individual and cannot be judged by these superficial signs. The rider who studies his horse will soon realise that he sticks to certain habits which may be recognised by the movements of his ears. Pricked ears reveal a greater interest for what is going on around him than for his rider's demands. If his ears are turned back towards his rider he will be paying attention and listen to him.

Horses whose ears are constantly going backward and forward will generally be nervous or unbalanced and not paying sufficient attention to their work. But it would be unwise to set too much store by these observations.

In this stage, work in the canter will increase in importance, as it improves the impulsion in the same way that the changing of pace and tempo improves the action of the rein going through the body. The correct execution of all turns and circles will be the proof of progress, if not of perfection. Perfection is the goal at which we aim, and at one moment we may approach nearer to it than at another. Frequent transitions into the canter from the trot and walk will establish the canter in its best form and improve the whole appearance of the horse; furthermore it will prepare him for the *flying change of leg.*

The old masters wisely advised that any attempt to teach a flying change should wait until the horse had acquired sufficient physical strength. As the flying change takes place in the moment of suspension, the horse should not be asked to attempt it until he is fully balanced and the hindquarters are strong enough for him to spring actively off the ground. In other words never ask for the flying change until the horse moves in the canter with regular and distinctly marked bounds, which means that a complete training in all the exercises, as explained in the previous chapter, will be required before the flying change is attempted.

These exercises must be reinforced by continually striking

off from the walk or trot on alternate legs on the large circle, on a straight line, and through the circle. This will improve the horse's proficiency and increase his understanding of the aids. His balance will become more established, but above all it will strengthen his hindquarters and perfect the action of the reins going through the body. When the rider is satisfied that sufficient progress has been made, he will demand alternating correct and "false" canter on the straight line, both from the walk and trot, in order to teach his horse to answer the most delicate aids. On any suspicion of anticipation the rider must change the order of his exercises, using his imagination to ensure that the horse executes only what is required of him.

When ready to try flying changes, the rider must consider the conformation of his horse and proceed in the way easiest for him. A good method is to change through the diagonal at the collected canter and apply the aids for changing the leg a little more emphatically at the moment the horse passes through the first corner. The aids are exactly the same as for the strike-off on the other leg and must be done without reducing the canter to a lower speed. The horse should follow the accustomed aids of the reins and legs together with the necessary shifting of the rider's weight, which should on no account be visible. The rider must avoid twisting his body in all directions, which is so often the case. It is for this reason that it is so important that the preparation for this exercise be carefully carried out to make sure that the horse will be able to follow the correct aids from the first attempt.

Another method of teaching the flying change is to do it at the point where the rein is changed when changing the circle. When this transition can be made without difficulty through a short and supple change at the trot and walk, the flying change can be asked by applying the same aids as described above. If the flying change has been correctly made, the horse should be immediately rewarded by a walk on the loose rein. If the change was not correct, the rider must go back to the preparation already explained. On no account must the horse be punished. This would not only increase the difficulties of this exercise but sow seeds for difficulties in the future training.

A horse sometimes will change his leg of his own accord when doing intensive training. The rider should take advantage of this and reward him, but only in the early stages of training, because later he must understand that he must wait for his master's commands.

The *counter canter* must be practised when preparing for the flying change. The counter canter is a "false" canter (cantering to the left with the right leg leading or vice versa) on a single track and is different from the canter in renvers which is a canter on two tracks. In some ways the counter canter is of greater importance in training than the canter in renvers, especially when teaching the flying change. It is also an effective means of straightening a horse that has a tendency to go crooked, as the wall of the school will prevent the quarters from flying out. But care must be taken that the horse does not defeat the rider's object by bringing the shoulder in because of his preference for going crooked.

In the counter canter the rider will employ the opposite aids to those for the correct canter. The inside leg behind the girth announces the movement, while the outside leg demands the strike-off, creates the bend to the outside, and ensures the smooth rhythm of the movement. The outside rein leads the horse along the wall, and is responsible for the correct position of the horse's head to the outside, preventing the shoulder from being brought in and the canter from becoming crooked. The inside rein limits the position to the outside and helps the outside rein in directing the horse. The movement of the counter canter must be just as smooth as that of the correct canter. The observer should not see any change in the rider's seat or any difference in the movement of the horse's body. A good counter canter with active bounds, with the hind legs following the tracks of the forelegs and no change in the tempo, will be an excellent proof of the suppleness of the horse, especially as he passes through the corners.

As soon as the horse understands the flying change, the

change should be alternated with the counter canter when passing through the corners to ensure the obedience to the aids especially with horses that are inclined to change of their own accord.

When first practising the counter canter it is advisable to describe a large arc when going through the corner and to increase the tempo slightly to make it easier for the horse. This will be the most likely way to prevent the horse from changing legs without orders. To perform the flying change from the counter canter, the inside leg is placed on the girth, the outside leg behind the girth. The position of the horse's head must be changed to the inside and the rider's weight shifted from the outside to the inside. All these changes must take place at the same moment. The inside leg acting strongly on the girth commands the change and must remain in its place—it must not be allowed to slide forward at the moment of the change—thus ensuring the smooth rhythm of the movement.

When the flying change can be correctly performed in the corner of the school or when changing the circle, it may be practised on a straight line, first in the middle of the diagonal when changing rein, then on the centre line, then after a turn and change of rein, and at last alongside the wall. It is more important in all these exercises that the hind legs spring smoothly under the body. The smooth rhythm of the movement must not be interrupted and the change must be absolutely straight and forward. Practising alongside the wall will help the flying change to remain straight, but this exercise should not be asked to begin with, as it needs greater proficiency.

A temptation that must be guarded against, especially by young riders, is that, overcome by the joy of having obtained the change, they practise it too often, forgetting the fatigue caused to the horse. This is the origin of many faults. In the same way faults will be caused by starting the exercise before the horse has acquired sufficient strength. The horse will change in front before he changes behind or vice versa, or the change will not be made with a full stride, especially of the hind legs. These faults will be difficult to eliminate, as horses often acquire great skill in performing them and even deceive their riders. This is why the ancient masters strongly advised never to start teaching the flying change too soon.

Many other faults may appear, such as deviation of the quarters to the side on which the horse is crooked; swinging the quarters to both sides at the moment of the change, because the horse had been allowed to strike off into the canter by bringing the hindquarters in; changing with the hindquarters too high because the joints of the hind legs are not sufficiently bent; changes without gaining ground to the front, the forelegs dipping into the ground because the horse is too much on his forehand. These last two faults may be corrected by a half-halt in an upward direction of what becomes the inside rein at the moment of the change. Some horses get upset and try to rush away when the change is asked, because they have been forced to do it before they are ready. Others carry the whole body to either side of the straight line, because they are not sufficiently collected or are lacking in impulsion. The great variety of faults that can be made is a distinct proof of the high degree of proficiency and suppleness required before the rider may demand this difficult exercise from his horse.

A correct change of legs in the air should be performed with graceful ease, every movement under the complete control of the rider, who should appear as part of his horse. The aids must be applied in the moment of suspension. The horse must change immediately without faltering and continue the canter on the other leg. The rider's control should be such that no aids should be seen; it would be as if he whispered "Now" and the change would take place.

If the horse does not obey the rider's aids to change in the next bound of canter, the change is far from perfection and any attempt to repeat the change after a prescribed number of strides will be not only premature but also harmful and lead to faults difficult to cure.

When the rhythm of the canter in the various tempos is thoroughly established, *work on two tracks at the canter* may be practised more intensively. At first, on a short line, that is to say a half volte and half pass back to the side of the arena or school; then on a longer line, i.e., a half pass from the centre line back to the side; and finally a half pass from one side of the arena to the other. The rhythm of the canter must be maintained as on the single track, which demands balance, suppleness, and proficiency.

The horse must maintain the same position on two tracks at the canter as he did at the trot. On reaching the wall of the school at the end of the half pass, he will either maintain the counter canter or perform a flying change. In either case the inside leg must ensure a smooth transition, without any hesitation, from two tracks to a single track.

In the first case, that is, when the horse stays in counter canter, the position will be maintained by the same inside leg as it was in the lateral movement. In the second case, when the horse changes leg, what was hitherto the outside leg becomes the inside leg on reaching the wall; a short half-halt in an upward direction by the new inside rein at the moment of the change will be necessary with a horse that is inclined to lie on the rein. Horses will have little difficulty in succeeding with a flying change after a half pass, a fact that riders should take advantage of.

In the thorough training of the school horse, the rider must never neglect the other paces as he concentrates on his programme of training. In this phase, the trot is of the same importance as in the earlier phase. It will gain even greater importance as the piaffe and passage are approached, as these two exercises of the High School can be developed only from a perfect trot.

For this reason, the work in *trot both on single and two tracks,* which was begun in the second stage of training, must be further developed and brought to perfection. The rider must always maintain a trot with a brisk cadence to meet the important demands to come. He must not only preserve but improve the paces given by nature. This is only possible if impulsion is maintained in all tempos, if the hind legs step well under the body to ensure the balance, and if the action of the reins going through the body responds to the most delicate aids. When this is achieved the horse will carry his rider with a swinging back and give him "the greatest happiness in the world."

The full harmony of these exercises will be reflected in the *carriage of the horse's tail.* The dock, or prolongation of the spine, should be carried straight and arched downwards, it should be carried well out from the hindquarters and should not be crooked. The carriage of the tail should not be over-rated but the observant rider will not overlook it. If the horse swishes his tail or still worse twists it, it will indicate an unbalanced character often seen with nervous horses. It may point to a lack of balance or a degree of tension. An exaggerated use of the spur will generally result in a swishing tail, thus detracting from the value of the rider's system of training.

As training proceeds, the extension from the collected trot may lose its fluent brilliancy; this will be the fault of the action of the hind legs, which may lose their activity, and will imply that the rider must go back to the previous phase of training. If, on the other hand, the horse starts to move his forelegs on a single track, or even cross them over each other, it is a very serious fault and forecasts trouble when starting the training for piaffe and passage. Some horses, by nature, move in this way; the trainer must try to overcome this fault by increasing the activity of the hind legs before teaching other exercises. The horse must first learn to move correctly. If this bad fault is neglected and becomes a habit, the rider will find it difficult or even impossible to eradicate.

We repeat that as training progresses the rider should observe his horse and himself with great care if he wants to develop his work into art. Every small detail must be registered. As another instance, the development of the muscles of the hindquarters will be proof of the correct activity of the hind legs, and the rider may gain valuable information about his work by noticing where the *sweat* appears on his horse's body. Those parts which have been made to work hard will sweat more profusely and often continue to sweat when the horse returns to the stable. Sweat between the hind legs will indicate that they are working correctly, especially if the forehand remains dry. On the other hand, if the horse sweats profusely all over it will indicate excitement or that the horse has been worked too hard rather than correctly.

For the improvement of the physical training of the horse, lateral work should now be developed with an increase in difficulty. The horse should now be able to go in half pass across the whole arena and this may be increased to three times. The greater the number of half passes that follow each other, the greater will be the difficulty, because the sideways movement will be increased and the forward movement decreased, which will require much impulsion.

When performing two or more consecutive *counter changes of hand* in half pass, the rider must be particularly careful that the horse remains straight before reaching the opposite side of the arena, that the movement is not interrupted as the direction is changed, and that the horse does not fall into the new direction, especially with the hindquarters leading, but waits for the aids of the rider.

When performing a sequence of half passes, the horse may anticipate his rider's aids and begin the next half pass with the hindquarters leading and reach the opposite side at an angle instead of being parallel. In consequence he will throw himself still more into the following half pass. On reaching the opposite side, the rein which was the inside rein in the lateral work must remain applied, just giving sufficiently to enable the outside leg, which now becomes the inside leg, to be placed on the girth to push the horse forward and produce the new position.

If the horse has improved in suppleness and responds to the aids equally on both sides, *short half passes alternately to left and right* may be practised on the centre line. By this exercise, the obedience of the horse and his attention to the rider's aids will be improved.

It is of importance with these short half passes, of two or

more metres on either side of the centre line, that the horse adopt the same position on both sides, that the forehand is always leading, and that the regular rhythm is maintained. The correct change from one rein to the other must be distinctly visible and the horse must be prevented from throwing himself into the new direction.

This exercise, when correctly performed, gives a good impression of complete relaxation, suppleness, regularity, and harmony. When teaching a sequence of short half passes the rider should begin these from the long side of the school. This will make it easier for the horse to keep straight when changing direction from that side. Later on, when performed on the centre line, the rider should take the horse straight for one horse's length before changing direction in order to prevent him from throwing himself into the following half pass.

It will be of benefit to make short half passes with horses that are inclined to hasten their steps and lose their rhythm when doing half passes across the arena, because they will have less difficulty in maintaining their balance—one more proof that every exercise will contribute towards perfection of the general training. The best exercise, however, will have little value if performed at the wrong moment. The successful rider must be able to think as well as ride.

Half passes should now be practised at the canter until they can be carried out across the whole arena. When this has been achieved satisfactorily, several counter changes of hand can be demanded following each other, but not before the horse can arrive straight at the farther side and make a correct flying change in a forward movement. The same rules for teaching the half pass at the trot will be utilised for teaching it at the canter. If the horse lies on the rein, the rider must give him a half-halt with the rein in an upward direction.

Up to now the counter canter has been practised with the object of making the horse straight. Now the *renvers* must be taught. There is a considerable difference between a correct canter in renvers and a crooked counter canter; in the latter the hindquarters are taken to the outside, the horse is not sufficiently bent throughout his length, and the hind legs drag. In the canter in renvers, the horse's body must be bent evenly from head to tail and the hind legs must spring with energy under the body.

As in the trot, the *canter in renvers* may be performed after a passade or a half pass or may be developed from the counter canter. The same aids as for the counter canter are applied for the canter in renvers, but the inside leg will be applied behind the girth to bring about the lateral movement. The inside rein leads the horse into the demanded direction, the outside leg on the girth must be applied with a stronger pressure to bend the horse laterally and in order to maintain the brisk bounds of the canter without which the exercise would be useless.

The rider should not demand an exaggerated position, but be satisfied with a slight general bend throughout the body. In order to ensure lively bounds, the canter must not be shortened too much to begin with, especially in passing through corners or performing a volte in renvers. In these two exercises the forelegs perform a smaller arc than the hind legs, which must be held by the inside leg behind the girth on the outside track. The outside leg on the girth stimulates the canter as in the case with the strike-off. As with the trot, so with the canter, the rider must not forget to keep up the pace when practising these various exercises. The shortened canter may induce the hind legs to lose their activity, either from laziness or fatigue, which will detract from the correctness of the exercise, or it may not succeed at all.

The regular sequence of the bounds should always be distinctly visible whether in the short, ordinary, or extended canter; if the horse loses his rhythm, he must be ridden forward in a changed tempo to ensure the liveliness of the short canter. The rider should not become so absorbed in the exercise that he allows his horse to become tense.

The correct execution of these exercises will depend on the correct canter. This will be still more the case when performing the *pirouette*.

In the pirouette—

180° in the half
270° in the three-quarter
360° in the full

the horse will turn according to his proficiency, with three to four strides in the half pirouette, four to six in the three-quarter, and six to eight in the full, with regular bounds around his hind legs, which turn on the spot in the rhythm of the canter. The inside hind leg is the centre of the circle which the forehand must describe; the outside hind leg moves in the same rhythm in a very small circle around the same centre. The inside hind leg must also maintain the rhythm on the spot. Pirouettes can be performed from a renvers, half pass, or on a single track. The pirouette from the single track is the most difficult to execute and is one of the ideals of the classical art.

The best method of teaching it is to develop it from the renvers. When performed from a half pass, it will increase the horse's attention to the rider's aids and will prevent the horse from moving sideways more than the rider demands. All three pirouettes must end in the manner in which they were begun, that is to say, in renvers, half pass, or on a single track.

The horse is taken into the turn by the inside rein; the inside leg on the girth is applied more firmly in order to maintain the canter, prevent the movement from dying down or the body from falling in. The outside leg behind the girth, supported by the outside rein, prevents the hindquarters from following the forehand, as in a volte. The outside rein should not be used against the neck or produce an incorrect bend. In the pirouette, the bend and the position must be to the inside for which the inside rein is responsible, but this position should not be exaggerated, which would lead to the hindquarters falling out. The rider can prevent the horse from lying on the rein or dropping on to his forehand by a half-halt in an upward direction on the stiff side. For a pirouette, the horse's hind legs must be correctly bent and they must spring well under the body. This will only be possible with a light contact which will be improved by the half-halt. The rider's weight rests on the inside seat bone with the upper part of the body upright.

The aids remain the same for half, three-quarter, or full pirouette. The exercise is brought to an end with a more firmly applied outside rein, the inside leg pushes the horse forward, and the inside rein must give sufficiently to allow the horse to follow the commands of the inside leg. The rider sits firmly on both seat bones and pushes the horse forward with his seat, being careful not to lean back. The rhythm of the canter must remain unchanged before, during, and after the pirouette.

At the Spanish Riding School, the stallions are taught the pirouette from the canter in renvers, as recommended by Guérinière. That is why the renvers plays such an important part at the School. Its advantages have already been mentioned, and its practical value can be seen in the figures performed by the Lipizzaner stallions.

One of the most frequently practised exercises is the *passade and renvers.* The exercise is to begin and to end on the wall or on the large circle. The renvers on the large circle is more difficult so it must be made easier for the horse by asking less position and a livelier tempo, and the forehand must be taken in slightly more at every bound to maintain the same angle on the circle.

When teaching the pirouette, a *passade and renvers with a pirouette* will be practised either in the corner or on the long side. The exercise differs from the ordinary passade and renvers by the fact that the turn in passade must be made larger and the hindquarters in the renvers remain on a track three yards from the wall. In the first two corners after the passade, the horse will execute a three-quarter pirouette to the outside and will pass the third corner in renvers. The rider will then straighten the horse and make a flying change. By the position in renvers, the pirouette in the corners will be made easier and passing the third corner in renvers will increase the horse's attention and prevent him from anticipating.

Teaching the pirouette on the large circle is another excellent exercise. It has the advantage of practising the pirouette from a straight forward position and not from the renvers, which might lead to a habit of crookedness. Even if the rider cannot control the hindquarters as well on the large circle as he can in the renvers, he will have better command than he would have on a straight line, as preparatory voltes can be ridden within the circle. When these can be executed smoothly, fluently, and without hesitation, the increased application of the outside rein, supported by the outside leg, at the commencement of the volte can reduce the volte to a passade and finally a half pirouette. The movement is continued in the counter canter and after half a circle a volte to the outside can be performed. If this volte is done correctly, it can be reduced to a passade, then to a half pirouette to the outside. The rider must continue on the circle in the correct canter and establish the impulsion by some changes of tempo.

When the horse can execute half pirouettes to the inside and outside of the large circle, the rider can start to practise full pirouettes to the outside. In order to make the exercise easier to start with, it may be done from canter in renvers instead of counter canter, but the object must be to perform the pirouette to the outside from the counter canter, which is a straight position.

Finally the pirouette will be performed within the circle. Experience has taught that a horse will have a greater inclination to fall in when doing a pirouette to the inside than when doing it to the outside. In order to avoid anticipation, the rider should alternate voltes with pirouettes so that the horse will not know what is coming next and will wait for his rider's commands.

To prevent the horse from falling in to the pirouette, he should be given a slight shoulder-in position before this exercise. At the same time, collection must be well established because, if the horse becomes "long" before starting the exercise, it will fail.

The rider's seat is of great importance in performing the pirouette.

Eventually full pirouettes will be executed in their most difficult form—namely, on a straight line, on the diagonal, on the centre line, after a turn, or any place in the school. The place should continually be changed to compel the horse to wait for his rider's commands.

As the pirouette requires impulsion, balance, proficiency, and the action of the reins going through the body, it is considered to be one of the most difficult exercises. If any of these factors are insufficient the pirouette not only will be short of perfection but may fail altogether. The performance in the pirouette will present the best picture of the standard of training and the abilities of the horse.

No detail must be overlooked in the training or numerous faults may appear. If the quarters deviate from the straight line and fall to the outside before the pirouette, it will deteriorate into a bad volte. It is an equally bad fault if the horse throws himself into the pirouette and makes an unbalanced turn over which the rider has no control.

A pirouette in which the hind legs turn on the spot, but lose the rhythm of the canter, is a worse fault than one in which the hind legs describe a larger circle but maintain the regular rhythm. In the ideal movement, the hind legs should turn on a circle the size of a plate. If the hind legs describe an oval or the horse sways, it shows that the balance is lost and the contact with the bit is too firm. It is an equally bad fault if the horse drops on to his forehand and steps back or throws himself into the movement and swings round his hindquarters with a few irregular bounds.

Should it seem that this subject has been discussed too minutely, it must be realised that the pirouette cannot be mastered by constant repetition. Success cannot be achieved unless every detail of the whole training is carefully considered. This work of art will appear in harmony and full beauty only when impulsion and the results of the action of the rein going through the body are equally balanced.

Nothing is more valuable for the training, and at the same time more impressive, than that the rider has such control over the horse's will to go forward that he is able to bring him to a *halt from the extended trot or canter,* or immediately strike off into one of the extended paces without the least difficulty or resistance. This is proof of the absolute will to go forward. These exercises are included in the more difficult dressage tests, to determine the degree of the action of the rein going through the body and the pushing aids. Although they may look easy, they are in reality very difficult and need the most thorough training of the horse. Even the non-expert will be duly impressed by the different movements direct from absolute immobility or from full speed to a well-balanced and smooth halt, the horse standing like a statue.

It is these achievements that give equitation the harmony and brilliance that in music are provided by fortissimo and piano. They will also be proof that the horse is ready to commence the passage.

Alternating *reining-back and going forward* is another good exercise. When the transition from the rein-back to forward and vice versa can be carried out without hesitation or any resistance it will be another proof of suppleness, obedience, the will to go forward, and the action of the rein going through the body. The difficulty of this exercise can be increased by naming the number of steps to go back and forward.

Progress in all these exercises will lead to the commencement of *flying changes after a given number of strides,* finally reaching the stage where the changes can be made at every stride. Under no condition must the continued changes be started until the single flying change is thoroughly established and the horse changes straight and forward upon the rider's most discreet aids without losing his rhythm. It will be much more rewarding to wait until the horse is ready for these changes than to try to force them by giving up all the principles of equitation and losing the correct position. Changing the leading leg after a certain number of strides, especially in one-time, may be considered among the most spectacular of exercises and tempt the rider to practise it more than necessary, although its value in training is relatively small. Flying changes can be performed with less collection and less suppleness, whereas pirouettes, passage, and piaffe will never succeed without the maximum of these qualities.

The rider must first practise changing the leg at every fifth and fourth stride and will have little difficulty in increasing the demand up to a change in every second stride. It is of importance that every change be performed correctly; if the movements are allowed to become slovenly, faults will creep in. Any sign of anticipation must be checked. During practice, intelligent horses will try to change on their own after a certain number of strides without waiting for orders. In this case, the only cure is to stop the exercise and go back to single changes.

Flying changes should be practised either along the wall or on the large circle. It will be easier on the large circle and will help to prevent the hindquarters from swinging to one side, especially to the outside at the moment of the change, but practice along the wall offers the best opportunity of keeping the horse straight. The wall prevents the hindquarters from swinging out and the rider can prevent the quarters from swinging in by taking the forehand to the inside at the moment of the change.

Changes at every stride are one of the most controversial exercises as a number of experts consider them circus movements and disapprove of them for this reason. Many arguments took place at the Spanish Riding School, without ever coming to a satisfactory conclusion. No one could give a reasonable explanation either for or against them. But the Fédération Equestre Internationale, as the ruling body on international equitation, declares that they belong to the classical exercises and demands them in the dressage tests at the Olympic Games. It is, therefore, superfluous to discuss the matter in this book. Their value for physical training has already been mentioned.

When the horse is able to execute flying changes in two-time with suppleness, correctness, and ease, the rider may start teaching changes at every stride. Begin by executing two consecutive changes along the wall, changing first into the counter canter and immediately back to the correct canter. If the horse has been correctly prepared in his previous training, he should find no difficulty in this exercise, which would appear to prove that changes from stride to stride are not an unnatural movement to the horse as the critics of this exercise contend. This is also endorsed by the fact that horses often perform changes in one-time when a fault is being corrected before they have ever been taught to do so.

When two successive flying changes can be performed on both reins in different places, three may be demanded. Some horses may find this exercise difficult. Once the difficulty is overcome and the horse is able to perform three flying changes on both reins, and after a few strides is able to repeat the exercise, the rider should find no further difficulty in performing any given number of changes.

It should always be the rider, never the horse, who decides the number of changes. Care must be taken that the horse remain absolutely straight and not decrease the length of his strides, which is liable to occur if this exercise is practised too often. This could also be the cause of the hind legs not making a full stride. The remedy for all these faults is to go back to single changes and then limit one-time changes to two correct ones.

The horse can now be practised in serpentines and half passes with a given number of strides to either side. This will complete his training at the canter and be a test of the degree of perfection reached.

Serpentines can be practised with a varying number of loops with a flying change when crossing the centre line. It becomes more difficult as the number of loops is increased and the exercise will serve to perfect the changes of leg especially if the loops are performed alternately in the correct and counter canter. This exercise, together with the figure of eight in correct and counter canter, will be further proof of the training.

The *zigzag* is a half pass on either side of the centre line with a given number of strides. The highest degree of proficiency is required in this exercise to maintain the even rhythm of movement throughout. For instance, three or four strides in the half pass at the canter are taken to the right of the centre line, followed, after a flying change, by six or eight strides to the left, another flying change and six to eight strides to the right, back to the left and so forth, until the exercise is brought to an end by three or four strides to the right and back to the centre line. The ground gained to the front and the side must be of equal value in each half pass.

When teaching the zigzag, it will be of help to start by performing a half pass of six strides from the long side to the centre of the school, change the leg, and return in half pass to the wall in the same number of strides. In this way, the rider can ensure that the strides cover the same distance to either side, which, to begin with, should not be taken for granted. When practising, care must be taken that the horse does not throw himself into the following half pass, which would allow the hindquarters to lead. He must be thoroughly under the control of his rider. The change of leg must be correct and maintain the same rhythm as the other strides.

If the horse attempts to lie on the new inside rein, he must be given a half-halt in an upward direction with this rein to prevent him from falling onto his shoulder and changing with unlevel steps. This is of great importance with horses inclined to leave one hind leg behind. The aids of the legs must be precise—the new outside leg behind the girth announces the change—but care must be taken not to make the hindquarters swing away. The new inside leg on the girth maintains the forward impulsion and prevents the horse from falling into the new direction.

The peak of training with the school horse is reached with the passage and piaffe. These two paces of the High School, already known in ancient times—Xenophon gives a description of the passage in his book—are not only the most effective movements to be performed by horse and rider but are the result of long and systematic training. Mindful of this fact, the rider will not try to teach passage and piaffe before his horse is ready. In spite of the evident truth of this teaching, the modern desire for quick success often disregards classical principles with the result that only caricatures of these wonderful airs are produced. A correct passage, and still more a correct piaffe, can rarely be seen by the enthusiastic onlooker and soon will appear only in old etchings and photographs. Many riders today do not realise that they can reach the top only by a gradual system of training in the same way that a student can reach the university only by first passing through lower schools. The ballet master, faithful to tradition, realises that perfection can be reached only after years of systematic training. Why should it be otherwise with the training of the horse, where not one but two elements have to be blended together in the perfection of movement?

The rider should never forget that all movements of the High School are born from impulsion. The piaffe is created by the desire to go forward, checked by the rider, and the passage by an exuberance of temperament, created and controlled by the rider. Even the capriole is a mixture of gaiety and impulsion. To control these movements, which are the gifts of nature, is the aim of equitation. When this aim is reached, equitation may justly qualify as an art. The power to prevent the horse from employing these movements against his rider might almost be included in the category.

In most cases, the horse is taught the piaffe before the passage, but this should not be looked upon as a rigid rule; much will depend on the individuality of the horse.

The *piaffe* is sometimes described as a trot or a trot-like movement on the spot, whereas the French riding masters of the past described it as a passage on the spot, which seems to indicate that the passage was taught first.

The rider should never attempt to teach the passage if his horse shows an inclination to do an over-suspended trot in the course of training. This would tend to lead to an evasion when asked for a collected trot and make it difficult to teach the horse to bend his hind legs correctly. In a passage of this sort the horse would hold back the impulsion. For this reason it is recommended that the piaffe be taught before the passage.

The horse can be taught the piaffe either under the rider or by work in hand, which is the method employed at the

Spanish Riding School and which is discussed in separate sections of this chapter.

When teaching the piaffe under the rider, the following factors must be present: perfect balance, the absolute will to go forward, and the action of the rein going through the body developed to the highest degree. These are the basic elements on which the piaffe and passage are founded. This knowledge will enable the rider to decide the moment when his horse is ready to commence the training for the piaffe and the method to be employed.

As a human being must learn to walk correctly before he is able to run or dance, so must the horse show his absolute balance by the regularity of his steps in all tempos and smooth transitions from collection to extension and vice versa before he is ready to be taught this movement. This balance will be the best guarantee that the hindquarters are sufficiently strong and active. The impulsion required for the piaffe to enable the horse to trot on the spot instead of coming to a standstill will show itself in the impulsion which appears in the liveliness of the steps in the collected trot and the immediate transition into extension. It is in the collected paces that this impulsion should be distinctly seen. The better they are executed, the more impulsion is present.

The degree of the rein going through the body, which is one of the most important requirements for the piaffe, will be revealed by the smooth transitions to the shortened trot brought about by the braced back of the rider with very light action of the reins. Only by a high degree of the action of the rein going through the body can the briskness and suppleness of the steps be maintained, which gives us the line on which the training must proceed.

The rider must start with changes of tempo at the trot alongside the wall, and gradually decrease the length of the steps until the horse goes forward only the length of a hoof. The practice should be alongside the wall because, in this preparatory work, every horse will try to avoid the increased shortening by crookedness, generally on the hollow side, and will try to evade the increased collection and bending of his hind legs demanded by the rider. The wall makes it easier to straighten the horse, which is of the greatest importance in this case. To start with, the rider should work on the rein on which the horse takes a firmer contact, because the wall will help prevent the hindquarters from swinging to the other side. At this stage the exercise should always be practised on the same rein to prevent the horse from being confused by any change.

The rider must be content with very few of these shortened steps—two to four will be quite enough to begin with—in order not to lose the rhythm of the movement. The horse will then be brought to a halt and rewarded to make him realise he has done what was required of him. But this practice must be employed only in the early stages, otherwise it might become a habit which would affect further training. Later, after a few of these shortened steps, the horse will be taken forward in the collected trot to ensure the impulsion and forward urge so necessary for the piaffe. Only after several successful changes of tempo will the horse be rewarded by a period at the walk.

When teaching the piaffe in this way, the rider may not always succeed with his pushing aids alone, as it is a recognised fact that the pushing aids are less powerful than those for the reduction of pace. He may require an assistant on the ground to help him achieve the necessary impulsion by the appropriate use of the whip. This assistant should never exceed his duties. It must always be the rider who produces the impulsion which the man with the whip helps him to maintain.

For this transition from the highly collected trot to the piaffe, the rider sits more deeply into the saddle and increases the pressure on the horse's back by bracing his own. At the same time he must press strongly on the stirrup with a low heel in order to brace the muscles of the calves and push the horse forward with his aids applied on the girth, thus maintaining the activity of the hind legs.

The regularity of the movement must not be impeded by an excessive influence of the reins. The best success will be achieved by repeated actions of the rein, which will also prevent the horse from taking a firmer contact and dropping on to his forehand. If the steps become slower and lose their cadence in spite of the increased pressure of the rider's legs, then the assistant on the ground must intervene with the long whip.

It cannot be emphasised too often that this outside aid must never be more than an admonition and a stimulant. It should be sufficient for the assistant merely to move a little faster towards the horse's hindquarters while showing his whip, but if this is not enough, he may touch him lightly just behind the girth. The whip must never be directed to the hindquarters in order to increase their activity, as this would only encourage the horse to raise his hind legs and would not produce the will to go forward. The result would be faults that would jeopardise the perfection of the piaffe. Using the whip on the hind legs has always been disapproved of in the Spanish Riding School as being inconsistent with correct training. If the rider relies on the assistance of the whip and neglects the influence of his back and legs, the piaffe will never achieve the necessary cadence and, when deprived of the assistance of the whip, will degenerate into an indifferent movement of the legs on the spot. The piaffe will only be successful and give the idea of a dancing movement if the horse is without tension and executes the movement with relaxed joints and muscles.

In the piaffe, the horse should spring from one diagonal to the other and should not just step from one leg to the other as the result of being tapped on alternate hind legs. It is of great benefit to supple the horse by trotting with short steps on a loose rein before practising the piaffe. Horses that have been taught by force and predominant use of the long whip will become irritated by this exercise because force does not allow their physical and mental tension to relax. Stiffness would make a long period of piaffe uncomfortable for the horse and he would evade by a bound forward or some other resistance.

Incorrect piaffes generally have their origin in the fact that the exercise has been taught too soon or by wrong methods. In most cases, it is the fault of the incorrect use of the long whip. By repeated action of the whip, the horse is made to raise his hind legs higher than necessary while the forelegs hardly leave the ground or remain on it. This kind of movement without balance is of no value. The result is that the diagonal is broken, the rhythm lost, and the horse appears to be fidgeting on the spot.

Sometimes the horse stiffens his forelegs against the movement and makes an incorrect piaffe which lacks the forward urge and would prevent him from making the transition into the trot. The reason for this may be too strong a contact on the bit or all kinds of fear complexes.

The following bad fault may also occur: the forelegs begin to cross over each other; the legs swing outwards, which is called balancé; the hindquarters become too high and the hind legs move stiffly without the necessary bend of the three joints. All these faults will be difficult to eliminate if allowed to become habits.

The assistant with the whip cannot alone be held responsible for these faults. It is the system of training that is to blame and the rider himself must bear the responsibility. He must, therefore, carefully consider the best method of training to be applied to each individual case, and at the same time keep a careful watch on everything that occurs in the course of training. This applies throughout the entire training but is of still greater importance when teaching the movements of the High School.

The most important principles in teaching the piaffe is to proceed slowly, be content with small progress, never try to force improvements. A few steps in regular rhythm will be of more value as a foundation than any amount of irregular stamping about on the spot. Success can only be achieved by gradually decreasing the length of the strides in piaffe movements. When executed on the spot, it is the absolute peak of perfection. Even when mastered, a change to a forward movement of a hoof's length, as practised at the Spanish Riding School, will maintain and improve the necessary impulsion and be a preparation for the transition to trot and passage, which are often more difficult than the piaffe itself.

It may prove necessary to allow the horse a lower position of the head and neck when teaching the piaffe. This does not mean that the horse should be allowed to lie on the rein or to shift his weight on to the forehand, or to overbend, thus losing his urge to go forward. When, by the aid of this temporary relief, the horse has again learned to execute regular rhythmic steps, he will be made to lift his forelegs higher and find the true sequence of the diagonals by raising his forehand. The raising of the forehand is achieved by activating the hindquarters and allowing the horse to go one hoof's length forward at each step. Activating the hindquarters does not necessarily mean applying the leg aids to such an extent that it tires out the rider and leads nowhere. The horse should be made more active, wound up as it were, to allow the rider to control the movements with a quiet seat. When the hind legs again step well under the body with regular activity and the horse follows the action of the reins by lowering his head, the rider can demand a higher position of the forehand even at the expense, for the moment, of correct contact and position of the head in order to render this High School movement more brilliant. The rider will then have succeeded in producing a piaffe with regular energetic steps which appear springy and effortless. The quarters will be lowered and the forehand correctly raised when the hind legs step well under the body with activity. The horse must never step backward because this would be a contradiction of the origin of this exercise, namely, the forward urge which has been checked. The piaffe backwards, together with the canter backwards and other such tricks, belong to the circus.

In the course of the training the rein will be changed, which will present the same difficulties as when changing the rein with the young horse on the longe. The next exercise will be to practise the movement away from the wall where the horse will again probably be just as unsteady as the young horse when he first goes on a straight line away from the wall.

In the first stages of practising the piaffe, the rider will find it of benefit to give the horse a slight shoulder-in position, especially if he is inclined to bring his hindquarters in when the collection is increased, which would prevent the hindquarters from stepping sufficiently under the body. The shoulder-in increases the activity of the inside hind leg and makes a good preparation for the piaffe.

A rider who wishes to enter the realms of equestrian art must realise that when teaching the piaffe he may meet with disappointments and find that slight setbacks may appear in his training. Knowing this, he must be patient and beware of rash actions which would be detrimental to the progress so far made. As with a ballet dancer, he must never forget the basic exercises. Continuing the practice or using force will not improve an unsuccessful piaffe. Improvement in the whole training, and especially in impulsion, will be required before the horse is sufficiently developed not only to understand his rider but also to be able to carry out his demands.

In exceptional cases, as for instance when the horse lacks the necessary impulsion by nature, or is inclined to cross his front legs, the passage should be taught before the piaffe. These drawbacks will be more apparent in the piaffe.

A correctly executed passage will increase the impulsion and help the hind legs to push the body more energetically off the ground. This will also increase the swinging of the back, help the piaffe to become more active, and prevent the inclination merely to step from one diagonal to the other. The passage, however, must be developed from forward movement and not from a holding back of the horse. When the horse has mastered the passage, and the rider can regulate the length of the strides without any change in the rhythm, he will be able to obtain the piaffe by controlling the forward urge and at the same time maintain the pushing aids until the length of the stride is reduced to a hoof's length and the horse finally moves on the spot.

As with other exercises, so with the piaffe, after the early setbacks have been overcome, the whole training will be improved. The balance and the action of the rein going through the body achieved in this movement of the High School will not only make the horse more beautiful but will also make

24 & 25 Ballotade in hand

26 Capriole in hand

27 Courbette in hand

28 Curb bridle with rein on the cavesson; after an engraving by Ridinger

all the other exercises more brilliant. The piaffe will develop and strengthen the hindquarters to the benefit of the other paces. For instance, a correct piaffe executed before an extended trot will make the movement more impressive.

The *passage* is a slow and highly cadenced trot with a long moment of suspension. Unlike the piaffe, it is taught exclusively under the rider. It demands the same preparation as the piaffe, but with even more impulsion and balance. The horse must be absolutely straight—a crooked horse will never step sufficiently under the body and the steps will probably be irregular. In this stage of training crookedness is generally an attempt by the horse to make things easier for himself by avoiding the increased bend of the joints of the hind legs required for this exercise.

The passage may be taught from the trot or the piaffe, or may even be begun from the walk. Which method is chosen will depend on the temperament and the degree of training of the horse. It will generally be easier to teach from the trot, as this pace provides more impulsion than the walk.

The *passage from the trot* will be best introduced by practising distinct changes of tempo. The horse must be ready to increase the tempo at the lightest pressure of the rider's legs and shorten it immediately upon the braced back of the rider accompanied by repeated short actions of the reins. When these changes of tempo can be performed perfectly, they will be repeated at shorter intervals to increase the obedience and balance of the horse.

The rider will then demand an energetic transition from collected to extended trot and check the forward movement at the moment when the horse commences the extension. This quick succession of two aids with a contrary effect will make the horse perform some floating movements. Reward him immediately by a period of walk and let him understand that he has carried out the rider's wishes.

The aids for the passage are the same as for the trot, but the increased pressure of the rider's back prevents the stride from gaining the full amount of ground to the front. The rider must sit upright in the saddle to apply the full influence of his back and must use his legs firmly to maintain the impulsion. The sequence of the steps of the trot will become slower and the firmer the rider applies his pushing aids, the more elevated will they become. If the rider raises his horse's head with his hands, even at the risk of temporarily losing the position of the head and the contact that has already been achieved, he will increase the brilliancy of the steps—provided always that contact is maintained and the rider can control with his seat the impulsion produced by the increased aids of his legs.

The length of the reins is most important. If they are too short, they will induce the horse to lie on them and throw his weight on to his forehand, or even to dash off. The passage would fail from the start. If the reins are too long, the rider will bring his hands back against his body which he would have to draw back, with the result that the correct influence of his back is rendered impossible and, again, the passage would fail.

The assistance of the long whip will be found to be of great advantage when teaching the passage. This aid of the whip should be applied only when the rider has demanded the transition into the passage by the increased influence of his back and legs, and should coincide with the aids of the rider. This fact is of the utmost importance. The whip must not be directed towards the hind legs, but closely behind the rider's legs. It must be dispensed with as the training progresses and be used only if the action of the hind legs cannot be maintained otherwise. If the rider allows himself to rely too much on the whip, the horse will acquire the habit of attending to it instead of following his rider's commands. The result will be that the horse will perform a tolerable passage when the man with the whip is present, but slack off immediately when the rider is left on his own.

The number of steps performed in the passage should be increased gradually, but be regulated by the strength and vigour of the horse, and the exercise should always be brought to an end before the horse tires, so that he recognises this as a reward for work well done.

Many faults that may appear will be traceable to the rider. The most frequent is the irregular movement of the hind legs caused by the difference in the length of the steps. This is due to insufficient influence of the rider's leg on the side on which the horse executes the shorter step. These irregular steps may also be caused by crookedness, or by the fact that one hind leg is more bent and held up longer than the other. This fault may result, too, from an uneven influence of the rider's legs. The remedy will be to straighten the horse and apply the leg more firmly on the side on which the hind leg is insufficiently bent. The aid of the leg may be supported by that of the whip.

An equally incorrect passage is one in which the horse lifts the forelegs but allows the hind legs to drag along the ground because he does not push himself off the ground. In this case, the diagonals will not come to the ground together, which proves lack of balance. This sort of passage can often be seen in the circus. In the so-called Spanish walk this movement is developed until the horse lifts and stretches out his forelegs in an unnatural manner, while the hind legs hardly leave the ground. It is a movement disapproved of in the classical art of riding.

Some horses are able to show a false swinging of the back and move on stiff legs, because they cannot do a correct passage, but have learned by incorrect training to make matters easier for themselves. It is another severe fault when the forelegs cross over each other.

All these faults can best be corrected by riding forward with longer strides in order to ensure the regularity and elevation of the steps when shortening the tempo. The horse will then give the impression that he floats above the ground with proud and slow steps.

Teaching the *passage from the piaffe* is more difficult, but has the advantage that it cultivates the transition at the same time, provided the horse can perform a faultless piaffe upon his rider's commands. First he must be made, by the rider's pushing aids, to do a perfect transition from the piaffe into the trot. This should be immediately rewarded, and after a short period at the walk, the transition repeated. When this preparatory exercise is well established, more impulsion will be created which must be absorbed by the rider's back until the horse executes some floating steps. At the same time the contact must be light and the horse's forehand raised by the action of the quarters. Immediate reward must be given to ensure that the horse knows what is required of him. Assistance with the long whip, as already described, may prove of benefit. The horse must commence the passage immediately with slow and elevated steps and with his head held proudly. When this transition is assured, the rider may correct the position of the head, if necessary, and gradually increase the number of steps. When the rider can maintain, in the transition to passage, the position the horse has learned in the piaffe, the steps of the passage will become more brilliant.

The passage will not succeed if the steps become faster instead of slower and higher. In this case it will lack the impulsion developed from the hindquarters. The rider must either allow the piaffe to mature to perfection before teaching the passage, or he must teach it from the trot or walk. It will be easier to teach from the trot than from the walk as the walk lacks impulsion, but both would be easier than from the piaffe. The walk has the advantage that the rider can apply his aids more correctly because the action of the walk is smoother. The method employed will be the same as when teaching the passage from the piaffe. The rider must be guided in his choice by the temperament, character, and conformation of his horse, and select the method which appears likely to be the easiest.

When the school horse has mastered these two paces of the High School, he must practise the transition from one to the other, which may prove more difficult than the paces themselves. Generally, the *transition from the piaffe to the trot*—the extension of the tempo—will be found to be easier than the transition from trot to piaffe—the shortening of the tempo. These transitions, when successful, will be the best preparation for the passage. The horse will lengthen his stride, but maintain the same rhythm as in the piaffe. The aids remain the same, the power of the aids of the back are slightly decreased and the reins given sufficiently to allow the forward movement to develop without loss of collection.

The *transition from trot to piaffe* requires a high degree of the action of the reins going through the body. When it succeeds it will improve the brilliancy of the piaffe. The rider must never forget that these exercises are an integral part of each other. The pushing aids must be increased at the same time as the tempo is decreased by repeated short actions of the reins accompanied by seat aids in order to shorten the steps until the horse trots on the spot without losing his rhythm.

The *transition from trot to passage* will be comparatively easy and is already practically mastered when the horse has learned the passage. Neither should there be any problem in *passage to trot* if there is sufficient impulsion. The pushing aids employed for the passage remain the same, while the pressure of the rider's back and the actions of the reins are decreased, allowing the horse to reduce the raising of his forehand. If the passage is correct, the rhythm of the subsequent steps at the trot should be longer and quicker, but if it remains slow in spite of the longer strides, it will signify an incorrect passage, and the steps at the trot will remain slow and tense.

The *transition from piaffe to passage* is more difficult. It is an excellent test of the impulsion and forward urge which exist in the piaffe, and, up to now, have not been released by the rider. The horse should move forward in a slower rhythm with elevated steps and appear to float in the air. The pressure of the rider's legs must be increased, and the forward urge released by giving the reins. The rider's hands, held slightly higher, will maintain a higher position of the forehand which is necessary to make the horse go into a passage instead of the trot. To make the transition easier to begin with, the piaffe should be allowed to gain a little ground to the front before starting the passage. This will best guarantee a smoother transition and the same rhythm of the steps. On no account should the horse be allowed to rush off; this would mean that he was lying on the reins, that he was too tense, and that the hindquarters were not sufficiently active.

The most difficult of all is the *transition from passage into piaffe*. It is the ultimate test of the training and the best proof of the reins going through the body. This transition to the piaffe will be produced when the elevated steps, executed with regularity and unbelievable control of muscles and joints, abandon without hesitation all ground gained to the front. Correctly executed it reveals the horse in all his beauty.

The aids of the legs maintain the movement while the increased pressure of the rider's back supports the repeated actions of the reins in order to decrease the forward movement until the horse passes into the piaffe. The rider's hands, which were raised for the passage, are now lowered to make the hind legs step well under the body and prevent tension. The smooth activity of the hind legs must not slacken and the rhythm must not be interrupted. These demands can only be fulfilled if the physical training of the horse is complete.

Even when the school horse has mastered these movements, the rider must always try to improve them. Once a work has been mastered, familiarity will bring the temptation to make matters easier. The horse will try to use his hindquarters less energetically, thus allowing the movement to become more shallow, or he will hasten the steps and move in a pace between trot and passage. The passage is never correct unless the onlooker can immediately recognise it.

Before the training is completed, the horse must be introduced to the *double bridle*—exactly when will depend upon the future requirements for the horse. If the rider has no ambition for more advanced training, the double bridle may be used at the end of the second phase; but as a rule the horse should learn all movements and exercises in the snaffle before being introduced to this more severe bit.

In some cases it may be of benefit to ride temporarily in a double bridle between the second and third phases of training and then go back to the snaffle. Even with a fully trained horse a snaffle should constantly be used when practising exercises in order to maintain the softness of the horse's mouth and to freshen him up.

The double bridle must be chosen with great care according to the sensitivity of the horse's mouth. It may be necessary, after the experience of the first week, to change the bit, or alter its position in the mouth until the horse appears comfortable and takes the same contact as on the snaffle.

The use of the double bridle may have an influence on the habits the horse has acquired. The rider must take this into consideration. To begin with the curb should be applied somewhat more loosely than customary, and the rider should ride more on the snaffle until the horse has become accustomed to this new bit and allows himself to be controlled by all four reins evenly applied.

On principle, during the first few days the rider should ride briskly forward, preferably in the rising trot. He will be helped by this impulsion to obtain a correct contact. Short periods in a shortened tempo should be alternated by periods in the normal tempo and even in extension to maintain the impulsion which has been developed so far.

When the double bridle is first introduced, lateral work and High School movements are not recommended as they will be inclined to make the horse hold himself back and lose impulsion. If this rule is not observed, faults, such as overbending, loss of action, irregularity of rhythm and incorrect performance of figures would be liable to creep in and be difficult to eradicate.

The rider must now recapitulate in a shorter time in the double bridle all the exercises he has performed in the snaffle. If he proceeds in this manner, the progress obtained by his conscientious work will not be lost. Patience and sensibility are the cornerstones of this phase.

When the long period of training that horse and rider have been through is completed, it will be evident that matters are not always as easy as they may appear in these pages. In all life there will be ups and downs, but the ups must exceed the downs, so that the direction of progress will always be upwards. The rider should not only be able to recognise unavoidable reverses in time, but he must know by what means they can be rectified. Before trying to overcome difficulties when they appear, he must never forget to re-establish the mental and physical balance of his horse. It will always be a bad sign if the rider upsets his horse, which, on account of the horse's long memory, may be the cause of unforeseeable consequences.

Horses that fear their riders or the whip will be proof of incorrect and rough work which does not comply with the classical conception of training. The fact that some horses trained in this manner may give performances probably lacking in brilliance is no contradiction of this statement.

The most important rule in training is that the gymnastic exercises never be neglected. Throughout the whole training, these exercises must be continued in order to maintain the standard reached. The more advanced training becomes, the more important it is to preserve the natural paces of the horse and keep in mind the basic training. Only through the perfection of the natural paces will riding develop into an art and the airs of the High School be performed in all their beauty. They will radiate joy to all, even impressing the non-expert who has an eye for beauty.

The motto of instructor and rider must always be *Forward.*
Forward in the movements of the horse entrusted to his care.
Forward in order to achieve his aim in the art of training.
Forward whenever difficulties appear.

The mountaineer striving to reach the peak pauses occasionally to look down and review the difficulties he has overcome, which will renew his strength and courage to continue. The rider must do the same, but be quite sure that he has overcome the difficulties and not overlooked any fault that, later, might be troublesome to eliminate. The necessity to go back to previous stages will enrich his experience and make him realise that riding forward, when necessitated by a temporary setback or when performing a new exercise, will never be a waste of time but always of benefit.

4. Work in Hand

Work in hand is a special branch of training practised at the Spanish Riding School. During the last half century this type of training has become so popular with dressage riders that it is no longer exclusive to the Spanish Riding School, but much as the popularity of this work in hand is to be welcomed, unless it is thoroughly understood, it is better left alone. Correctly executed it is of great value. Nevertheless, this training often proves to be the reverse when practised by inexperienced and ignorant people. If a trainer thinks that this work is going to require less effort and make matters easier for himself, he will be making a great mistake, and, if it is approached from this point of view, it will do more harm than good. He must realise from the beginning that this work, if correctly done, is very tiring.

To perform the piaffe, which is the basis of the movements of the High School, the impulsion of the horse must not only be maintained but also be developed to a high degree. For this work in hand the horse will be brought into the arena with a saddle, snaffle, and cavesson. In rare cases, when the rider wants to mount immediately after the exercise, he may come with a double bridle. Work in hand must be practised in an enclosed arena, so that the walls would prevent the horse from evading to the outside. The horse should be taken into the middle of the arena and the side reins attached as for longeing, and not shorter than is required by the position of the horse's neck. It is advisable to fasten them lower to begin with, as most horses have the inclination to raise their heads when they are excited. These adjustments should be made in the middle of the school as then the horse has more room all round him, which is an advantage in case of difficulties.

The trainer must observe the attitude of his horse when fastening the side reins; if he does not stand still it will mean nervousness and excitement caused by the unaccustomed proceedings. This fact must not be neglected and every effort made to calm the horse down and prevent tension, which would make difficulties in this work.

The trainer will take the leading rein, fastened to the caveson, in his left hand and the whip in his right hand, lead the horse to the track, and go on the left rein. Experience has taught that, as with longeing, the left rein will be found easier. The trainer will place himself at the shoulder of the horse and ask him to go forward. If he does not respond willingly, he will be encouraged by a click of the tongue and a touch of the whip behind the girth. When the trainer has succeeded in leading his horse quietly along one or two lengths of the wall, he may break into a trot. This transition should be made as quietly as possible without causing any excitement. The trainer should never forget the importance of first impressions, and work in hand is a new exercise. The trainer must begin to run slowly, thus making the horse break into a quiet trot. He should not pull on the leading rein, but if the horse does not comply, the whip must be applied behind the girth. If the horse tries to rush off, he must be brought back to a walk by repeated short actions of the leading rein, and another attempt made after the horse has calmed down. If after several attempts the trainer does not succeed in obtaining a quiet trot, the exercise should be discontinued for the time being and on no account should the horse be punished. The same applies if the horse will break into a trot only after a strong action from the whip. In the first case the action of the rein does not go through the body, and in the second, the horse lacks impulsion which shows he is not yet ready for work in hand.

At times, when starting this work, the horse will show a deterioration in other exercises. In this case the work in hand must cease and the rider go back to the previous phase.

Suppling up and bringing the horse in balance may be compared to tuning up the instruments before the concert. Unless the instruments are properly tuned, there can be no good performance. It is the same with work in hand; the result will not be good if the horse is not supple and the action of the reins does not go through the body.

When the horse trots calmly and without excitement between his trainer and the wall, he will be taken into a walk and rewarded.

When repeating this exercise the trainer must now take care that the horse remain perfectly straight, which is one of the basic requirements for successful work in hand. If the horse becomes crooked by bringing his hindquarters in, the leading rein will take the shoulder away from the wall to make him straight, as with a young horse. If the horse leans his forehand in and tries to avoid placing his hind legs under the body, the trainer will press the hand that holds the rein against the horse's cheek and push him back on to the track.

When these short periods of trot can be made without difficulty, the tempo will be reduced by repeated short actions of the leading rein until the horse trots with short, active steps with the trainer walking beside him. As a pushing aid, the whip should be used behind the girth; the click of the tongue should be used sparingly as an encouragement or to make the horse trot, otherwise through familiarity the horse will cease to respond to this very useful aid.

After a period in the very collected trot, the horse should be taken into a walk as a reward and in order to regain new strength before repeating the exercise. Later he will be brought to a halt and rewarded. The trainer must always stand in front of his horse when halted to show him the difference between coming to a halt or continuing at the walk. The horse should stand quiet and relaxed which will not always be the case to begin with. Nervous horses will try to step sideways or backward, so the trainer should limit the halt to a short period but demand that this short period should be a proper halt and prolong the length gradually. On no account should nervous horses be punished.

When demanding the trot from the halt, the rider takes his position at the shoulder of the horse and by a click of the tongue makes him break immediately into an energetic trot. Should he not react to this, the whip must be brought into action but, in order to preserve confidence, must cease the moment the horse moves off. Work in hand without confidence is impossible.

The trainer must not forget the power of his horse, for if the horse becomes aware of his own power, the trainer will be more or less helpless with the leading rein fastened to the caves-son. To make up for this helplessness by rough usage would not only offend the rules of classical riding but also be unwise.

When the procedure explained above has been carried out, the horse should move off the moment the trainer steps to his side. And when the horse has become familiar with this new work, the steps will gradually be shortened still more until the horse performs a few steps on the spot, which are the piaffe.

This success will be obtained more quickly with high-spirited horses than with lazy ones, because at first the latter will go back to the walk when the steps are shortened. When this is the case, the tempo must be increased in order to ensure the action of the trot. These changes of tempo, assisted by the pushing aids of the whip, will increase the agility of the horse so that he will be able to execute a few steps at the trot gaining only the length of a hoof to the front. Although the aim is a trot on the spot, gaining a little ground to the front is preferable to unlevel steps or stepping back. If the horse executes unlevel steps in the piaffe he must not be brought to a halt, which would indicate reward, but must be pushed forward at the trot.

At this stage the horse should be made more familiar with the aids of the riding whip and the long whip. As already explained, in longeing the trainer should be able to pass the whip over the horse's back and hind legs without his moving or becoming nervous. Rewards will increase his confidence and make him stand quietly.

The greatest fault that an ignorant rider can make when working in hand is to create piaffe-like steps by touching the horse with the whip without making him go forward, in other words, trying to take a short cut by beginning with what should be the ultimate phase. As already explained, the piaffe has its origin in the forward urge which has been restricted, as can be seen with horses at liberty. Therefore, the urge to go forward, the desire to trot, must be present in the horse before the trainer should try to obtain this movement by demanding less ground gained to the front until the piaffe is produced.

If the trainer takes his horse along the wall and demands the piaffe by touching the hind legs with the whip before allowing him to develop this movement from the trot, he will produce the false piaffe so often seen today. The horse will step too far under the body with his hind legs and be unable to raise himself from the ground; he will step from one leg to the other, or use his hind legs very actively while the forelegs remain on the ground, or give an outline of a piaffe-like movement without properly lifting his legs.

Work in hand may be considered successful when the horse begins to piaffe upon the click of the tongue and performs the movement without restraint. How long it will take to obtain this success depends on the individual. The trainer must be prepared for several weeks of systematic work.

Work in hand is very tiring for the horse as well as for the trainer and should be limited to five to ten minutes. It may be practised before or after the daily work under the rider. If done before the normal work, it will have a suppling effect, but with horses that have difficult temperaments it should be practised after riding during the first days of this work.

This work may also be performed with the aid of an assistant who leads the horse on a leading rein. He must take care that the horse remains alongside the wall and goes straight forward; he must not pull the horse forward or hold him back. The trainer will direct the horse with the longe rein fastened in the outside ring of the cavesson and taken over the pommel of the saddle to the inside, the trainer standing either near the hindquarters or one step behind the horse. He will hold the longe in his left hand when the horse is on the left rein, and with short actions of the longe make the horse shorten his steps while, with the whip in his right hand, he pushes the horse forward to ensure the liveliness of the steps. By this co-ordination of the pushing and holding aids the horse's steps will become more active and the hind legs will step well under the body, which will enable the horse to raise himself from the ground. The trainer must avoid directing the whip to the hind legs, which would make the horse step too much under the body, especially when he has insufficient urge to go forward, but apply the whip behind the girth, on the spot where the legs act.

When the steps of the hind legs in the piaffe are established —two or three will suffice to start with—the horse may if necessary be made to raise his forelegs higher by a touch of the riding whip behind them at the precise moment at which the forelegs are raised from the ground; at the same time he is pushed forward with a long whip. Or the riding whip can be brought to meet the foreleg above the knee as it is raised. These aids should be used only as auxiliaries as the forehand must always be raised by the impulsion coming from the hindquarters.

If the horse loses his rhythm or his steps become lazy or unlevel, the remedy will be to go forward for a few steps at the collected trot and then again come back to the piaffe. To try to correct this irregularity with the whip would only irritate the horse and not help him to find his rhythm.

Up to now the horse has been worked on the left rein only in order to make work easier for him and not to confuse him. The moment has now come to change the rein. This moment must depend upon the individual and will be decided by the behaviour of the horse. In all cases work on the right rein must begin in exactly the same way as on the left rein. Progress should, however, be obtained more quickly because the horse will now understand what his trainer wants. The rider should not be disappointed if at first he finds difficulties on this rein. He must not be annoyed with his horse, let alone inflict punishment. This would, in all probability, undo much of the work already done and lose more time than if he quietly made his horse familiar with work on this new rein.

When changing the rein the trainer and assistant must change the side, as they must always be on the inside. The change of rein is done by a turn towards the wall (half circle in reverse and change). The horse is first led away from the wall, the trainer then goes to his other side and leads him in a small circle back to the wall and on to the other rein. If the trainer leads the horse on the longe, the assistant acts as explained, and the trainer, having changed the longe rein to the other side, directs the horse back to the wall.

It must be remembered that during work on the longe, the horse must have contact with the leading rein or the longe, which plays the role of the reins. If the horse were taught these exercises without a correct contact, the rider would find difficulty because the horse would not go forward and perform the piaffe when the reins are applied.

Towards the end of the work in hand, it would be of advantage for the rider to mount and accustom the horse to perform the piaffe under the weight of the rider. The pushing and rein aids will remain the same as those employed in the training so far, as the work in hand is only the preliminary training for the piaffe mounted, and to help the rider to produce this movement by his own aids. He should prepare the piaffe mounted in exactly the same way as it was done in hand, and on no account should he rely on an assistant, because this would annul to a great extent the success achieved by the long and difficult work in hand. The horse would only perform the piaffe as long as the assistant was present.

Work in hand may cause a setback to the current training, as mentioned before, and may even affect the paces adversely, because in this work the horse is required to make shorter and higher steps and he may try to show higher and quicker steps when asked to lengthen his stride under the rider. As long as this is only a transitional stage, the rider should be able to compensate by riding the horse forward, but if he realises that this setback continues he must discontinue the work in hand and ride his horse forward for longer periods at the rising trot with a lowered position of the head and neck.

When the horse moves well forward again, the rider may commence the sitting trot, just as he did with the young horse. Impulsion and rhythm must remain the same as when rising, and the horse must arch his back, which the rider should feel in the smooth movements that prove that the steps are slower and longer.

Alternating work in hand with the normal training will prove of great benefit provided the rider has sufficient knowledge and experience; if not, it would only be harmful to the horse and more or less degenerate into tricks.

The object of work in hand is not only to teach the piaffe but also as preparation for the airs above the ground as practised at the Spanish Riding School. More about this may be found in Chapter VI (3), *Work Between the Pillars.*

CHAPTER IV

THE TRAINING OF THE RIDER

The object of the training of the horse is to make him obedient and submissive to the rider's will. The object of training for the rider is to give him the physical and mental proficiency to be able to understand his partner, to execute with him all movements, to be able to follow them with skill and power, and to be able to resist them if necessary.

The best-trained horse would be useless without a potential rider. A well-trained horse will certainly be an excellent hack, but in this case the activities of the rider will be no more than those of a passenger. Both horse and rider must contribute an equal share to the work of art which is the goal. Even when presenting a fully trained horse, a rider must have considerable knowledge and experience. How much more he will require to train an untrained horse, and still more to retrain a badly trained one.

The training of the horse and that of the rider are very closely related, and many important references may be found in the chapters about the training of the horse.

Three basic requirements are necessary for the training of the rider:

(1) A mental picture of the goal to be reached.
(2) An understanding of how it should feel.
(3) The development of the physical ability to reach the goal.

The mental picture will in most cases be easiest to fulfil. Many riders will develop the physical abilities more quickly than the correct feeling, which will take the longest time to develop. The feeling of the rider may be compared to the hearing of the musician. Both must have sufficient talent to be able to play the instrument, whether a living creature or an inanimate device.

Besides, every rider who strives after a successful training must submit unconditionally to the school he has gone to and give himself up to the teacher. Nothing is worse than a rider who tries to excuse his own shortcomings by putting the fault on his teacher. The teacher gives the line of training that the pupil must follow. Only at the end of the training will the pupil be able to tell whether it was successful or not. If he is not prepared to follow his teacher's advice, he will not achieve any success.

Instructors have different methods and different lines. The pupil will only be able to judge the standard after he has followed the teachings loyally. So the first essential for every student is to believe in his teacher unconditionally or else leave the school. There is no halfway solution.

Having passed through a school, the rider may try to find his own methods. The experience of hundreds of years has taught us, however, that the principles of the classical art of riding have their imperishable value, because they deal with a creature of nature and not with a machine devised by the technical mind of man.

The training of the rider commences with the teaching of the correct seat, which is the basic requirement for any kind of riding and especially for dressage riding. The rider's seat must be supple and flexible, upright and deep in order to be able to give the correct aids without disturbing the balance of the horse, especially in difficult exercises. It is also necessary for aesthetic reasons.

In the outward appearance, riding should present itself as an art. Horse and rider in all movements should give the impression of two living creatures merged into one.

1. *On the Longe*

The best way to obtain the correct seat, especially for a dressage rider, is longeing without stirrups. During this work, the rider need not pay attention to guiding his horse but can concentrate on controlling his own movements in the various paces. This is the quickest way to achieve the necessary independent seat, if the legs and reins are to be employed as aids and not as a means to regain lost balance. Absolute self-control is the basic requirement for every rider. He must not only be able to control his body but also his temperament. Only then will he be able to make the other creature submit to his will and develop his natural abilities.

When *mounting for the first time* the rider must stand close to the left side of the horse, facing him, place his left hand on the pommel and the right hand on the cantle of the saddle, and spring up with his weight on his hands. The trainer will stand in front of the horse to make sure he does not move. The rider then transfers his right hand to the right flap of the saddle, swings his right leg over the horse's back and lets himself down lightly into the saddle. If he suddenly dropped his weight onto the horse's back he would upset him or might even injure him.

While the horse is standing still, the trainer explains the correct position to the rider. This begins with the foundation, namely *the seat.* This should be pushed well forward into the centre of the saddle. Both seat bones should rest firmly in the saddle so that the coccyx (the prolongation of the spine) points to the centre line of the saddle. The seat should be open and not be pinched together in order to allow the rider to sit as deep as possible in the saddle. Both seat bones resting in the saddle together with the coccyx, which does not touch the saddle, form the "triangle of the seat" mentioned in many old books about riding.

Both hips, which decide the position of the upper part of the body, must be vertical to the saddle and the triangle of the seat. If the hip comes behind this vertical line, the rider will sit as if he were in a chair, the back would be rounded, the knees would

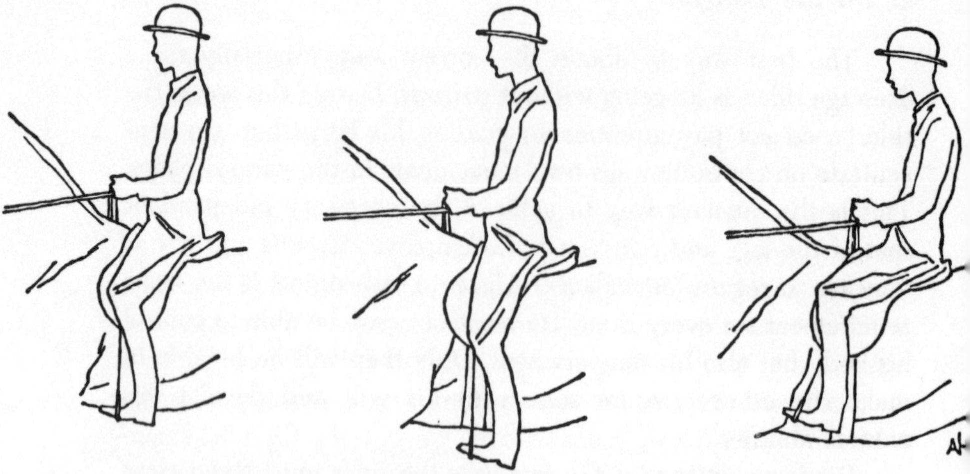

LEFT: *correct seat* **CENTRE:** *seat on the fork* **RIGHT:** *"chair" seat*

come off the saddle, and the legs would slide too much forward. This seat would be as much a fault as *sitting on the fork,* which comes about when the hip comes in front of the vertical line with the consequence that legs and knees would be taken too far back. The effect of this seat is even more harmful than the *"chair" seat* because the rider sits more on the thigh than on his backside. The upper body would become unsteady and the rider would easily lose his balance, besides which any pushing aid of the weight would be impossible.

It is a fault if the rider collapses his hip because the natural aids of the weight would be annulled, the balance would be badly influenced, and the rider would drop his shoulder of the same side. In most cases, this fault is formed by the fact that the seat bones have slipped to one side and the upper part of the body can only be made upright by collapsing the hip of the other side.

The rider's back must be upright with the small of the back braced. The spine must not be hollow and the back must remain supple and flexible. This is necessary to enable the rider to follow all movements of his horse as if he were part of his own body. The back must remain firm and upright to allow the rider to use the small of the back as an aid; otherwise he would not be able to prevent the horse from pulling him out of the saddle when lying on the rein.

Here we have another example of how much contrasts combine to make harmony. The rider should sit upright but not stiffly, and he should be completely relaxed without slouching. This harmony can only be the result of a long and systematic training of the human body of which ballet dancers give an excellent example.

The shoulders must be so taken back that the chest is arched without tenseness, and the shoulder blades must be flattened against the back. The shoulders must not be drawn up and should not be dropped forward, making a round back, nor should they be taken back so much that the chest arches in an exaggerated way and makes the rider stiff. A line drawn through the shoulders of the rider should form a right angle to the spine of the horse.

The head should be carried with a firm but not stiff neck. The chin should be slightly drawn back. It should not be pushed forward and the head should not look down. The result of this fault would be a round back which would disturb the balance and annul the back aids. The rider should look straight forward over the ears of his horse. If the rider looks down when he gets absorbed in his work, he will lean his head forward and drop his chin.

The thigh should turn inwards from the hip and lie smoothly and firmly on the saddle without being clamped to it, which would lead to tenseness. The flatter the thigh, the firmer will be the rider's seat. The flat thighs will make the seat open, which gives him a wider base. The thighs must be at an angle to the hips to enable the knees to lie forward on the flap of the saddle.

If *the knees* are raised and too far forward they will provoke the "chair" seat. If they come too far back, the leg will be nearly vertical to the ground and throw the rider onto his fork. The knees must lie flat on the saddle and must never move from it. A gap should never be seen between the knee and the saddle.

The lower legs should form a wide angle with the thighs and lie close to the horse's body, hanging down by their own weight without tension. They should be on the girth. The foot, parallel to the horse's side, is the prolongation of the leg turned inwards throughout its whole length. The heel should be the lowest point of the foot.

A vertical line drawn from the shoulders of the rider to the ground should touch his heel and a vertical line from the knee should touch his toes.

After considerable practice, the rider will be able to maintain this seat even when the horse is moving, and the trainer will be able to judge the character and temperament of his pupil.

In *the correct seat*, the seat and thighs down to the knees lie close to the horse's body. The upper part from the hips upwards and the legs from the knees downwards are moveable. Their movements must co-ordinate with the movements of the horse. The rider must not fall back as the horse starts to move, or fall forward when he reduces the speed.

The rider must now learn to maintain the correct seat in all paces. The demands on him will gradually be increased. The rider will have more difficulty sitting at the trot than he has at the walk or the halt; therefore, the horse should go at an easy trot to start with so that his movements are not too strong. It is also a matter of importance whether the horse moves with suppleness or with hard stiff movements. A well-trained horse will be the best teacher. If the rider finds difficulty in sitting, he may hold onto the saddle, that is, pull himself into the saddle. He should not balance on the top of the saddle, but grip the horse with his knees.

On the longe, by riding on the circle which the horse describes, the rider will learn *how to sit in the turns.* He will learn to sit more on the inside seat bone and prevent the outside shoulder from dropping back, or being lowered or raised up. Once more, a line drawn through the rider's shoulders should be at right angles to the spine of the horse and continue to the trainer in the centre of the circle.

When the rider holds onto the saddle, his outside hand will hold the pommel and his inside hand the cantle. If the position of the hands were reversed, which might be done as a correction, his outside shoulder would fall back and would not be at a right angle to the horse's spine.

When the rider has become accustomed to the *trot* and is able to sit in the saddle, he will first take his hand from the cantle and later from the pommel of the saddle. He should now be able to remain quietly and independently in the saddle without losing his balance by the movements of his horse.

If the seat is not firm enough and the rider loses his balance, he must again hold onto the saddle, which will make him more comfortable and help him to turn his legs in so that they become flatter on the saddle and give him a better grip.

If the seat is sufficiently firm, different exercises should be practised to improve his suppleness and avoid stiffness. Seat, thighs, and knees must remain firmly on the saddle during these exercises.

The first *exercises* demanded from the rider on the longe should encourage the loosening of the muscles and the improvement of the necessary suppleness, but above all the balance. These exercises may be developed into gymnastics, especially with young riders who have had little or no contact with horses. This will help them to become more familiar with their mounts and increase their self-confidence, and make the more or less tedious work on the longe gayer and more interesting.

Swinging the arms forward and backward will loosen the muscles of the upper body and improve the carriage of the shoulders. The arms are stretched to the side and made to perform a circle either together or one after the other. The position of the upper body must remain unchanged and the seat remain firmly in the saddle. It is better to swing the arms backward because it encourages the rider to sit more firmly in the saddle while swinging forward would induce him to lean his body forward and to lose his seat. Bending forward towards the right and left forefoot of the horse will prevent the body from becoming tense and increase the rider's confidence in the balance he has gained. On the longe, the rider should bend to the inside foreleg, but the seat must not be lifted from the saddle and the grip of the knees must not be lost. The rider should caress his horse on the shoulder or the breast, so that he does not become irritated by the weight being shifted.

Turning the body is another good exercise to increase the suppleness and to test the firmness the seat has achieved; both arms are stretched out to the side at the height of the shoulders and the body is turned from the hips as far as possible to both sides without changing the position of seat, thighs, or knees.

Turning the head while the position of the body remains unchanged will improve the relaxation of the muscles and prepare the correct position of the rider's head.

Swinging the lower legs backward and forward will prevent stiffness and incorrect immobility, but thighs and knees should not change their position. Circling the feet will prevent stiffness and improve the necessary suppleness for the correct position of the foot. Bending the body back until the back of the head touches the hindquarters of the horse is another good exercise.

All these exercises are only of value if the position of the seat, thighs, and knees remains unchanged in the saddle. They must not be over-rated as they are only a means to obtain a correct seat.

The following exercises may be used for gymnastics on horseback:

The legs are alternatively taken slowly over the horse's neck and the rider sits as if on a sidesaddle with the back of the knee resting on the pommel of the saddle.

The rider holding the horse's mane or the pommel with one hand stretches the corresponding leg back along the side of the horse and leans down as far as possible on the other side.

The rider leaning with both his hands on the pommel lifts his seat from the saddle and tightens the grip of his knees. He stretches his body upright then sits down again slowly.

The rider leans with both hands on the flaps of the saddle and swings the legs backwards and upwards until the heels meet above the horse's back.

The rider leans with both hands on the cantle of the saddle and, keeping his seat firmly in the saddle, swings his legs forward till they meet over the horse's neck. Care must be taken not to touch the horse's head and frighten him.

Vaulting on and off at all paces and many other exercises will complete the gymnastics on horseback. As already stated, these exercises serve only to make the young riders familiar with the horse and to increase their proficiency and courage.

When the rider has obtained a firm seat in an energetic trot, work at *the canter* may commence. As this work, to begin with, may be found more tiring than work at the trot, it should only be done for short periods as fatigue is the enemy of progress and may annul any success that has already been obtained. It must, therefore, be begun as systematically as work at the trot. It is important that the rider should sit in the movement of the canter as he was taught at the trot and that his seat should not slide backward and forward in the saddle. The legs, especially the inside one, may be inclined to swing by the movement of the canter, which must be avoided from the beginning without, however, teaching a stiff position of the leg. Further progress will gradually be obtained by appropriate exercises and by correcting the seat constantly in the same way as in the trot.

When the rider can control his seat in all movements without ever holding the saddle, the trainer may begin to teach the correct position of the arms. *The upper arm* must hang freely from the shoulder along the upper body, the elbow must neither be pressed to the body nor stick out. Elbows in this position would make the rider's hands unsteady and when pressed to the body would induce a tense position, besides which the shoulders would be hunched.

The lower arm should form nearly a right angle with the upper arm and the hands should be at the same level in front of the middle of the body.

The hand and wrist should be in a straight line with the lower arm, the wrist should be slightly bent towards the body and not bent back, which would annul the elastic effect of the joint. The fingers should be closed with the thumbs stretched facing each other. The little finger should be directed towards the body so that the rider can just see the fingernail on looking down.

If the position of the hand is correct, the position of the shoulders, elbow, and wrist will allow an elastic connection of the reins with the horse's mouth.

During this stage, the trainer will control the firmness of the rider's seat in the transitions. When breaking into a trot or striking off into a canter, the rider should stretch his arms to the side at the height of the shoulder, and the body should not fall behind the movement. It is by the upright position of the body, from the vertical position of the hip, that the rider will obtain a firm seat with the correct grip of the knees.

When reducing the speed, the same exercise is employed and care taken that the body does not fall forward, following the laws of inertia.

Experience has taught that it is much easier to teach the correct seat to a rider who has never ridden than to one who has been accustomed to ride with an incorrect seat. It is always more difficult to eliminate faults. The experienced trainer will help his pupil with his correction which will differ considerably from instructions given to a novice. While it is sufficient with the latter to demand the correct position, with the rider who has established faults it will be necessary to demand exaggerated corrections. For instance, if the rider has been in the habit of riding with his body leaning backward and his knees raised, the trainer will require him to bring his body forward and lower his knees more than the correct position would require. The same method would be employed in the opposite direction if the rider sits on his fork. When straightening a crooked stick it will be necessary to bend it more in the other direction before it is made straight.

The duration of the training on the longe will depend on the ability of the rider as well as on the training of the longe horse. The better the horse is trained and moves in balance, the better the progress. The better the horse, the sooner and more easily will the novice learn the correct position. Besides which the young rider will become acquainted with the correct paces and acquire the correct feel from the beginning. First impressions are lasting in riding, as in life.

Horses with strong movements will be of more value to the advanced rider to improve his balance, but would hamper the progress of a beginner who would be unbalanced by the movement and find greater difficulty in acquiring the correct position.

It is sufficient to ride on the longe for thirty to forty-five minutes a day. Periods of walk should be interspersed in order to allow the rider to fulfil the demands of his trainer with renewed strength and good-will. The trainer must not forget that it requires a great effort to work for the correct seat, and so he should not overtire his pupil.

The lesson should come to a close in a set pattern. The trainer brings the horse to a halt with the longe and stands in front of him while the rider vaults off to the left side by taking his weight on his hands on the flaps of the saddle and swinging his legs backward.

At the Spanish Riding School, the riders are trained on the longe until the correct seat is obtained and established. In most cases this will take six months to a year. During the later stage of the training the young rider will ride a well-trained school horse, as well as his longe horse, in order to become gradually accustomed to independent work.

Even an experienced rider will periodically return to be longed in order to eliminate faults that may have crept in and that will be harder to get rid of while riding his own horse.

Before beginning work on the school horse, the rider will *take up the reins* and continue to ride on the longe in order to learn how to guide the horse himself. Longe and whip will now be used as a stimulant and for correction and the horse will be guided by his rider who need no longer concentrate exclusively on his seat. The side reins must be fastened underneath the reins of the snaffle in order not to interfere with the guiding reins.

The rider will take the reins, one in each hand, flat between the little and third finger and the slack should come out over the first finger. The loop of the rein hangs down the right side

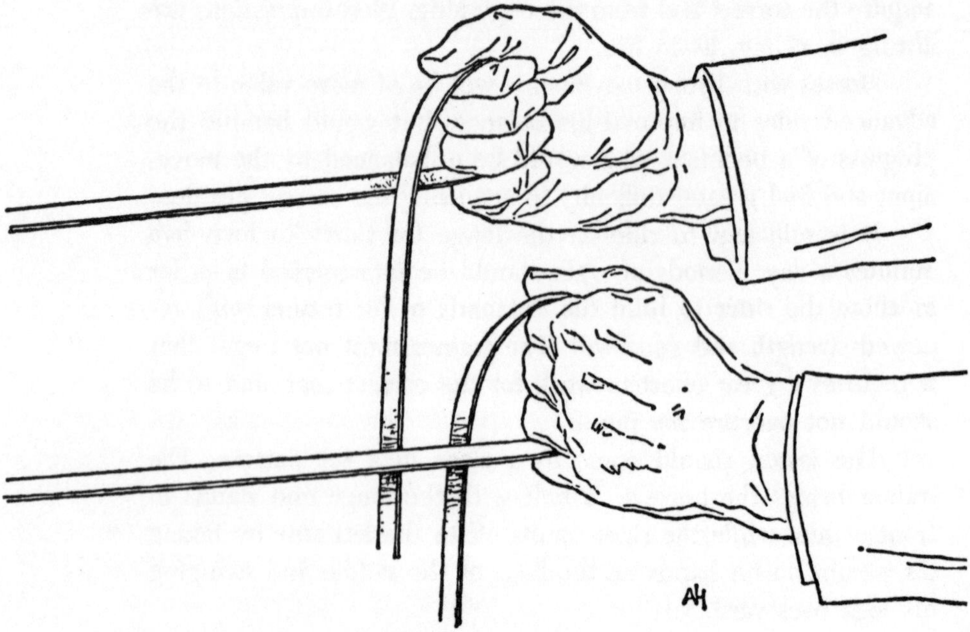

Correct way of holding the reins of the snaffle

between the horse and the right rein. As the rider's hands must maintain a light contact with the horse's mouth through the reins, the correct length of the reins is important. With a well-trained horse a slight turn of the hand, bringing the little finger nearer to the body and in the direction of the opposite hip, will increase the pressure on the horse's mouth and act as an aid.

The length of the reins depends on the length of the lower arm. If the reins are too long, the elbows will stick out, the whole body be brought behind the vertical line, and the rider's seat be behind the movement of the horse. Neither arms nor body should be drawn back, so the reins will be shorter with riders with longer arms and vice versa.

Both hands, thumbs uppermost, should be held with slightly rounded wrists, close together, at the same level, about one or two hands above the withers. They should not be held too high, which would make them unsteady and lose the correct angle of upper and lower arm. Neither should they be held too low with the back of the hand up, nor leaning on the horse's neck, in which case the rider's hands would become hard and light contact would become impossible. Furthermore both hands should be at the same distance from the horse's neck, which should be looked upon as a barrier and never crossed by either hand, otherwise the reins would be used as a lever over the neck which is a serious fault. With a fully trained horse, the upper arm of the rider should never take an active part in the rein aids.

In the last stage of training on the longe, the rider will learn, together with the correct seat, the proper use of the aids of the reins, legs, and weight, the preparation for further training on a school horse.

2. *On the School Horse*

The work on the longe may be considered as the preparatory training for the real purpose of riding, namely to train the horse to submit willingly to the demands of his rider. The young rider, having been given a strong and correct seat by work on the longe, will now have to learn the language of the aids and how to make the horse submit to his demands. This, however, will only be obtained by degrees.

The tutor will be the school horse who will make him understand the correct use of the aids which, later on, the rider, in his turn, will teach to a green horse. The preparation on the longe alone will not be sufficient, the student must now reinforce his physical ability with theoretical knowledge. The theory must comprise a knowledge of anatomy and the natural habits of the horse. For this reason the old riding masters apportioned a large space in their books to hippology.

During this stage of training the student will learn many things which have already been explained in the chapter on the training of the horse. Therefore, it must again be emphasised that the training of the horse and that of the rider cannot be separated.

The trainer must have a profound knowledge and a steadiness of character which does not give way to moods or humours. Besides which he must be able to understand the mentality of his pupil. The qualities necessary for an instructor have already been explained in the training of the horse.

The school horse is a very important, almost indispensable, assistant to the instructor. But he will be of full value only if the instructor is thoroughly acquainted with his movements and his temperament.

The chief asset in the training at the Spanish Riding School is the fact that the instructor trains the young rider on a horse that he, himself, has trained, so that he knows all his strong and weak points. When the instructor has not trained the horse himself, he should ride the horse himself, before starting to train his pupil, in order to get to know his capabilities. This will give the pupil confidence that he will not be asked to do anything that the horse cannot perform, and it will not only strengthen the authority of the instructor but also give him ideas how best to remedy difficulties that are sure to occur in the process of training.

The lessons begin with *mounting*. If the training is to be built up on a sound foundation, the pupil should not be presumed to have any knowledge of riding. Instruction at high school will commence with subjects which have already been superficially taught at grammar school.

Before mounting, the pupil, under the supervision of the instructor, should make sure that his horse has been correctly saddled and bridled, as described in Chapter V.

First the stirrups, which are pulled up when the horse is brought into the school, are let down, and adjusted to the necessary length. For this purpose, the horse must stand squarely on all four legs and the saddle must be in the middle of his back, not more on one side than the other. This can best be seen when standing directly behind the horse. The rider places the tips of his fingers on the stirrup bar and the tread of the stirrup in his armpit with his arm outstretched; this will give him approximately the correct length of the stirrup. Both stirrup leathers must be of the same length.

The rider will stand as close as possible to the left side of his horse, facing the saddle, place his left hand, holding the left rein and the whip, on the withers and, with the right hand, pass the right rein into the left hand. The reins should have a light contact with the horse's mouth in order to make him stand still. The left hand now grasps the mane or the horse's withers and, holding the stirrup in his right hand, the rider places his left foot "home" into the stirrup so that the tread is up against his heel. The left knee is pressed well into the horse's side, taking care that the toe does not touch the horse's body, which would be liable to irritate him. If necessary, the tip of the toe may be pressed on the girth. The right hand grips the cantle of the saddle and the rider, pushing himself up with his right foot and leaning his body slightly forward, will lift himself up until his right foot is level with his left. He then transfers his right hand to the flap of the saddle and, bending his knee, swings his right leg over the horse's back and lets himself down gently into the saddle. On no account must he drop into the saddle with his whole weight.

The rider then turns his right foot inwards and places it in the stirrup without looking down and takes the reins in both hands. If the saddle has slipped to the left side, the rider must tread firmly into the right stirrup and, if necessary, pull it into position with his right hand. To prevent the saddle from slipping when mounting, an assistant may hold the right cheekpiece of the bridle to make the horse stand still and press down on the right stirrup with his left hand.

When the pupil rides for the first time, the instructor will adjust the stirrups to the correct length. He will then stand behind the horse, see that he stands square, and make sure that the saddle is in the centre of the horse's back. He will now order the student to take his feet out of the stirrups and sit in the saddle as he was taught to do on the longe. The stirrups are now adjusted so that the tread is two fingers above the seam of the heel.

The correct length of the stirrups is as important for a correct seat as it is for correct aids. If the stirrups are too long, the heel will be drawn up, the seat will become less firm, and the rider will find it more difficult to apply his leg aids. If the stirrups are too short, the knees will be raised, they will lose their grip on the saddle, which would encourage the "chair" seat, and the seat will slip back in the saddle.

Together with the correct seat, the rider must learn to carry his whip correctly. As with everything else in riding, this should be done in an elegant way. Today details are inclined to be neglected and deviations from the rules may be seen which in no way improve the rider's appearance. When saluting, whip and reins are held in the left hand and the hat taken off with the right hand.

With the snaffle *the whip* should always be carried in the inside hand. The rider must hold it at the end and not in the middle, as too many riders do, and it must be carried parallel to the horse's flank. An exception may be made with young horses when the aids of the whip are applied on the shoulder. The whip, carried in this way, will look natural and elegant and, at the same time, offer the best control for the correct position of the rider's hands. The whip can only be carried correctly when the rider's thumb is uppermost, as already explained. The rider should remember that the whip is to be employed only when all other methods fail.

The whip may be called the sceptre of the rider which should always appear with dignity. It was the ideal and the aim of the art of riding with the old masters that the whip should be carried vertically in the right hand with all the reins in the left hand.

The further training of the rider will be built up in much the same way as it was with the school horse; therefore, many references, especially about the aids, may be found in the chapter about the training of the horse, with the difference that the school horse which knows how to perform the exercises will now teach them to the rider.

The instructor will explain the aids to be employed and concentrate on maintaining and cultivating the shape of horse and rider. During the whole training, it will be seen how closely the performances of horse and rider are interlaced. Only on a well-trained horse will the rider be able to sit pleasantly in all

29 Riding in the curb only, after an engraving by Ridinger

30 Double bridle

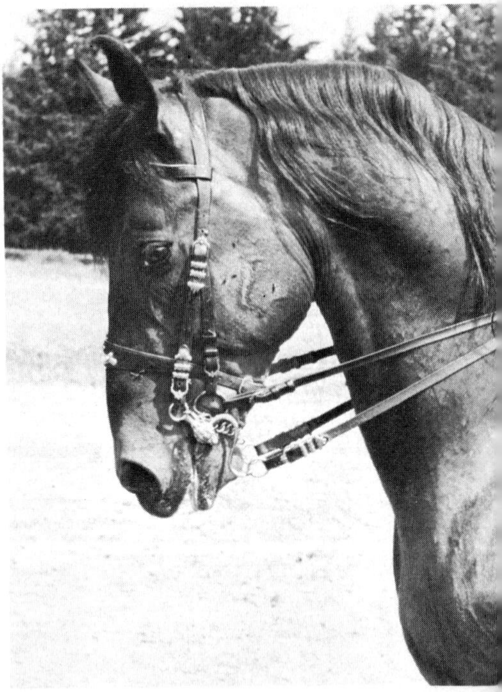

31 Double bridle used at the Spanish Riding School

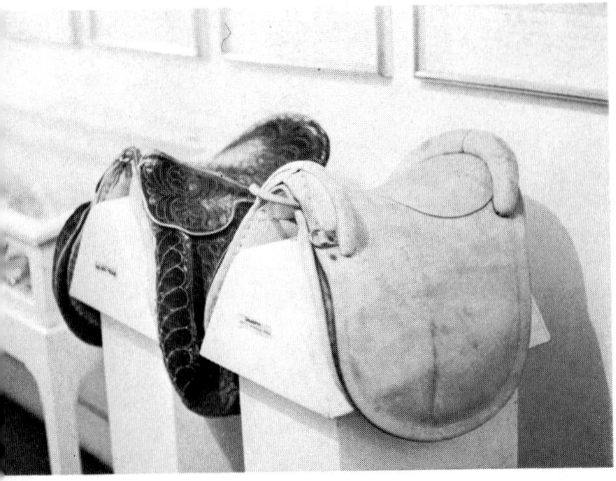

32 Left: English saddle
Right: school saddle used at the Spanish Riding School today

33 Piaffe between the pillars

34 Levade between the pillars

movements; on the other hand, the ability of the rider is reflected by the movements of the horse. When inspecting troops, experienced officers have been able to deduce the degree of training of the horses from the seat of the riders, and the progress of the riders from the movements of the horses. Although Army riding now belongs to the past, it would be wrong to reject the knowledge and experience handed down by the military riding masters, for the cavalry, after all, was the basis from which the art of riding was developed.

When the young rider has settled in the saddle at the halt, he should try to maintain his seat in all movements in spite of having to apply the necessary aids. The instructor must take care that the horse does not try to make work easier for himself but continues to move as he was taught. He should begin the movement in a state of collection and particular attention must be paid, when moving off at the walk for the first time, that the rider does not fall back with the upper part of his body and seek support with the reins.

At first the young rider should merely try to make his horse go straight and maintain the correct position. This will best be done *on the large circle* where it will be easier to keep the horse in the best position and the instructor will be able to observe his pupil in all phases of the movement and make the necessary corrections. The instructor should not always remain in the centre of the circle but occasionally go to the outside in order to control the outer side of his pupil. From this position he will be able to see whether the rider sits squarely in the middle of the saddle and does not pull up his outside shoulder by collapsing his inside hip, a fault that will also occur when the rider's seat is allowed to slide to the outside by the movement of the horse and he tries to sit upright on this displaced base.

As in the turn, so in the circle the horse takes a shorter stride with the inside legs than with the outside ones, which will encourage the rider to sit more to the outside. In the same way a horse that is hollow on one side, say on the left, will make the rider sit more to the right side and collapse his hip on the hollow side. The instructor must treat these faults with consideration and be able to recognise their cause before he will be able to eliminate them.

The position of the lower leg on the outside will also be controlled from outside the circle. It should be applied slightly behind the girth with a lowered heel. From within the circle the instructor will best be able to judge whether the rider brings his inside shoulder forward and whether the inside leg remains steady on the girth throughout all movements. From there he will also be able to judge the correct position of the horse, which should not be bent more in the neck than in the whole body. At this stage it is most important that the few exercises demanded from the rider are executed correctly. Careful attention to detail will bear fruit later.

The instructor must remember that even the simplest exercises may be difficult for the beginner. He must proceed systematically and gradually increase the demands. Work should begin at the walk, at which pace the rider can better maintain the position he has been taught on the longe. Later the greater part of the training will be done at *the trot*, as this pace is the backbone of the training of the rider in the same way as it is with the horse. Once more the chapter on the training of the horse should be referred to for a fuller description of procedures indicated here.

As the rider will find it more difficult to sit at the trot, either a school horse with smooth paces should be used, or the tempo shortened until the young rider is able to maintain his seat. As progress is made and the correct seat developed, the tempo can be increased.

A good instructor will not try to correct more than one fault at a time; otherwise he will confuse his pupil and create mental and physical tension. It is the complete relaxation of both horse and rider that develops riding into an art. Nor should the instructor shout at his pupil, but quietly try to make him understand what is required of him. Instructive explanation will enrich a lesson and make lessons in theory unnecessary—another proof of the value of practice over theory.

The instructor should approach his subject as a sculptor

would. He first eliminates the basic faults, then he can deal with the minor ones, and finally add the finishing touches. Concentrating too much on detail will interfere with the general line of instruction and consequently with the success of training.

The instructor must not be carried away by the fact that results are more easily obtained on the large circle and neglect *working in the whole arena,* which is the main object of training. The large circle should alternate with "going large." At first only simple turns and circles should be practised and the horse taken correctly through the corners, which should be large and round to begin with. To be able to perform these simple exercises properly will take longer than one may suppose. That is why officers who were already excellent riders used to be surprised to find, when they were sent to the Spanish Riding School, that they could only execute these simple exercises correctly after weeks of training; once they had mastered these, it was relatively easy to execute the more difficult exercises, and with greater perfection, because they had been built up on a solid foundation.

The exercises must first be executed at the walk and trot, and later at the canter, and the instructor should take care that they are performed exactly as already explained in the chapter on the training of the horse. Furthermore, he will control the correct seat and the proper application of the aids and help the rider to get the correct feeling in the different tempos plus the regularity and briskness of the steps in all paces. He must not always speak about faults, but take every opportunity to give appropriate praise which will be a great stimulant to the pupil. Even if perfection is far off, an occasional word of praise works wonders.

Bringing the horse to a halt and moving off again will further enrich the experience of the pupil and make him familiar with the effect of the aids. These *transitions* must first be made from the walk and later demanded from the trot and canter. The position of the rider remains unchanged, but the strength of the application of the aids must be increased in proportion to the pace.

The reins, controlled by a slightly rounded wrist, should be repeatedly applied by turning the hand so that the little finger comes nearer to the body until the horse comes to a halt. The correct length of the reins is of major importance to this delicate aid; therefore, the rider should repeatedly shorten them as they will tend to slide through the fingers with the movements of the horse.

The following faults are the most frequent and should be watched for and immediately corrected: producing the action of the rein by sticking the elbow out or bringing the upper part of the body backward; allowing the legs to slip forward or stiffen against the movement, instead of being used to push the horse forward; letting the upper part of the body fall forward as the horse comes to a halt or raising the seat instead of keeping it firmly in the saddle. These faults not only diminish the balance of the rider but also disturb the balance of the horse.

When *moving off*, the little finger should be turned away from the rider's body in the direction of the horse's head and the reins given just sufficiently to allow the horse to move forward without losing collection. The pressure of the legs should be increased until the horse moves off in the demanded pace; this pressure will be lighter for the walk and stronger for the other paces. The leg aids must never be applied with a sudden action.

Again the upper body of the rider plays an important role. It should not fall back at the moment of transition, making the application of the aids unsteady and disturbing the balance of the horse, and the rider should neither lean forward nor raise his seat from the saddle, which would have the same effect.

The rein aid influences that side of the horse to which it is applied, therefore, precise riding is made impossible if the rein is taken over the horse's neck, thus becoming an indirect rein. From the beginning of training up to High School, the instructor must check the rider for this prevalent fault. In a turn or circle the inside rein should not be taken away from the horse's neck for it would mean that the rider was riding with a faulty contact or in a wrong position. The instructor must make the pupil understand the smooth and elastic contact that is required to prevent the rein aids from degenerating into a steady pull, which would harden the mouth of even the best trained horse.

The instructor should see that the rider's head is carried with the chin slightly drawn back. A man can walk straight only by keeping his eye on a mark ahead; in the same way he will only be able to ride his horse straight—one of the most important demands in equitation—if he keeps his head up and his eyes on a mark straight in front. As the rider progresses in training and becomes more absorbed in his work, he will be inclined to look down at his horse's ears, a fault that will make it more difficult to keep straight and have a bad influence on the balance of the rider as well as on the application of his aids.

While constantly correcting the seat, the instructor should not overlook the rider's legs. There is no great problem when the leg aids are not being applied, but when they are, the rider will be inclined to raise his heels as he may feel that the horse will be pushed forward better in this way. This would, in fact, weaken the pushing aid. The raised heel of the outside leg behind the girth would make it lose its effect and encourage the rider's seat to slip to this side, a common fault often seen in the half pass.

When the rider has obtained the necessary firmness and independence of seat, especially in the increased tempo of the trot, *work at the canter* may begin. This work should not be considered until the rider's seat is sufficiently firm, because the canter demands a stronger application of the aids than the other paces. For the strike-off the rider must maintain the collection of his horse throughout the transition to ensure that the canter will begin with a full stride.

If collection is lost before the strike-off the transition will be rough and make it difficult for the rider to maintain the correct seat, which is necessary if a true canter is to be obtained. In order to keep the correct canter, the rider must repeat, at every bound, the same aids as for the strike-off. For the same reason the rider must sit deep in the saddle and not raise his seat. The inside leg applied on the girth with a deep heel will help him to maintain this seat and prevent it from sliding to the outside, which would disturb the balance. At the same time the inside leg must be prevented from swinging and remain quietly applied in order to repeat the aid.

There are different methods of beginning the canter with the young rider. The strike-off may be taught from the walk or the trot; both methods have their advantages and disadvantages. At the walk the rider will have less difficulty in controlling his body and giving the necessary aids because at this pace the movements of the horse are smoother than at the trot. He would only have to concentrate on not leaning back at the commencement of the movement and taking too strong a hold on the reins. For this method, however, the horse must be more advanced in training and be able to strike off easily into the canter from the walk. This is the method employed at the Spanish Riding School where trained horses are available.

When striking off from the trot—the method employed in the Austro-Hungarian Cavalry—the transition is easier for the horse and the rider will be able to follow the movement better because the impulsion is ensured. But he will find it more difficult to apply the leg aids correctly if he is not sufficiently firm in the saddle.

The further training will now follow on exactly the same lines as for the training of the horse, including lateral work, changes of leg, pirouettes, and High School movements. But special attention must be drawn to the following points:

With the *shoulder-in,* the most important of all lateral movements, it must be impressed on the rider that he sit to the inside, apply the inside leg on, and not behind, the girth in order to push the horse forward, and the outside leg behind the girth to prevent the quarters from swinging out. The horse's shoulder must be brought in by the action of both hands at an equal distance from the horse's neck, and the rider's eyes must be directed forward over the outside ear of his horse. The aids for the other lateral work and exercises have already been explained in the chapter on the training of the horse.

With the *flying change,* the rider must be warned that on no account should he try to obtain it by throwing the horse from side to side with the weight of his body, a method often seen, and not a very attractive sight. If he is not able to obtain the flying change by the correct aids, either the rider is not advanced enough in his training or the horse does not move forward with sufficient impulsion; in short, one or both partners are not ready for this exercise. Another incorrect application of the aids when making a flying change which detracts from the beauty of the movement is when the rider lifts his seat out of the saddle to make his aids more effective and looks down to make sure the change has taken place.

The choice of horse is most important in the training of the rider, and the instructor should have an exact knowledge of the temperament and ability of both in order to obtain the best results. If possible, the horse should not be changed during the early lessons, for the rider should have the chance to get to know his partner and become acquainted with his good and bad habits. This will make it easier for him to control his horse and will increase the self-confidence which is essential for successful training. Just as the trainer must prevent the young horse from throwing his rider lest this become a habit, so he must prevent his pupil from being thrown lest his confidence be shaken.

When the rider is sufficiently advanced, he may perform the simpler exercises with the horse in a *double bridle*. The correct handling of the reins must first be explained and carefully supervised in order to prevent the rider from adopting an incorrect position of the hands. Periods of riding in the double bridle and the snaffle will now alternate.

As the FEI have issued no directions on the correct way of holding the reins, it is left to the individual rider to select his own method. This has not always proved to be for the welfare of riding or in the best interest of the horse. The Spanish Riding School has adopted, and teaches, the method demanded by the classical art of riding since time immemorial and the same method was taught in the Austro-Hungarian Army. This method is known today as "three in one," that is, the left hand holds three reins and the right hand one. Both curb reins are held in the left hand, divided by the third finger, and the right hand is used to draw them through the fingers until contact is established;

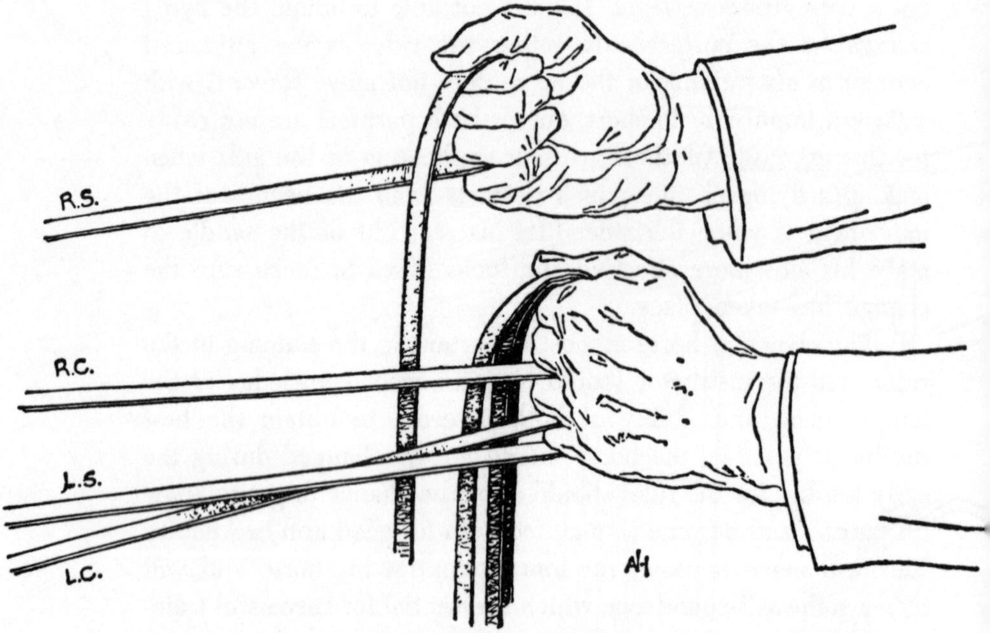

Correct way of holding the reins of the double bridle (FROM THE TOP DOWN: *right snaffle rein; right curb rein; left snaffle rein; left curb rein*)

the left snaffle rein is held in the same hand, separated from the left curb rein by the little finger; the right snaffle rein is held between the third and little finger of the right hand. The closed left hand should be held in front of the body with a slightly rounded wrist. It should be carried above the pommel of the saddle without leaning on it. The right hand should be held close to the left with a rounded wrist so that the thumbs of both hands face each other and the rider is able to see the fingernails when looking down. The ends of the reins should hang down on the right side of the horse inside the right snaffle rein. With this method of holding the reins of the double bridle, the whip must always be carried in the right hand. It is important that all four reins should be evenly applied, therefore, the right hand must now and then correct the length of the reins, especially when the left hand is not closed firmly enough so that the reins become

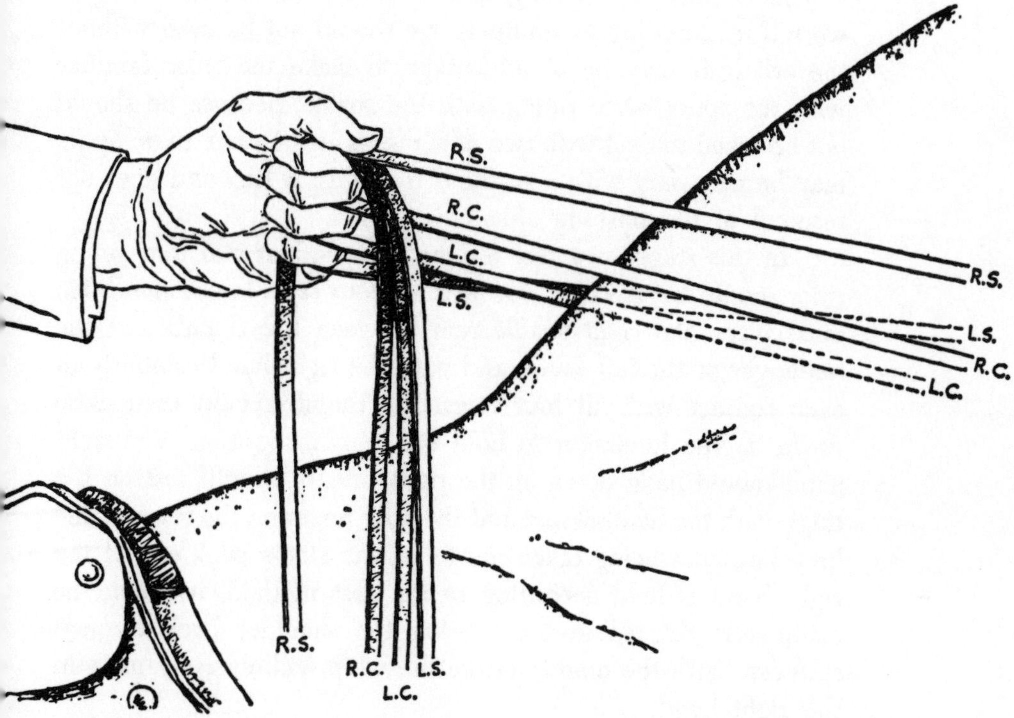

Holding all four reins in one hand (FROM THE TOP DOWN: *right snaffle rein; right curb rein; left curb rein; left snaffle rein*)

longer by slipping through the fingers. This would make an uneven contact which must on no account be allowed.

The reins are incorrectly held if the left hand is on the left side of the horse's neck instead of being directly in front of the rider, for then the right rein would cross the horse's neck and the left rein would have no contact. When giving an aid with the left reins, the left hand must be turned to the right so that the little finger points to the rider's right hip; at the same time the rider's right hand gives the rein by a slight forward turn. The aid of the reins to the right is brought about by a turn of the left hand to the left, which would make the little finger move away from the body of the rider; the right hand will be turned to the left so that the little finger points to the rider's left hip.

As a rule when riding with a double bridle *spurs* will be worn, for according to tradition one should not be used without the other. It may be of advantage to make the rider familiar with the spurs when riding with the snaffle, because he should not be asked to deal with two new things at the same time. Spurs may be necessary with a snaffle if the horse is lazy and does not respond to the pushing aids.

In this stage, as a test for the independent seat, the young rider should be asked to ride with *all four reins in one hand.* He must place the right snaffle rein between the thumb and the forefinger of the left hand, and with the right hand establish an even contact with all four reins; the thumb should then close down on the forefinger to hold the reins in position. The right hand should hang down on the right side, or should rest on the thigh with the hand closed and the little finger on the seam of the breeches, care being taken not to let the elbow stick out. If the right hand is held according to the first method, it should be completely relaxed and not bring the shoulder back through stiffness. With the double bridle the whip will always remain in the right hand.

Holding all four reins in one hand and *riding on the curb only* is the height of perfection in the classical art of riding. All four reins are taken into the left hand as described above, the snaffle reins are then loosened until they hang down on either side of the horse's neck so that only the buckle is held with the curb reins. The rider's hand has contact with the horse's mouth just by the curb reins and must direct the exercises with the most delicate aids. The right hand, held close to the left hand, will carry the whip proudly upright. The aids of legs and weight remain the same as when riding on all four reins.

During the first part of the training the instructor will designate each exercise, as this is the best method to build up the work systematically and according to the ability of the pupil. But when the young rider has acquired sufficient knowledge, the instructor should allow him to work out his own programme and merely correct him when necessary. In this way the pupil will learn to work out the order of the exercises himself and practise them with precision. The instructor should be able to recognise the movement and the tempo of the pace and estimate the logical procedure of his work.

Only after this thorough training should the young rider be initiated in the *airs of the High School.* A well-trained horse will be necessary to teach the young rider the correct feeling, but the piaffe, passage, and other spectacular exercises should be reserved as a reward for good work and to increase self-confidence and ambition rather than to satisfy the vanity of the rider, who might be easily spoiled for important but less exciting work, thus jeopardising his future career. Moreover, the horse would become tired by the constant repetition of these exercises, their brilliance would be lost, and the rider would not get the correct feel for these movements of the High School.

Although discipline is of the utmost importance for instruction, the lesson should be brought to an end at the right moment so that the pupil never becomes overtired or listless. During the lessons correction and reward should be sensibly apportioned and the lessons brought to an end on a good note, the last impression being a pleasant one for rider, horse, and instructor. If these methods are employed throughout the whole training they will bring happiness on horseback to the rider.

It is always difficult to set a measure of time for the training of a rider. The greatest masters realised that they could never reach the end of learning, and it is this realisation that enabled them to join the select company who could be called great. There are two different objects in training. The ability to ride a trained horse and show all the exercises of the High School with brilliance and beauty is one. This will take from two to four years, including an appropriate period for the High School. But it will take from four to six years before the young rider can train his own horse from the beginning to High School, and, even after that, it may still be necessary to seek advice from an experienced instructor.

Now that the development of technique has speeded everything up, this time for training may appear too long. But the rider should remember that the object is the greatest perfection. The only direct comparison might be to the classical ballet.

George Balanchine, the famous ballet master, rejected the idea of shortening the time for training with the horrified exclamation: "Human beings have the same two arms and two legs as in former times!" Why should it be different for horse and rider?

An instructor should never try to determine the time required for the training of either horse or rider. But there is one principle that should never be abandoned, namely, that the rider must learn to control himself before he can control his horse. This is the basic, most important principle to be preserved in equitation. In the words of Rittmeister von Oeynhausen in 1845: "Man can only be master of his horse when he is master of his own deeds and actions."

CHAPTER V

SADDLES AND BRIDLES

Every craftsman must know his tools and how to use them correctly and to their best advantage. Certainly the sculptor must know his material and be able to fashion it with the proper tools. The rider alone is the exception and often has little knowledge of how to fit his saddle and bridle. He will probably try to make up for lack of knowledge by making experiments that would be harmful. In former times this knowledge was expected of a rider, but today, when there is no cavalry, inexperience is alarmingly widespread. This knowledge, however, is of great importance for conscientious work. The description here of the "tools" is to remind the rider of the importance of these auxiliaries, namely, grooming, saddling, and bridling.

1. *Saddles*

Many changes have taken place in the development of the saddle, from a fur rug through the high arched saddle favoured in times of chivalry to those in use today. Man's inventive powers and the requirements of the day have decided the shape of the saddle. The military saddle, with its high pommel and cantle designed to carry the greatcoat and equipment of the soldier, is now rarely used outside the Army.

The *English saddle* is most widely used, and has been adjusted to the various forms of riding. With the jumping saddle, the flaps must be carried farther to the front, as with the shorter stirrup the rider's knees will be nearer to the horse's shoulder.

For dressage, the older type of saddle is used in which the flaps are not so far forward, but far enough to enable the rider to sit comfortably in the required position. In order to fix the knees, which is necessary for the leg aids, the front of the flaps are padded or more shaped, so that the knee can be bedded in. It is important for the rider that the saddle should be correctly shaped so that the lowest part of the seat should be just in front of the central point. If it were farther to the rear, the rider's seat would slip back, the legs would come up, and the "chair" seat would be adopted. If the saddle is padded too high behind, the lowest point would be too far forward and the rider would be encouraged to sit on his fork. For riders with long legs, the flaps should be sufficiently long to prevent the top of the riding boot from catching in the bottom of the flap.

The saddle must be chosen not only from the point of view of the rider but also, and above all, it must fit the horse. A badly fitting saddle will disturb the balance and irritate the horse, in the same way that a tight or ill-fitted suit would be uncomfortable for a man.

The saddle must not touch the withers of the horse where it would cause injuries that take a long time to heal. When the girths are fastened the saddle should lie not less than two fingers' breadth behind the withers.

If the saddle is placed correctly on the horse's back, the weight of the rider will not disturb the balance. This means it must be placed in the middle of the back so that the girth lies on the true ribs. Sometimes the saddle is placed too much to the front or it will slip forward when the horse moves; for this reason it should be inspected frequently and replaced if necessary.

When the saddle is placed on the horse's back, the girths should never be on the false ribs as this would cause difficulty in breathing when tightened and upset the horse.

The *girths* may be made of leather, linen, or web. The latter are the best as they prevent the saddle from slipping forward. When longeing, the side reins should be fastened to a *surcingle* placed over the saddle. If fastened to the girths or the D's on the front of the saddle, they would be inclined to pull the saddle forward. The surcingle can be made of hemp or leather; it should be about six inches wide and have two buckles to fasten it over the saddle. In the front, at each side of the withers, are fastened three equally spaced D's to which the side reins can be attached. In this way the saddle is maintained in its place by the saddle girth as well as by the surcingle, and the latter absorbs the action of the horse on the side reins.

Besides the English saddle already described, a *school saddle* is in use today which is mainly used at the Spanish Riding School. It is larger and heavier than the English saddle and has thick pads on the panels and cantle. This saddle is chiefly used for the traditional performances, whereas the English saddle is preferred for the training of the Lipizzaner stallions and the young riders.

With the school saddle the horse must wear a breastplate, crupper, and saddle cloth. The *breastplate* was used by the cavalry in former times to prevent the saddle from slipping back. It consists of a strap, fastened to the saddle by two buckles, which goes over the shoulders into a ring on the breast of the horse; another strap goes from this ring between the horse's forelegs to the girths. It should be fastened in such a way that the rider can pass his fist between the ring on the horse's breast and the horse. If too tight, it would bring the saddle forward and hinder the horse's action; if too long, it would not prevent the saddle from slipping back. At the Spanish Riding School it is gold plated and used only on gala occasions.

The *crupper*, too, was designed to hold the saddle in place. It is fastened to the cantle of the saddle and follows the top of the horse's back to end in a loop through which the tail is placed. It should not be fastened too tightly as it would cause a sore and interfere with the carriage of the horse's tail. If it is too long, it would flap on the horse's back and disturb him.

The breastplate and the crupper are of little practical value today in the practice of classical horsemanship, though the former is commonly used on hunters and jumpers, but have been preserved as an ornament to the school saddle.

The *saddle cloth* was originally intended to prevent the

rider's coat from being soiled by the horse's sweat. Decorated with braid and emblems, it has also been preserved as an adornment to the saddle. According to tradition, the saddle of the Chief of the School is decorated with three gold bands and a gold fringe; that of the head rider with three gold bands and no fringe; that of the rider with two gold bands; and that of the assistant rider with a single band, so that the decorations denote the ranks of the riders. The colour of the saddle cloth is traditional and in keeping with the bridle. For ordinary days black bridles and green saddle cloths are used, but for gala performances the gold bridles and red saddle cloths come out.

2. *Bridles*

There are two bridles at the disposal of the rider: the snaffle and the double bridle.

The double bridle is the more ancient, as can be seen from statues, pictures, and old books on riding. Beside the illustrations of horses being ridden on the curb bit only, there are ones of horses being ridden only on a rein attached to the cavesson. Later this rein was attached to the snaffle bridle and used in conjunction with the curb, until finally the snaffle alone was used for the training of the horse.

There are two types of *snaffle*. For dressage and training the horse the snaffle used at the Spanish Riding School which has cheekpieces and a dropped noseband is the better, whereas for hacking and hunting a snaffle with rings (sometimes called the English snaffle) and a cavesson noseband are generally employed. The former is more suitable for training because the noseband, fastened under the bit, prevents the horse from opening his mouth and crossing his jaws, a bad habit often found with young horses. It also prevents the horse from yielding with the lower jaw instead of at the poll in order to evade the discomfort of bending. With the snaffle the seeds for successful riding with a double bridle are sown.

To obtain full success, the snaffle must be carefully selected and fitted. The correct width is important: it should not be so wide that it can be drawn backward and forward through the mouth, and not so narrow that it pinches the horse's lips.

The rider should remember that a thin bit has a stronger effect and, therefore, should be used only on horses with hard mouths. Horses with sensitive mouths and those that have difficulty in finding a contact should be fitted with a thicker bit as it has a softer effect. The cheeks on either end of the mouthpiece will help to keep the bit quiet in the mouth, which is necessary for correct riding. They will also prevent the ring from being drawn into the mouth, which can happen when there are difficulties with the horse, especially if the rings are small and there are no cheekpieces. When the snaffle has been chosen and correctly fitted, it must be fastened to the cheekpieces of the bridle and pulled up as high as possible without crinkling the corners of the lips. The noseband must be on the nosebone and not on the cartilage. The chin strap must be fastened under the bit and be loose enough to allow the horse to accept titbits from the hand; it should be tighter with a horse that opens his mouth or crosses his jaws and looser for one with a quiet mouth.

With the ring snaffle, the cavesson noseband should lie above the corners of the horse's mouth, and, therefore, higher on the nosebone. A snaffle with cheeks should not be used with this bridle as they could get caught up in the noseband.

With a fully trained horse a *double bridle* is used. By its sharper effects it enables the rider to guide his horse with very light aids. But its use requires a thorough preparation on the snaffle, as already explained in the chapter on the training of the horse. The correct choice and fitting of the curb demands a thorough knowledge of all possible consequences.

The double bridle consists of two parts, the curb bit and the snaffle. To the curb belong the mouthpiece and the curb chain as well as the headpiece, to the cheekpieces of which the curb bit is fastened. The snaffle bridle is also composed of head- and cheekpieces. The important effect is that of the curb which will depend on the thickness of the mouthpiece, the size of the port, and the proportion of the upper cheek to the lower. The effect can also be varied by the adjustment of the curb chain.

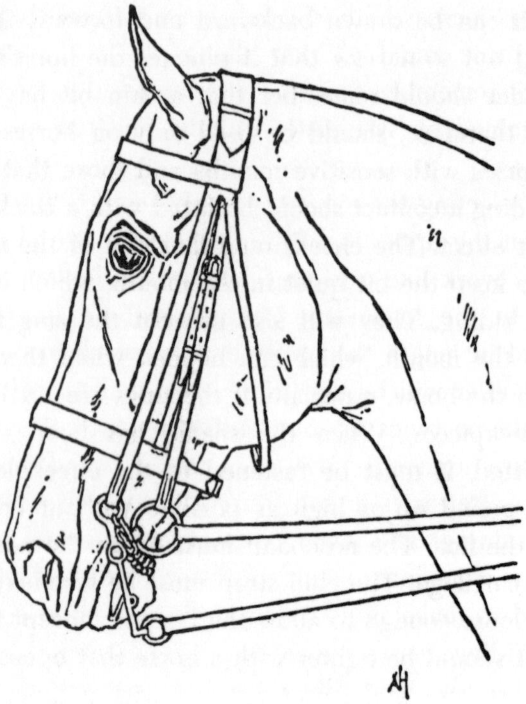

Correct double bridle

The size of the horse's mouth must be measured; if the bit is too narrow the lips of the horse will be pinched, which will cause pain and disturb him, and his lower jaw will not move freely. If, on the contrary, the mouthpiece is too wide, it will slip from one side to the other with the action of the reins and interfere with their effect. Besides which, the curb chain would not lie steady in the chin groove.

It is important to emphasise that the severity of the mouthpiece will depend on its thickness. The thinner it is the sharper it will be. Therefore, a thin mouthpiece should be selected for a horse with fleshy bars and a thicker one for horses with more sensitive bars. The size of the port must be selected with great care. The origin of the port was to give freedom to the tongue, so the size of the tongue must be considered when making a selection—a low port for a horse with a thin tongue and vice versa. The effect of the curb becomes more severe as the height of the port is increased. For a dull horse with a hard mouth, a thin mouthpiece and high port should be used, but the rider must always remember that the correct position of the horse's head is obtained by systematic training and not by use of the curb bit.

When selecting the mouthpiece of the curb bit, the proportion between the upper and lower cheeks has to be considered, too, as they work like a lever. The shorter the upper cheek in proportion to the lower, the sharper will be the effect. The nearer equal in length the upper and lower cheeks are to each other, the milder will be the bridle. As a general rule the lower cheek should be twice as long as the upper.

There are numerous varieties of curb bits and the inventiveness of man often tries to substitute them for his lack of knowledge and training. The many types of antique bits which, to a great extent, were instruments of torture, prove that men have always tried to make brutality triumph over knowledge. An experienced riding master once said: "The more metal in the horse's mouth, the more the rider lacks the art of riding."

The actions of the curb will depend on the chain and its power will depend on its adjustment. The chain, therefore, is of greater importance than is often supposed. A horse will generally yield to pressure. This is the case with the snaffle, but it is much more so with the curb, the power of which is increased by its lever-like action. This action will be possible only when the curb chain holds the mouthpiece so that it will exercise a pressure on the curb groove. Because the curb groove is covered with hair, it is less sensitive than the bars of the mouth and care must be taken that the curb groove is not made more sensitive than the bars by a twisted or badly fitting chain. The horse will always yield to the stronger pressure, so that if the curb chain is the stronger, he will throw his head up and lose contact instead of lowering his head by responding to the pressure on the bars of his mouth. Therefore, a horse with a sensitive skin should have a curb chain with large flat links, or one fitted with a leather or rubber curb guard. The curb chain should lie evenly over the whole chin and not just touch it in places, as would occur when the mouthpiece is too wide and the first links, attached to the curb hooks on either side, do not make contact with the chin. The length of the chain is important: when correctly adjusted there should be two spare links on one side and one on the other.

When the correct bit has been selected, it must be fitted to the horse. The length of the cheekpiece must first be adjusted so that the mouthpiece does not touch the eyetooth. This will generally be the case if the mouthpiece lies on the bars exactly opposite the chin groove. The effect of the bit may be further regulated by the height at which it lies in the mouth. The lower it lies, the more severe it will become. Careful attention should be paid in fitting the bit until it is in the perfect position.

A ring snaffle, which is thinner than the ordinary one, will be used with the double bridle; it should lie above the curb and near the corners of the mouth without wrinkling the horse's lips.

When fitting the curb chain, fasten it to the left curb chain hook, turn it to the right until it is flat, and then fasten it to the right hook so that the cheek of the bit forms an angle of forty to forty-five degrees with the horse's mouth when the reins are applied; if this angle is larger the curb chain will be too loose and vice versa. A curb chain which is too loose would be the lesser fault and sometimes is advisable when using a curb for the first time with a sensitive horse. There would be little value in using the curb bit without a chain because the straight mouthpiece could not replace the more flexible snaffle.

The cavesson noseband completes the curb bridle. This must be fitted sufficiently high so that the horse's lips are not pinched between the bit and the noseband. At the Spanish Riding School the curb bit is used without a throat latch. Both buckles of the cheekpieces should be at the level of the horse's eyebrows. The curb reins are sewn together, whereas the snaffle reins are joined by a buckle.

In addition to the bridle just described, in which the noseband and buckles are richly ornamented, there is at the School a gala bridle with cheekpieces, noseband, snaffle, and snaffle reins covered in gold and black curb reins.

3. *Auxiliaries*

In the last decades a flood of new inventions has appeared with the hope that they would benefit equitation, but only those in use at the Spanish Riding School will be mentioned here because it is considered that they are all that is required by a serious rider. They are only auxiliaries to assist the rider in reaching his goal more easily and quickly, and he should always endeavour to attain his object by the traditional means.

The first to be mentioned is the *cavesson* because it is most widely used in training. It is used for working the horse on the longe or leading him in hand. The employment of the cavesson may be traced back through several centuries. In earlier times it was more than an auxiliary as it was used to break in young horses. In those days the curb bit only was used, but it was too severe for early training, so reins fastened to the cavesson which acted by pressure on the horse's nose were employed. This original cavesson did not have the same mild effect as today because the part that rested on the horse's nose was made of iron and sharply dented.

The cavesson used today is a form of headpiece with a shaped noseband made of three pieces of iron hinged together, padded, and covered with leather. A strap and buckle, at the level of the horse's eye, is attached to the cheekpieces and is fastened tightly round the jawbones so that the cavesson is firmly fixed into position and cannot be displaced. The noseband is fitted with three rings for the longe or leading rein and is connected by two rings to the chin strap, which is buckled either above or below the snaffle, according to the requirements of training. The cheek strap must be tight in order to prevent the noseband from being displaced, which would reduce its effect. The noseband should merely exert a pressure on the horse's nose but not rub the skin or cause pain.

The leading rein or the longe is fastened into the centre ring of the cavesson or the ring on the same side to which the horse is going. When performing work in hand with an assistant, the leading rein is fastened into the centre ring and the longe into one of the side rings.

The cavesson is of great advantage when leading the horse, because should difficulties occur, the leader can do much less harm to the horse's mouth than when leading with a snaffle rein.

The *leading rein* is made of hemp, about one and a half metres (four and a half to five feet) long and about two inches wide, with a loop at one end and a buckle at the other to fasten into the rings of the cavesson. This rein is used for leading the horse and work in hand.

The *longe rein* is made of the same material and is fastened into the cavesson in the same way. The usual length of a longe rein is eight metres (eight and a half yards), but for work in hand six metres (six and a half yards).

The *side reins* are made of leather of the same width as those of the bridle. They are fastened by buckles to the snaffle at one end and to the girths or a ring on the saddle at the other. The length must be decided according to the requirements. In order to make it easier to find the same length on both sides, the holes should be numbered or the necessary length marked. As the length of these reins must be selected according to the length of the horse's neck, it is advisable to possess side reins of different lengths. There should be at least twelve holes on each rein. Side reins should be used when the horse is working without a rider, or when the rider is being longed without taking up the reins. In the first case the side reins are fastened to the snaffle above the reins and in the latter, below. When unfastening the side reins, the trainer should stand in front of the horse's head and should unfasten both reins at the same time in order to avoid pulling the horse's head to one side.

The *running rein* is another auxiliary rein and one that must be used with extreme care. It was originally employed by the Duke of Newcastle who ruined his reputation with his contemporaries because, by the use of it, his horses became overbent. It must be strongly emphasised that this rein should be used only by extremely skilled riders and always in conjunction with a snaffle rein. And it should only be employed when learning new exercises to maintain the correct position of the head and neck which has already been taught. It must never be used to force the horse's head into the correct position.

The running rein is adjusted in the following way: one end is fastened to the girths of the saddle and the other passed through the ring of the snaffle, from inside to outside, and back to the hands of the rider. On no account should this rein be passed through the snaffle rings from the outside to the inside, in which case it would not pass freely enough through the rings in an emergency and might cause an accident.

When using running reins, the rider must always remember that by their lever-like action their power is double. The lower the ends are fastened into the girths, the more severe will be their action. The rider should always employ them in conjunction with the snaffle reins and their use should be gradually decreased until taken over by the snaffle reins.

The *riding whip* is included in the auxiliaries of the rider. At the Spanish Riding School a long switch of natural wood is used which the rider employs as a pushing aid behind his legs.

The *spurs,* which reinforce the leg aids, should be fastened to the boots in such a way that the rider should be able to touch the horse behind the girths without raising his heel. At the Spanish Riding School the traditional spur is turned upwards as the Lipizzaners are relatively small and a spur turned down might induce the rider to raise his heel in order to touch the horse.

The *long whip* should be long enough to enable the trainer to reach his horse with the end of the lash. It should not be too heavy as this would make it clumsy and unsuitable for more delicate aids. A shorter whip is used for work in hand.

This equipment will be found sufficient for any rider who relies more on his knowledge and less on the various auxiliaries. Thus he will not be tempted to offend the principles of the classical art of riding.

CHAPTER VI

THE SPANISH RIDING SCHOOL

An institution that is unique in the world and can look back on a tradition of four hundred years has a moral obligation to its past. This obligation must bow to the irrevocable regulations which have been the reason for the success of the School, thanks to those outstanding men who have handed down their knowledge and experience, even though chiefly by word of mouth. Now it seems important that these principles and regulations should be recorded in a book; otherwise, what has taken centuries to build up would be forgotten and lost forever in the fast-moving rhythm of our time. Tradition is the Alpha and Omega of the Spanish Riding School, but tradition cannot be built up by words alone.

The Spanish Riding School is the oldest in the world. Little is known about its foundation and history. While masters of the School have left few and incomplete records behind, their pupils have published voluminous books, but mostly in foreign countries. Only from papers preserved in the archives of the Imperial Court can any light be thrown upon the darkness that surrounds its foundation.

It can be stated with certainty that the newly awakened art of riding came to the powerful Imperial Court in Vienna in the sixteenth century. Records in the archives show that money was expended to provide an arena for riding within the premises of the Imperial Palace in 1565. In the year 1572 the "Spanish Manège" was mentioned for the first time. This shows that, years before Pluvinel's manège in France was heard of, there was an indoor school in Vienna.

It was in those days that the School obtained its name. It originated from the fact that Spanish horses were trained there because of their special abilities for the classical art of riding. Today this art is practised at the Spanish Riding School exclusively with Lipizzaner stallions, the descendants of this ancient Spanish breed.

The Spanish Riding School gradually awakened a new interest in riding which spread to other countries. The system employed in Vienna was adopted by Baron von Sind in Cologne in 1770, at a time when the French riding masters were influencing the whole of Europe. But the School was at its greatest and playing a leading role in Europe when it was under the head rider Max Ritter von Weyrother.

Unfortunately, apart from two small books, Weyrother has left no publications; it was his pupils, in their valuable books, who conveyed his principles to future generations. Today Weyrother's teachings are still practised at the School, which is, in effect, the greatest monument to his memory.

Wars, revolutions, and even the disruption of the Austro-Hungarian Monarchy have failed to destroy this unique institution, which is proof that it is not merely a relic of the Court but an establishment of great importance even today. If the School remains faithful to its tradition and the teachings of the great masters, it will continue to set the standard for riding in general and the performances will serve as an example of the harmony between horse and rider which is demanded by the classical art of riding. Above all, it will stimulate the dressage rider to strive for this ideal.

The history of the School would be incomplete without mention of the wonderful Riding Hall which, for over 225 years, has provided such a unique setting. Any visitor must be rapt in admiration when entering this hall for the first time. In spite of the fact that since the sixteenth century the royal courts of Europe have erected magnificent halls, that of the Austrian Court at Vienna has never been transcended.

The hall was built in the centre of the city alongside the Imperial Palace. The outside gives no clue to its use, which makes the interior all the more overwhelming. Untouched by the centuries, the hall rises before the eyes of the visitor, a huge building filled with natural light, a wonderful symphony in white. Opposite the entrance, on the first gallery, is the Royal Box in which hangs the portrait of the founder Charles VI mounted on a Lipizzaner stallion. It provides the only colour in this huge white hall.

In the year 1729 the Emperor Charles VI gave the order to the architect, Fischer von Erlach, to build a riding hall. He wanted to raise a dignified home suitable for the special art of the Spanish Riding School which, up to then, had been housed in a wooden arena. Although the measurements of fifty-five metres by eighteen metres and a height of seventeen metres are unusual, the hall is so beautifully proportioned that the harmony leaves upon the visitor an impression that lasts for life.

Through the course of centuries, the hall has witnessed numerous festivities of a pomp and ceremony difficult to imagine today. From the beginning of the twentieth century, however, the doors have been opened exclusively for the performances of the Spanish Riding School. The admiration of the spectator is no longer aroused by the splendour of the decorations but by the brilliance of the performances of horse and rider.

The work in the School consists of the daily training and the occasional performance. Both are open to the public. The fact that the riders are continually under the spotlight before the public carries with it an increased obligation to stand unflinchingly by the customs and live up to the heritage of the old, historical tradition. This will not only keep the tradition alive but also give the visitor a sense of the dignity of this ancient Riding School.

1. Protocol

The traditional protocol must be observed as much during the daily training as in the performances. This deportment, indoctrinated by personal example, must be handed on to the younger generation. Every individual rider should look upon it as a duty to guard the reputation of this unique Institute by his correct behaviour and strict submission to discipline. Equestrian tact demands that every rider should be able to ride his horse without being disturbed by the others.

In accordance with protocol, every rider on entering the hall salutes the portrait of the Emperor Charles VI, which is a symbolic gesture of gratitude for the privilege of riding in this magnificent hall. After dismounting at the end of work, the pupil salutes his instructor and all salute the commander before leaving the arena.

The riders mount in the arena, or in the horse corridor alongside the School. If they mount in the arena, the horse must be parallel to the short side of the School so that the rider never turns his back on the portrait of the Emperor when mounting. Before mounting, the rider must inspect the saddle and bridle of his horse, for which he remains responsible as long as he rides; any defects should immediately be put right. After mounting and before starting to work, the rider must adjust his dress, avoiding the unsightly performance, as is so often seen, of making adjustments when moving off.

When riding with a snaffle the whip must be carried by the inside hand with the point down and altered to the other hand when the rein is changed. When changing through the diagonal the change must be made at the pillars or in the middle of the School. When changing the whip, for instance from the left to the right hand, the point of the whip should be brought up by turning the left wrist outwards and bringing the right hand over the left so that the thumb is alongside the little finger of the left hand. The point of the whip is then brought over the horse's head with the right hand.

When riding with a double bridle, the whip is always carried in the right hand, with the point down. When riding with the curb rein only, the whip must be carried upright in the right hand.

When mounted, remarks should be reduced to a minimum, and, when necessary, made with a low voice. Replies from horseback should always be avoided. If there is any reason for an objection, it should be made only after dismounting and the correct protocol should be observed.

The riders must always begin their work on the right rein. The senior rider will take the lead and he will set the pattern of the work; the remainder will conform as long as it does not interfere with their programme.

When riding on both reins, the following rules must be observed: when two riders meet, the rider on the right rein yields the right of way in time by taking his horse one or two yards away from the track and remaining parallel to the wall until he reaches the next corner.

The rider practising shoulder-in, renvers or counter canter, no matter on which rein, must always give way to the rider coming towards him on a single track. If two riders meet in shoulder-in, renvers or counter canter, the rider on the right rein should give way.

Periods of walk, unless very short, should be done away from the track, so that other riders have room to work on the track.

Riders practising hindquarters-in (travers), piaffe, passage, or any other special exercise will have the right to remain on the track on both reins. When two riders meet in these exercises, the rider on the left rein will have the right of way.

It is contrary to etiquette to overtake another rider, and this is avoided by the rider in the faster pace turning across the school to the opposite long side. Work on a large circle should be practised in such a way that there is enough room left for riders to work on the track.

When an instructor gives a lesson to several students at the same time they will have the right of way. In this case individual riders will either ride on the same rein or yield. Trainers practising work in hand will always remain alongside the wall. When two meet, the same rule will apply as for riders.

As a general rule, only paces, exercises, and figures authorised by the School will be practised. Any instructor, rider, or spectator should be able to recognise these movements at first sight.

No rider should become so absorbed in his work that he sees only the ears of his own horse and interferes with the work of others. His eyes should take in the whole school so that his movements will conform to those of the others, besides which looking down is considered a fault in the art of riding.

2. *Traditional Figures*

The following exercises and figures are practised in the Spanish Riding School.

Go large: Means follow the outside track round the entire school. The corners must be passed on the arc of a circle the diameter of which is six yards. With young horses and when in the extended paces, the corners will be larger.

Half the School: On receipt of this order, the rider will turn across the school at the centre of the long side, thus dividing the school into two sections, and will continue in this way until the order "go large" is given. The corners must be ridden in the same way. At the Spanish Riding School much of the work is done in the half-school.

Turn left or turn right: On this command the simple turns are practised from the long sides. The horse is turned across the school in an arc of a circle of six yards diameter and is turned onto the same rein on reaching the wall on the opposite side.

Down the centre: This command demands a simple turn from the centre of the short side down the centre of the school. After the turn the command may be given to change the rein on reaching the opposite wall.

Change through the diagonal: The rider will turn diagonally across the school six yards after the corner into the long side and reach the opposite long side six yards before the corner into the short side. When two riders meet on the diagonal line they will pass outside rein to outside rein.

The large circle: (diagram) Can be performed in each half of the school. It should have a diameter of at least eighteen yards and leave sufficient room for riders working along the wall. Work on the large circle must continue until the order "go large" is given.

A volte: (diagram) Is a small circle with a diameter of six yards. It may be practised in the corners as well as on the sides of the school. Contrary to the rule when on the large circle, the volte will be performed only once unless a repetition is demanded by the command "double volte." At the School, voltes are much practised in the corners as they are considered to be very important exercises.

Renvers-volte: Is a volte performed in renvers, that is to say, the hind legs perform a larger circle than the forelegs, and the bend and position of the horse are to the outside.

The square volte: (diagram) Is a figure in which the horse describes, instead of a circle, a square in which the corners are passed in small turns. The size of the square volte will depend on the ability of the horse and may be from six to twelve yards square.

Figure of eight: (diagram) This should be practised between two long sides and one short side. Commencing from the long side perform a small half circle to the centre line. Change the rein and perform a small circle of the same diameter back to the centre line and complete the figure by a small half circle on the original rein back to the point on the long side where the figure commenced.

Half volte and change: (diagram) A half volte followed by a straight line back to the track on an angle of forty-five degrees to the wall. The position should be changed on reaching the wall. This exercise must be begun and finished on the same wall.

Change out of the corner: (diagram) This exercise is executed in the corner of the school before the short side and consists of a half volte just before reaching the short side and returning to the long side at an angle of forty-five degrees.

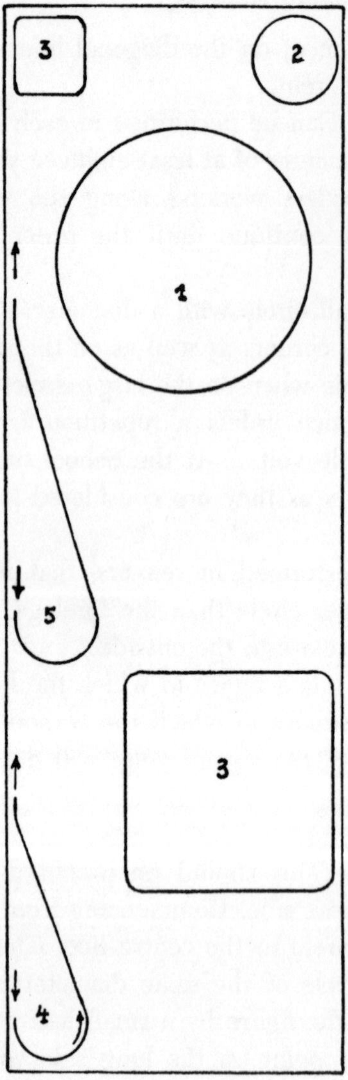

1) *Large circle*
2) *Volte or small circle*
3) *Square volte*
4) *Change out of the corner*
5) *Half volte and change*

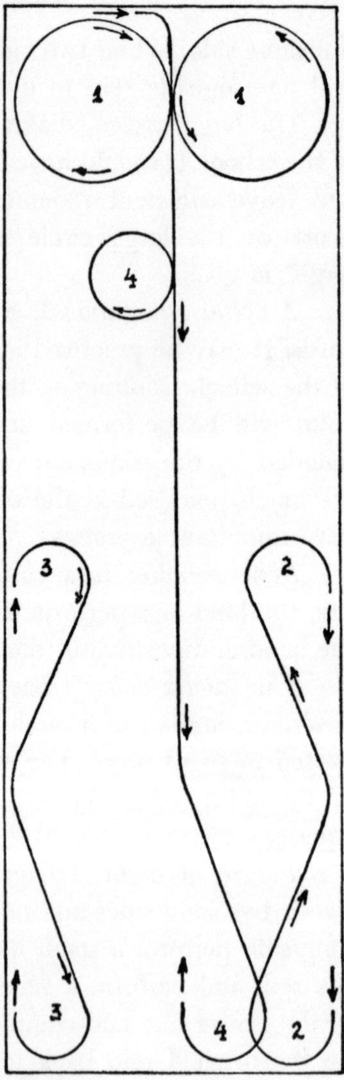

1) *Figure of eight*
2) *Change out of the corner and change in a half volte*
3) *Half volte and change and change into the corner*
4) *A volte performed off the centre line followed by a change in a half volte from the centre line*

35 Levade

36 Capriole

37 Courbette

38 Quadrille

Change into the corner: (diagram) This exercise is executed in the opposite direction, that is to say an oblique line is taken away from the wall on the long side and a half volte is performed into the corner and back to the long side. The change of position is made before the start of the half volte.

A good exercise is to perform a change out of the corner, and on reaching the long side take an oblique line away from the wall and perform a half volte back to the long side.

Change in half volte from the centre line: (diagram) Turn down the centre line; on approaching the opposite short side move away obliquely and return to the centre line by a half volte. This exercise is the same as the change into the corner, but performed on the centre line. A volte may be performed off the centre line before the half volte from the centre line is made. The position is changed after the half volte.

Change direction from the centre line: (diagram) Turn down the centre line, move on a single track back to the centre of the long side, where the position is changed. This exercise may be continued by returning to the centre of the short side of the opposite wall to which the exercise started, and returning on the same rein. (diagram)

From the wall to the wall: (diagram) The horse is taken on a diagonal line away from the long side to the centre of the school and back again to the same long side. The position is changed at every turn.

Change the circle: Perform a circle in half the arena, from the long side move on a diagonal line to the long side in the other half of the arena and perform the same-sized circle on the other rein.

Change the circle in a figure of eight: (diagram) Starting in the centre of the school, perform a circle in one half of the school, on returning to the centre, change the rein and perform a circle in the other half.

Change within the circle: (diagram) Perform a small half circle from the circumference of the large circle to the centre and make another half circle of the same size on the other rein-

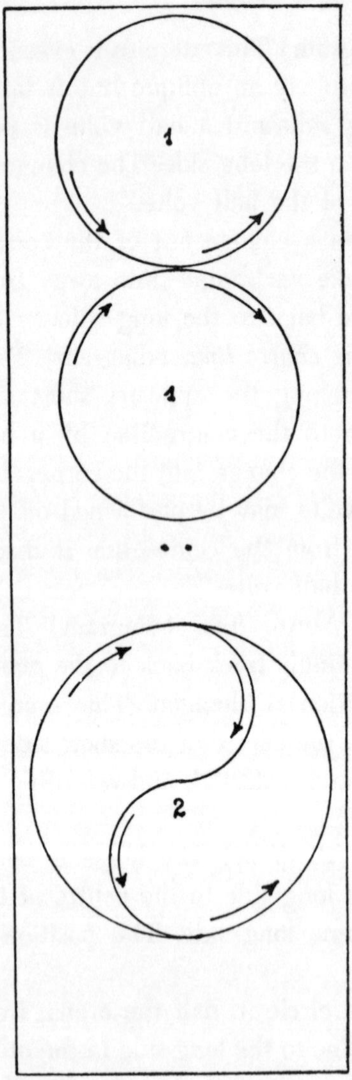

1) *Change the circle in a figure of eight*
2) *Change within the circle*

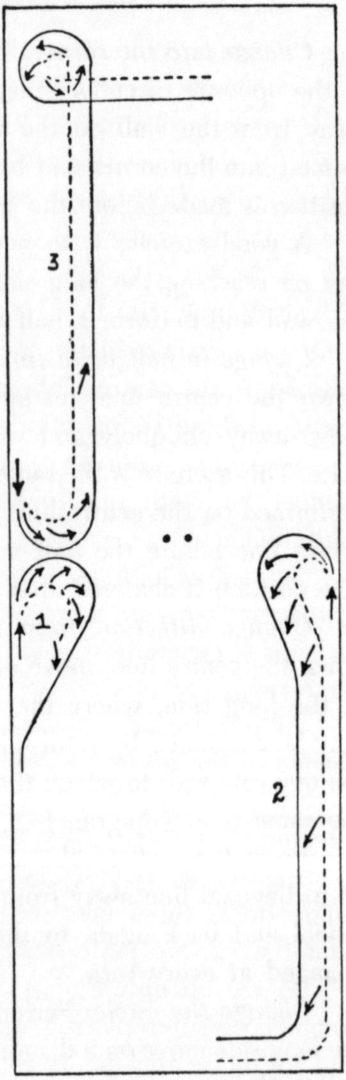

1) *Passade*
2) *Passade and renvers through the corners*
3) *Passade and renvers with pirouettes in the corners*

back to the circumference of the large circle at a point opposite where the movement commenced.

Simple serpentine: (diagram) Make a small loop from the centre of the short side, after crossing the centre line, make a large loop past the centre of the long side and, after re-crossing the centre line make a small loop back to the centre of the short side.

Serpentine with three half circles: (diagram) Start from the centre of the short side, make three half circles of the same size, finishing in the centre of the opposite short side. Change the rein every time the centre line is crossed.

Serpentine with five half circles: Performed in the same manner but with smaller half circles, approximately of seven yards diameter.

Serpentine with five loops: (diagram) Differs from the above in that the loops are narrower at the open ends. An odd number of loops is generally selected as this finishes the exercise on the same rein.

All serpentines at the canter can be performed without change of the leading leg when crossing the centre line. Every second circle can be ridden in counter canter or renvers as directed.

Figures on two tracks: In addition to the exercises on a single track, those on two tracks, that is to say, exercises in lateral work, are performed.

In the Spanish Riding School, the *shoulder-in* is generally commenced after passing the second corner of the short side, and the horse remains in this exercise until the order "straight on" is given. The corners are passed by slightly holding back the forehand to enable the hind legs, which have to cover the greater distance, to pass through the corners. Only when teaching this exercise should the shoulder-in be practised on the large circle. The shoulder-in may be interrupted by a volte on a single track, after which the exercise can be continued.

Hindquarters-in (*travers*) should also be commenced after the second corner of the short side, and be brought to an end on the command "straight on." When passing through the cor-

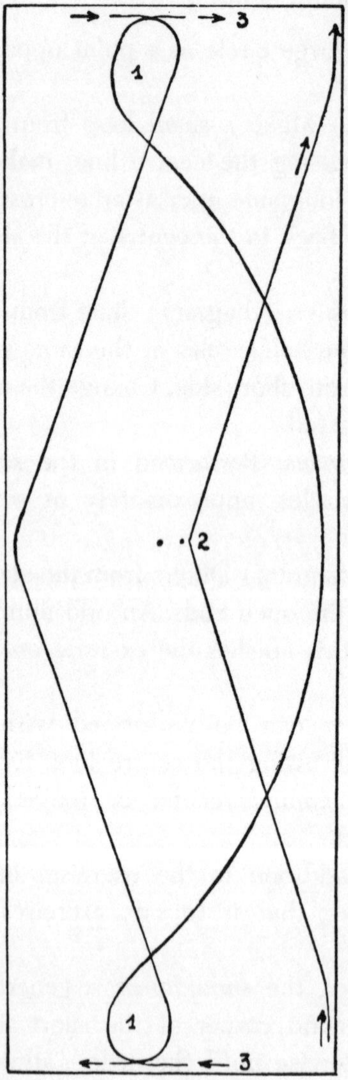

1) *Change direction from the centre line, continued to the opposite short side of the school*
2) *From the wall to the wall*
3) *Simple serpentine*

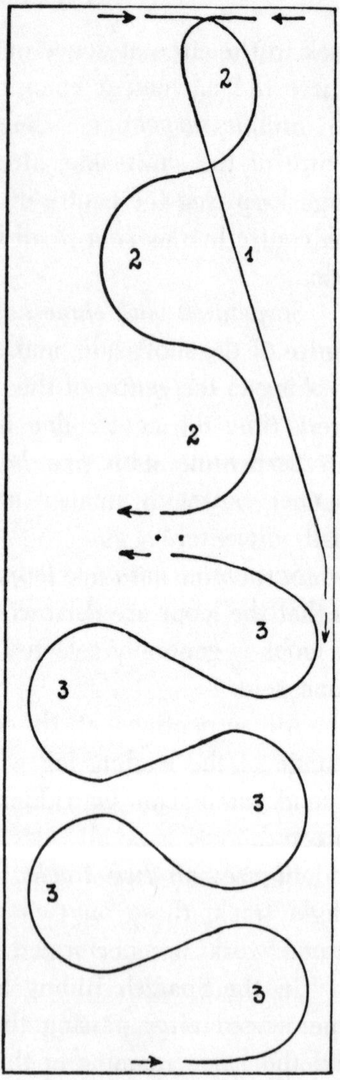

1) *Change direction from the centre line*
2) *Serpentine with three half circles in half the school*
3) *Serpentine with five loops in half the school*

ners, the quarters must be slightly held back to allow the forehand to go through. This exercise is rarely practised at the Spanish Riding School and never on the large circle.

Half pass from the centre line: Turn down the centre line; when one horse's length has been covered, take the horse in half pass to the centre of the long side where the position is changed.

Half volte and change in half pass: After the half volte the horse is taken back to the wall in half pass.

Renvers (tail to the wall): The forehand is taken away from the wall as in the shoulder-in, but the position and bend are in the direction to which the horse is going, which is the opposite to that of the shoulder-in. The renvers may begin after a half pass by checking the forehand before it reaches the wall while the hind legs are taken on into the track. The corners are passed as in the shoulder-in except that the position of the horse is to the outside. Voltes can also be performed in renvers. The transition from shoulder-in to renvers and vice versa in which the sequence of steps and angle to the wall remain the same, is another good exercise.

Passade: (diagram) A small half volte and change on two tracks and is generally performed from the centre of the long side in the half-school. The hind legs turn on a very small circle, nearly on the spot, while the forehand circles round them. The passade may also be practised on the large circle.

Passade into renvers through the corner: After a passade the horse remains in renvers and continues in this position through one or two corners. The rider can pass from shoulder-in by a passade into renvers without interrupting the movement.

From the centre to the centre: (diagram) This exercise is performed in the half-school. Turn from the long side to the centre and perform a half pass back to the long side and then in renvers to the centre of the short side where the position is changed. A renvers-volte may be performed in this exercise when changing from the half pass into the renvers.

Counter half passes: (diagram) As many as three half passes can be performed in the half-school. This exercise begins after

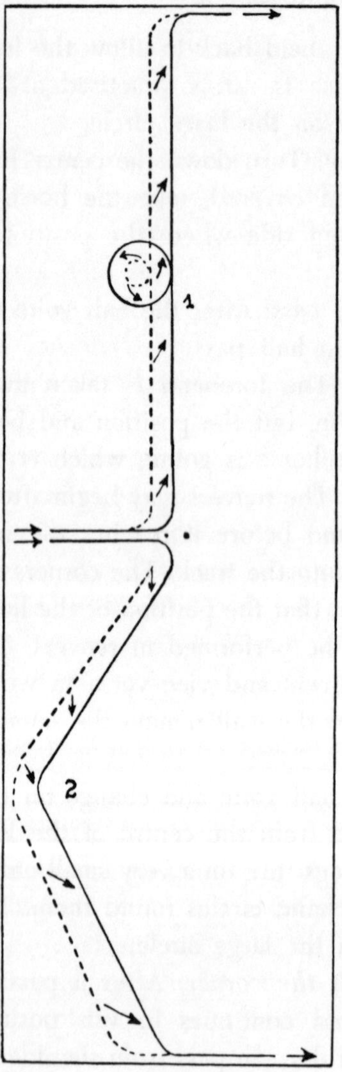

1) *Travers on the centre line with pirouette*
2) *From the centre to the centre*

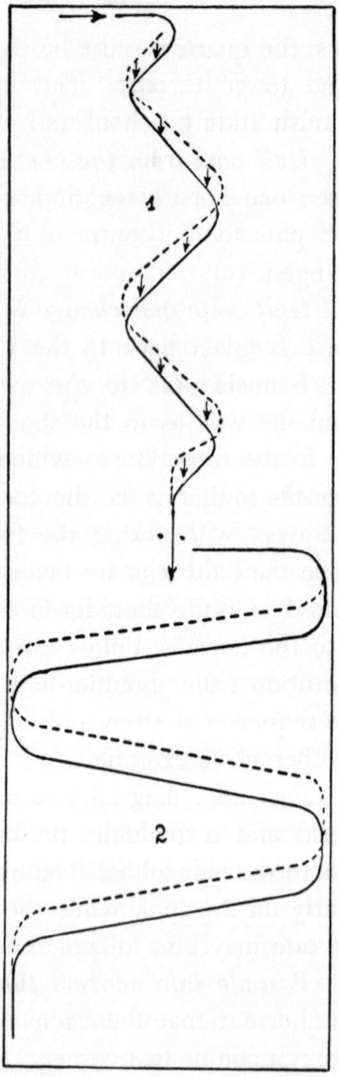

1) *Zigzag on the centre line*
2) *Three counter changes in half pass in the half-school*

the second corner of the short side, and the angle of the pass will depend on the number of half passes to be performed. The exercise must be performed with the forehand distinctly leading and the hind legs catching up each time before reaching the wall, so that the horse is parallel to the wall before the position is changed and the new half pass begins.

As a rule half passes should be performed in such a way that the spectators see them from the front.

Zigzag: (diagram) Short half passes on either side of the centre line. The position and direction are changed after a given number of steps or metres.

Travers on the centre line: (diagram) The horse is turned from the long side to the centre and turns down the centre line in travers with the forefeet on the centre line. As the horse approaches the short side, the angle to the wall will be decreased so that, when he arrives at the short side, he is parallel to the wall. When this exercise is performed at the canter it may be interrupted by a pirouette, for which the horse is well prepared by the position of the hindquarters.

Passade and renvers with pirouettes: (diagram) Perform a large passade in the half-school, after which the horse is not taken back to the long side, but remains in renvers at a distance of three yards parallel to the wall; in the following two corners of the short side, three-quarter pirouettes will be performed to the outside. If no other command is given, the next corner is passed in renvers and then the position of the horse is changed. It is important that the horse goes on a straight line before and after the pirouettes.

All these exercises may be performed alongside the wall, at a distance from it, or on the centre line, and some of them on a large circle.

The *turn on the haunches:* Performed at the walk only. The hind legs maintain the rhythm of the walk nearly on the spot, while the forelegs perform a circle round them. When this turn is performed at the canter it is called a half pirouette.

The *turn on the centre:* May be practised from the walk or on the spot. The horse must be taken away from the wall. The rider's inside leg is the centre round which the forehand moves to one side and the hindquarters to the other.

The *full travers:* May be practised on the centre line or in the centre of the school. The horse moves sideways with his body parallel to the wall and with both fore and hind legs on a track parallel to each other. The forehand must always lead.

The *rein-back:* For this exercise a place must be chosen of sufficient distance from the wall so that the rider does not interfere with the other riders.

All these exercises may be used in the performance as the figures of a Pas de Deux or a Quadrille.

3. *Work Between the Pillars*

Work between the pillars, as it was performed by the old masters, can today be seen only at the Spanish Riding School. The Cadre Noir have pillars at Saumur, but they are used only to strengthen the rider's seat by the powerful movements of the horse.

Pluvinel is generally recognised as the inventor of pillars, but the Greeks must have had a knowledge of them because Eumenes, the defender of the fortress Nora in Cappadocia, is reported to have kept his horses fit by moving them between two pillars. However, it was Pluvinel, first with one pillar and later between two, who cultivated and employed them systematically as an important means of training. This is revealed by Pluvinel's book written in 1623 and many etchings handed down to us.

Although work between the pillars may be important and of great advantage for training horses in High School movements, its great difficulties must not be underestimated as it necessitates rich knowledge and experience on the part of the trainer. H. E. von Holbein states in his *Directives* that work in the pillars must not become a torture, which could easily happen if practised without experience.

In the last fifty years this work has to a large extent lost favour as a training exercise at the School. Today it survives more as a traditional spectacle, whereas in former days it was used as a gymnastic exercise to strengthen and supple the horse and increase the power of his hindquarters so that he could lift himself from the ground.

Work between the pillars will, however, assist the trainer to detect talent given the horse by nature and to develop it for exercises above the ground. This work, as already mentioned, demands great experience, knowledge, and patience on the part of the trainer. If these factors are not present, work between the pillars will do more harm than good. The greatest mistake that a trainer can make is to think that he can put his horse between the pillars and demand a piaffe with the whip. The horse would break away from the pillar reins by jumping forward or running back or would lean against the pillars. The horse must first have learned the piaffe in work in hand before he is introduced to the pillars.

The trainer will then put on the pillar reins and lead the horse through the pillars at a walk. This should first be done at the end of work in hand with side reins fastened. When the horse has passed quietly through the pillars from both sides without shying, he should be brought to a halt between the pillars and rewarded. When he has stood still for some time, the side reins can be unfastened and the horse taken back to the stable. After this has been done two or three times, the horse will have gained full confidence and the proper work can begin.

At first a short description of pillars, reins, and halters is necessary.

The pillars, 1.45 metres apart, are made of hard wood fixed firmly in the ground so that they will resist any pressure. Four rings are fastened to each pillar at a height of 1.05 to 1.75 metres.

The pillar halter must be loose and comfortable and is made of two cheekpieces joined at the poll. A throat latch, a padded noseband, and a strap are attached to the top of the headpiece which goes underneath the browband and prevents the noseband from dropping. The chin strap is loose, only tight enough to prevent the horse from slipping out of the halter.

The pillar reins must be made of very strong leather with a

clip on one end which fastens into the rings of the noseband while the other end is buckled into the rings of the pillars.

To begin with two leading reins will be fastened to the rings on either side of the cavesson. Two assistants will take the horse with the leading reins down the centre line so that he stands with his shoulders between the pillars. They will lengthen the leading reins and step backward to the pillars so that they can lean against them with their outside shoulders. Their inside hands, which hold the leading reins, should rest against the pillars at the height of the rings into which the pillar reins are fastened and hanging down. The horse should take a light contact with the leading rein and stand still. On no account should he step back. The trainer should stand at the level of the horse's hip and with a click of his tongue and by raising his whip ask the horse to move. If he tries to go forward he will be prevented by the leading reins. It will be quite sufficient if the horse moves between the pillars or makes a step sideways or forward.

In spite of the preparation of work in hand, the horse will make a piaffe-like step only in rare cases. On the contrary he will most likely not react at all to the command but remain motionless. It would be wrong to try to force the horse with the whip, as finding himself in this unaccustomed position he might try to jump forward, a movement that neither the leading nor the pillar reins could prevent. The two assistants will give with the leading reins and then try and get the horse under control again. If the pillar reins had been fastened to the pillars there would have been a fight and the horse, being the stronger, would have been the victor. That is why to begin with the leading reins are used instead of the pillar reins.

When the horse remains motionless, the trainer will try to make him move to the side as there is more room to the side than to the front. When the horse has obeyed this command willingly, he may be made to move forward by an increased aid with the whip from behind. The trainer must be satisfied with a few steps and mainly demand the repetition of the suggested movements until the first steps of a piaffe are produced, which the horse has already learned in work in hand. In between the attempts to move forward the horse should stand still and take a quiet contact on the leading reins, which shows that he has gained confidence and is free from excitement.

If he remains quiet and does not attempt to rush off or run back, but willingly responds by the movement and comes back to a standstill, the moment has come to fasten the pillar reins. They should be fastened to the rings on the noseband of the pillar halter and the leading reins unfastened from the cavesson. Noise must be avoided when fastening the clips as this might upset the horse. The leading reins will now be fastened to the centre ring of the cavesson and lightly applied by a man standing in front of the horse. The leading rein will prevent the horse from moving back and should make him take a light contact on the pillar reins. These should be of such a length that the girth of the horse is on a line with the pillars when the horse begins the movement.

The assistant with the leading rein will help to make the horse straight, as work between the pillars can only be successful if the horse is absolutely straight. If, for instance, he tries to come away with his quarters to the right, the trainer will touch him with the whip on this side to make him step to the left. The assistant must reinforce this aid by an action of the leading rein to the right.

When the horse has become accustomed to responding to this demand by immediately beginning the movement and by performing a regular, even piaffe, the duration of the exercise can be increased. The trainer will then do the work without an assistant, but he must not change the order of his actions.

He will take the horse by the leading rein into the pillars, fasten the pillar reins, and bring the horse forward until a contact with these reins is obtained. The leading rein is placed over the horse's neck and tucked into the halter so that it does not slip. The trainer will step sideways and backward so that the horse can see his movements. He will then demand the piaffe by a click of the tongue and a touch of the whip. If the steps should flatten or become irregular, they should be livened up by the aid of the whip in the same way as was done when working in hand. After some good steps of piaffe, the trainer should walk back to the horse's head and reward him, and after an interval, repeat the exercise.

The result of correct work in the pillars will be an energetic and regular piaffe. The lowered hind legs, pushing elastically off the ground, will relieve the forehand and allow the forelegs to be lifted higher.

As this work makes the horse lower his hindquarters he may raise his forehand or perform a jump by which he will reveal his talent for levade or school jumps.

4. Exercises Above the Ground

The exercises in which the horse raises himself off the ground with his forelegs or with both fore and hind legs are known as exercises above the ground. In former times these exercises and jumps were a most important part of the High School. According to Steinbrecht they represented the "Peak of perfection of Dressage."

From the sixteenth to the eighteenth century they were cultivated in all countries in Europe and pictures of them have been handed down in numerous etchings and paintings. Today they are preserved in pure classical style only at the Spanish Riding School. In spite of wars this institution of the Austro-Hungarian Empire has been able to keep alive this testament to the highest equestrian culture.

Today only Lipizzaner stallions, because of their physical abilities which combine power with suppleness, are used for exercises above the ground. But even with this breed few have the necessary talent combined with proficiency and intelligence. Only after completing all the stages of training, including that of the High School, will the stallions be ready for these exercises. If taught too soon, they would make use of them as evasions to defeat their riders.

As previously mentioned, the Lipizzaner is prepared for this work above the ground by the exercises in hand and between the pillars in which he will reveal for which of these exercises he has the necessary talent. Only by the gift of instinct, observation, and understanding will the trainer be able to detect this latent talent within the stallion. It must not be expected that the stallion will manifest the talent by a regular levade or capriole; on the contrary, the smallest hint must be noticed and the talent furthered by understanding and patient work. When the Lipizzaner has acquired the necessary proficiency in performing these exercises without the rider, they may be tried mounted.

The trainer will be better able to judge the ability of his horse in work in hand and still more between the pillars than when riding. Some horses other than Lipizzaners will show a tendency to leave the ground when they are made to place their hind legs energetically under the body as they are practising work in hand. This proves that the weight has been correctly shifted to the hindquarters. A horse with a lively temperament might be tempted to jump from this position, performing a regular school jump, because he is no longer able to remain on his bent hind legs, or is frightened by his own audacity. The trainer will not only be able to recognise the talent of his horse for certain exercises above the ground, but also be given the line of training. In any event, the thinking trainer would never try to teach his horse an exercise upon which he has set his own mind rather than one to which the talent of the horse points.

The levade and pesade are the introduction to the exercises above the ground. They are also the preliminary stage for the school jumps. Up to the nineteenth century the riding masters knew only the *pesade* in which the horse lifts his forehand off the ground with lowered hocks, his body forming an angle of forty-five degrees to the ground. Beginning with the twentieth century an exercise was introduced in which the height of the body from the ground was reduced and the body held at an angle of thirty degrees to the ground. This was called the *levade* and used as a model for many equestrian monuments. If the horse lifts himself higher from the ground at an angle of more than forty-five degrees and does not bend his hind legs, he does not perform any classical movement but simply rears up.

When the stallion understands the levade he will often produce it without command, but this should not be allowed because it might be used as an evasion against the rider. The levade must be performed only to order; therefore, it must be asked only when in contact with the rein, or, when doing work in hand, when in contact with the leading rein, and be brought to an end at the rider's command. Horses that run back may produce a levade behind the bit.

To obtain the levade from work in hand, the piaffe is demanded with more energy and less ground gained to the front. The whip, applied underneath the hock, will make the hind legs work more under the body and repeated actions of the leading rein in an upward direction will make the horse raise his head and neck and eventually his forelegs, which will be tucked under the body. When the stallion does not come off the ground with his forehand, he may be made to understand by touching his forelegs with the whip, and, if any response is amply rewarded, this should soon bear fruit. The stallion may even be taken straight back to the stables.

In the further course of work the exercise should come to an end only on the command of the trainer. He should be able to decide, according to the conformation of the horse, the duration of the levade and how long the horse is able to stand on his hind legs without losing his balance. This duration will increase as the training progresses until the stallion can stand like a statue for some seconds.

If the stallion tries to raise his forehand too high, the side reins may be fastened lower and the trainer may attempt very carefully to hold his head down with the leading rein. In most cases this will also lower the hindquarters.

The levade should be practised along the wall, which will prevent the outside legs from falling out. The success of the exercise will depend on an equal bend of all three joints of the hind legs at the same time. For this reason a crooked horse will never be able to perform a correct exercise above the ground.

Only when progress has been established on the left rein should the rein be changed. The trainer must avoid anything that might irritate or confuse the stallion; therefore, levades in the pillars or at any other point in the arena will not be performed until later.

When the horse has attained the necessary proficiency in work in hand, the levade may be practised under the rider along the wall to begin with. Again the levade will be asked from the piaffe. The rider will slightly increase his leg aids and raise his hands which should lead to the raising of the forehand. The click of the tongue will help the stallion to understand the aids, but this should be resorted to sparingly. Care must be taken that the stallion does not come off the bit and during the levade he should wait on his rider's commands in contact with the bit. When the exercise is brought to an end he should come down with graceful ease and not drop down suddenly. When demanded he should be able to go forward immediately, which is proof that the levade was not produced by the horse holding back.

The behaviour of the rider must not disturb the balance of the horse, which means that he must not put more weight on the forehand by leaning forward, but should contribute to the weight on the hindquarters by sitting firmly in the saddle. The position of the rider is correct when the upper part of his body remains vertical to the ground.

By sitting as still as possible, he should try not to disturb the balance of his horse which is so necessary in the levade. He should act only in order to re-establish the balance. If the weight is too much on the forehand, or if the stallion tries to bring the levade prematurely to an end, the rider must increase his contact with the bit. But, if there is too much weight on the hindquarters and the horse tries to step back, he must increase the pressure of his legs and give with the reins to prevent the balance from being lost.

Caprioles, courbettes, etc., are developed from the levade. Experience has taught that a quiet horse is better for the levade, but that a stallion should have a lively temperament for the school jumps. Which jumps the stallion will be selected to do will depend on the way he jumps away from the levade. If he pushes his whole weight off the ground with his hind legs so that his back and hindquarters are horizontal, he will reveal talent for capriole, ballotade, or croupade. If he lifts his hind legs only a little from the ground with his body remaining in the position of the levade, he will show more talent for the courbette.

In the *capriole,* the horse jumps off the ground and kicks out with his hind legs at the moment his body is horizontal to the ground. This effective school jump demands much power and courage and is first taught without a rider in the work in hand.

The assistant will take the stallion on the leading rein in the required direction, while the trainer holds the longe as explained in the chapter on work in hand. The assistant must take care that the stallion remains straight alongside the wall and does not try to avoid the increased action of the hind legs by swinging the hindquarters to one side. He must apply the leading rein only when necessary and hold it in such a way that it does not hinder the movement at the moment when the horse jumps off the ground. With the longe rein lightly applied, the trainer will make the horse perform some piaffe-like steps, gaining very little ground to the front. With the longe rein the trainer will make the steps even shorter and, by increased action, will encourage the forehand to rise. When the stallion begins the levade, a click of the tongue accompanied by the aid of the whip behind the girth should make him take off and the longe rein must be let out appropriately. When all four legs are in the air the application of the longe will prevent the horse from going forward and his forelegs from dangling. If he does not kick out with his hind legs, he should be touched with the lash of the whip on the hindquarters. Some stallions may be too good-natured to kick out at this aid; the lash should then be tried on the hocks or on the fetlocks. It may even be necessary to apply the whip on the hind legs from front to rear. If this produces no result the horse must be taught to kick when standing on the ground by applying the whip on his hindquarters and rewarding him when he kicks.

The capriole is the most difficult of all the exercises above the ground and will be obtained only after the other exercises related to it have been taught. The first phase will be the *croupade* in which the horse jumps off the ground in a position similar to the pesade and tucks his legs underneath his body. Because of this position, which is not horizontal to the ground, the croupade can also be taken as a preliminary to the *courbette* in which the horse lands on his hind legs. Experience has taught that the lower the forehand is in the levade the higher will be the jump because the spring from the hind legs will be stronger. The higher the school jump the more horizontal will be the horse's body to the ground, and in this second phase, which is known as the *ballotade,* the hind legs are tucked under the body so that the shoes may be seen from behind but the stallion does not kick.

The development of the capriole is thus outlined and gives an indication of the line of training. Even stallions that have already learned the capriole may sometimes perform a ballotade instead. This will be the case when the horse lacks the necessary strength, or when he feels uncertain in the moment of suspense. This is no reason for punishment.

When the stallion has understood these exercises and the performance is improved, they may be performed without the aid of an assistant. The trainer will lead his horse on the longe as he did before, but the horse must be absolutely straight and go forward so that the trainer can direct him with the longe while walking behind him. When using the leading rein, the trainer had to stand at the shoulder of the stallion, from which position it was easier for him to direct the horse, but where he would not be able to apply the whip with sufficient effect necessary for school jumps which demand much impulsion.

When first performing the capriole under the rider, it should be practised in hand with the rider acting as a passenger. Later an assistant will help with the whip when the rider demands the first capriole himself.

Before attempting this difficult exercise, the rider must be sure that the stallion takes contact with the bit in the correct position. A stronger contact is preferable because horses that are inclined to get behind the bit are not suitable for school jumps.

The strong action of the movement should not make the horse

throw up his head, because from this position he would drop his back and lose his balance, making it difficult for the rider to remain in the saddle. The rider must not disturb the balance of the horse but sit upright and not lean forward.

The rider, by his seat and reins, should prevent the stallion from gaining too much ground to the front, which would occur if he were pushed too much by legs and spurs and which would develop the pushing powers of the hind legs rather than the spring. As the development of the capriole on the spot is improved, the more the forelegs will be tucked in and the more the hind legs will kick out. The rider must remain upright, even leaning slightly back and, at the moment of suspension, apply the reins firmly to prevent the horse from landing on his forelegs. Then the forelegs should be correctly tucked in, the kick-out ensured, and the horse should land on all four legs almost on the same spot or even with his hind legs first. The capriole is incorrect if the stallion kicks out and leaves his forelegs dangling. This is sometimes called a reversed capriole. But, if the forelegs remain on the ground and the hind legs kick out, it cannot even be considered a classical movement.

The *courbette* as it is practised at the Spanish Riding School today differs much from the exercise of the same name practised by the old masters. A school jump known to the Spanish Riding School as a mézair was then called the courbette. This consisted of a series of short levades in which the forehand touched the ground for a moment after each jump, with the horse gaining little ground to the front. This exercise, which has not been practised at the School for the past thirty-five years, was never taken seriously, although it counted among the classical school jumps.

The courbette now is a series of jumps on the hind legs without the forelegs touching the ground. There are three phases: the piaffe, the levade developed from the piaffe, and the jump landing on the hind legs in the position of the levade. According to the ability of the stallion, these jumps are repeated from two to five times until the forelegs again touch the ground. The courbette is also first taught from work in hand. To start with three assistants will be required. The first leads the stallion with the rein fastened to the centre ring of the cavesson and is responsible for keeping him absolutely straight along the wall; the second walks behind the horse and maintains the contact with the two longe reins fastened to the side rings of the cavesson. He helps the stallion to keep the direction and regulates the length of the stride in the piaffe. The third walks near the hindquarters with the whip to make the hind legs step well under the body and ensure the bend of all three joints of the hind legs, the forward urge, and the take-off. The trainer either assumes this latter part or directs the stallion with both longe reins. Both these functions are of equal importance, and the trainer must also direct his assistants.

As the stallion is unaccustomed to having three men busy around him, he should be taken two or three times round the school at the walk until his confidence is established. Piaffe-like steps may then be demanded, gaining much ground to the front in order to secure the necessary impulsion. When these have been obtained the trainer and an assistant will demand, with both longe rein and whip, an energetic piaffe gaining little ground to the front. When this has been reduced to a piaffe on the spot, the moment has arrived to demand the levade with repeated actions of both longe reins. The longe reins must be held very low and firmly applied when the forehand is raised. The whip will then be placed underneath the hocks in order to prevent the stallion from stepping back, and to ensure that the hind legs, stepping well under the body, are placed side by side. Only when the hind legs are placed side by side is the utmost spring, necessary for any school jump, guaranteed. When the stallion is in the levade, the assistant, holding the longe reins with deeply lowered hands, must take care they do not come away from the horse's body, which would produce a wrong effect. For this reason the longe reins should be passed through the stirrups which are drawn up. When the stallion is in the position of the levade, the leading rein must be held very lightly in order not to disturb the jump-off. The trainer will now demand the take-off with a click of the tongue and a touch of the whip on the hind legs. The longe reins must be firmly applied to make the horse jump into the air, and not forward, and land again on his hind legs. He should then remain in the position of the levade before touching the ground again with his forelegs.

When the stallion understands and is able to follow his trainer's commands without nervousness, a second jump may be demanded before the forelegs come to the ground. According to the ability of the stallion, these courbettes may be repeated three or more times.

When all these jumps can be executed on very light aids and with power and regularity upon a click of the tongue, a rider may be mounted as merely a passenger at first, before bringing the work in hand to an end. He must not disturb the balance of the horse and his body must be vertical to the ground. He may hold on to the pommel to prevent himself from slipping back.

Before practising the courbette under the rider alone the leading rein should be unfastened and the rider, holding the reins, sitting very quietly and gripping with his knees and legs, must not be tempted to make use of the reins to retain his balance. It is better to hold on to the pommel than to disturb the stallion by a misuse of the reins. In the next stage, the longe reins will be unfastened and the rider will be responsible for guiding the horse. This will demand great knowledge as the leg aids will now be reinforced only by the aid of the whip, which must gradually cease until the rider works entirely alone.

The rider must first demand the piaffe by his leg and back aids and repeated actions of the reins. He then proceeds to the levade by increased aids and finally commands the take-off with still increased leg aids and the riding whip, if necessary. At this moment the reins must be firmly applied so that the stallion does not jump too much forward as he would then be unable to keep his balance and repeat the jump.

The influence of the legs, equal on both sides, must ensure that both hind legs stand side by side. If this is not the case, the stallion, instead of jumping, would run on his hind legs which may often be seen in the circus. As this is much easier than making a school jump, the stallion would try to adopt it to make work easier for himself, and this practice must of course be prevented.

In the exercises above the ground the Lipizzaners are transformed from four-legged ballet dancers into athletes from whom great ability, courage, and power are demanded. More than a hundred years ago riding masters complained that the number of horses showing sufficient talent for the school jumps was gradually decreasing. This trend, which has been observed with the Lipizzaners during the past fifty years, is even more in evidence today.

5. *The Performance*

The performances of the Spanish Riding School were originally reserved for the guests of the Court and were only made accessible to a larger part of the population after the beginning of the century and for special occasions.

The programme for these performances was somewhat modest to begin with. It consisted of the head rider presenting a few stallions in the paces and exercises of the High School, exercises above the ground and on the long reins. There might have been a Pas de Deux and the performance was brought to a close by a Quadrille of four riders.

After the end of the Austro-Hungarian Empire in 1918, the School had to contribute to its upkeep by taking in students and opening the performances to the general public. For this reason the performance had to be enlarged in order to increase the public interest in this precious Austrian institution.

The performances have a solemn effect. The riders wear the traditional uniform: brown coat, white buckskin breeches, and two-cornered hat. With the exception of slight concessions to the fashion of the various epochs, such as the height and width of the hat and collar of the coat, this uniform has not changed during the past two hundred years. It seems to have been made especially for the wonderful Riding Hall. The traditional saddles and gold-plated bridles complete the spectacle, bringing back memories of the glorious past.

The course of the performance is governed by tradition. When entering and leaving the arena the riders make their salute from the centre line facing the Royal Box, except when presenting the young stallions or the work in hand and on the long rein. The spectator will see examples of all the different phases of training and is thus able to follow the course of the whole education of the stallions.

Today the programme of the performance comprises the following items:

(1) *The young stallions* which came from the stud farm at the age of four represent the young generation. They must be seen to go forward and accept the aids willingly, a principle which should be followed by every young horse and every riding horse.

(2) *Exercises and paces of the High School.* To the strains of music the fully trained stallion performs all the difficult airs and paces of the High School. These include the pirouette, the flying change, piaffe, and passage, and all exercises demanded in the Olympic Dressage Tests. Riding on the curb only, with the whip carried upright in the right hand, the rider blends in harmony with his horse and reminds us of the golden age of the classical art of riding.

(3) *The Pas de Deux or Pas de Trois.* In these figures the riders guide the stallions to work together with the greatest precision in the execution of the movements.

(4) *Work in hand.* Shows the preparation of the stallions for the exercises above the ground, including the piaffe alongside the wall and between the pillars as well as levades, caprioles, and courbettes in hand.

(5) *On the long rein.* The rider walking behind his horse shows all the exercises performed by the stallions under their riders. The stallion must be thoroughly trained and respond to the most discreet aids in order to allow himself to be controlled by rein aids alone.

(6) *Exercises above the ground.* In this section the stallions

remind us of many an equestrian statue as they stand motionless in the levade, or jump high into the air in caprioles, courbettes, and ballotades. All exercises above the ground are performed without stirrups.

(7) *The School Quadrille.* Performed by four, eight, or twelve riders, the Quadrille is the traditional conclusion of the performance. The onlooker is reminded of the ancient horse ballets. To the sound of old-time music, the stallions, with the greatest precision, perform in unison the exercises of the Quadrille.

The graceful ease with which this Quadrille is performed seems almost unreal to the onlooker and requires exceptionally well-trained horses submitting willingly in full harmony with their riders. This Quadrille provides, as it were, a testimonial to the well-trained horse.

EPILOGUE

When I was entrusted with the direction of the Spanish Riding School in 1939, I was fully conscious that I was undertaking the hardest task of my life. The great difficulty in directing an institute of this kind consists in maintaining the standard at the same high level and in preserving the tradition, which plays such an important part at the Spanish Riding School, without making concessions.

This difficulty has been increased by the fact that the regulations of the Spanish Riding School, the method of training and the traditional customs, have always been handed down by word of mouth and there is no written record.

A strong personality is required to preserve and continue these traditions. Without such a personality important experiences and knowledge might be lost, tradition would be replaced by complacency, and the gradual decline of the equestrian standard would be the unavoidable consequence. If this has not been the case during the existence of the Spanish Riding School through the centuries, it has been due to the merit of those truly great horsemen who have preserved the art of riding at this institution. We bow in admiration and gratitude before these great masters of equestrian art.

In spite of this acknowledgment, the need to record in writing the regulations and the system of training has become apparent and I have considered it my major duty to collect all relevant information from the Spanish Riding School so that it could be preserved in a book. I was fully aware of the difficulty of this task and might never have had the courage to undertake it had it not been for the fact that for many years I trained my own horses according to the principles of the School and over a long period had considerable success with them in dressage competitions at numerous international horse shows.

In producing this book of the Spanish Riding School instructions which have been handed down by word of mouth, I had the benefit of the experience and rich knowledge of the three great head riders, Zrust, Polak, and Lindenbauer. We decided to write down the essential rules during regular conferences. Unfortunately, the work was interrupted at its inception by the outbreak of the Second World War. In 1940 head rider Zrust died; he was followed by riding master Polak in 1942. Although head rider Lindenbauer remained active until 1950, he was unable to help as he was engaged in other work.

Now this work of compiling the rules of instruction has been completed after twenty-six years of experience at the Spanish Riding School. Maybe there is an advantage in the fact that the production has been delayed so long. After all these years of activity as Director of the School, which included instructing the riders and personally training many Lipizzaner stallions, I may now be even better qualified than before to lay down the traditional principles, reinforced by personal experiences, and so make them universally understood and accessible to everybody.

Because of their simplicity and clarity, the principles of the classical equestrian art are of value for any kind of riding. They came into being at a time when the horse was a part of everyday life and when riding was a means of expressing a certain form of culture. In those days man tried to penetrate the secret of the harmony between two living creatures—horse and rider. Today, when motors and mechanics have replaced the horse in our lives, we are not likely to find new methods of training in this field. When anyone thinks he has found out something new, he may be sure that some old riding master has had the same experience and that it has been only temporarily forgotten.

It is my hope that this book based on the principles of the classical art of riding as they have been practised for generations at the Spanish Riding School will be found of value for instruction and as a reference for riding in general and for dressage in particular.

INDEX